THE PRACTICAL ENCYCLOPEDIA OF
ASIAN COOKING

THE PRACTICAL ENCYCLOPEDIA OF
ASIAN
COOKING

SALLIE MORRIS & DEH-TA HSIUNG

LORENZ BOOKS

First published in 1999 by Lorenz Books

LORENZ BOOKS are available for sales promotion and for premium use. For details, write or call the sales director, Lorenz Books, 27 West 20th Street, New York, NY 10011; (800) 354-9657

Lorenz Books is an imprint of
Anness Publishing Inc.

ISBN 0 7548 0193 4

Publisher: Joanna Lorenz
Executive Editor: Linda Fraser
Editor: Jenni Fleetwood
Indexer: Dawn Butcher
Designer: Nigel Partridge
Production Controller: Wendy Lawson
Photography: Nicki Dowey (recipes) and Janine Hosegood
Food for Photography: Becky Johnson (recipes) and Annabel Ford

Printed and bound in Italy

3 5 7 9 10 8 6 4 2

CONTENTS

INTRODUCTION

*Everything you ever wanted to know about Asian foods and
cooking is contained within this fascinating book, from
essential information on hundreds of ingredients to authentic
recipes from every part of the region.*

SOME OF THE WORLD'S most exciting cuisines come from the Far East and South-east Asia. From the vastness of China to the island states of Indonesia and the Philippines, food is prepared with pleasure and keen attention to detail. Each of the countries in this broad sweep has its own unique style of cooking, colored by climate, local crops, cultural mores and the impact of historical events such as invasion or war, but there are common threads too. Throughout this region, the emphasis is always on serving food that is as fresh as possible. Presentation is paramount, particularly in Japan and Thailand, and the sharing of food is so fundamental to the faith of each culture that honored guests are precisely that.

Rice is the staple food of the whole of this region. Cultivated in southern Asia for over 5,000 years, it is eaten at every meal, including breakfast, and is the basis of both sweet and savory

Above: A variety of crops and grains are grown on the terraced fields on river banks in southern China.

Below: A chef preparing a variety of fresh fish, meats, vegetables and herbs at a roadside stall in Hong Kong.

snack foods, as well as
a being a source for both wine and
vinegar. In Japan, vinegared rice is used
to make sushi, those delicious titbits
that consist either of shaped rice
topped with fish or vegetables, or rice
and other ingredients rolled in thin
sheets of edible seaweed.

Fish forms an important part of the
diet. Every country, with the exception
of Laos, has miles of coastline, as well
as rivers, lakes and ponds, all of which
yield plentiful supplies of fish. The
lower reaches of the Yangtze River are
traditionally known as the "Land of Fish
and Rice", a term that is used to
indicate the well-being of the local
inhabitants. The first king of Siam
expressed similar sentiments when, in
1292, he wrote of the value of having
"fish in the water and rice in the field".

The Japanese cooks' skill in
preparing and serving fish is legendary.
This is partly due to the fact that the
country has abundant fish stocks and
only limited land for grazing, but is also
because for many years, meat was off
the menu, due to a government decree
that prohibited its consumption by any
but the sick, on the grounds that it

*Below: Fresh red chiles being sold at a
market in Myanmar. Chiles give a hot
spicy flavor to many dishes.*

increased aggression. As a result,
Japanese cooks became extremely
adept at preparing fish in a wide variety
of ways. Very fresh fish is sliced thinly
and served raw, or marinated, but this is
by no means the only way of preparing
it. Fish is also poached, broiled, cooked
on skewers and battered and fried in the
famous tempura.

In Thailand, too, fish is of enormous
importance. As elsewhere in Asia, it is
always served as fresh as possible. In
restaurants it is usual for diners to

*Above: Planting rice in a paddy field in
the Mekong Delta, Vietnam. Two crops
are harvested each year.*

choose their own fish from tanks, a
serious business that demands
considerable deliberation, and nobody
objects to waiting while the grouper or
snapper is despatched, prepared and
cooked in the manner the host has
selected. Fish bought at market is often
live and is carried home in a bucket of
water for preparation by the cook.

The Asian preoccupation with the
freshest possible food, be it animal or
vegetable, can be a little disconcerting
for the Western visitor. Before enjoying
the famous Hong Kong dish Drunken
Shrimp, for instance, the diner must
first watch as the live shrimp are
marinated in Shao Xing rice wine, then
cooked in fragrant stock.

At the other end of the spectrum,
salted and cured fish is a valuable
source of food throughout the area, but
particularly in South-east Asia. All sorts
of fish and seafood are prepared in this
way, either in brine or by being dried in
the sun. Dried fish and shellfish also
furnish the raw material for fish sauce
and shrimp paste, essential ingredients
that go under various names, and
contribute a subtle but unique signature
to so many dishes.

Fish sauce is not the only condiment to play a seminal role in Asian cooking. Even more important is soy sauce, which was invented by the Chinese thousands of years ago. Beancurd (tofu) is another soybean product that was originally peculiar to the region, but is now widely used in the Western world, as are noodles, another valuable food.

As well as having many ingredients in common, the countries of the Far East and South-east Asia share a similar approach to food. All prepare, cook and serve their daily meals according to the long-established principle the Chinese call *fan-cai*. The "fan" is the main part of the meal, usually rice or another form of grain, while the "cai" includes the supplementary dishes such as fish, meat, poultry and vegetables. These elements must be balanced in every meal, as must the ingredients in

Above: The colorful floating market in Bangkok, Thailand, sells a wonderful selection of fresh fruits and vegetables.

every supplementary dish, so that aromas, colors, textures and tastes are all in perfect harmony.

Harmony dictates that all the dishes be served together, buffet style, rather than as separate courses. Guests begin by taking a portion of rice, and then one

beautifully served. Thai girls learn the art of fruit carving from a young age, and fruit (and vegetables) are cut into fabulous shapes of birds, flowers and butterflies. They are, of course, fortunate in having such wonderful raw materials. Visit the floating market in Bangkok—or, indeed, any market in this part of the world—and you will marvel at the array of vegetables and fruit on offer, many of them relatively unknown in the West until recently, when Asia became such a sought-after travel destination.

Tourism is one of the major reasons why Asian food has become so popular in the US, Europe, Australia and elsewhere. Travelers discovered that Chinese food was not a single cuisine, but many, ranging from Peking cooking

Below: Asia is a vast region, from China, through Japan and Korea, down to the South-east Asian islands of Malaysia, Indonesia and the Philippines.

in the north, to the hot and spicy Sichuan-style in the west and Cantonese in the south. Visitors to Vietnam and Thailand learned to enjoy —and distinguish between—the cuisines of those countries and, when they returned home, they wanted to be able to continue eating the meals that had been so much a part of their holiday. In major cities the world over, it is now possible to enjoy authentic Thai, Vietnamese, Indonesian, Malayan and even Filipino food, and it is only a matter of time before lesser-known cuisines are equally well represented.

Home cooks are eager to experiment with this quick, healthy and sensual style of cooking too. Ingredients such as lemongrass and galangal, which could once be bought only in oriental markets are now readily available in many supermarkets. There's never been a better time to discover or extend your repertoire of Asian recipes, and this book is the very best place to start.

of the supplementary dishes on offer, relishing it on its own before taking another portion of rice and a second choice. Soup is served at the same time as other dishes, and is enjoyed throughout the meal.

Harmony extends to presentation, too, an art which reaches its apogee in Japan, where food is valued as much for its aesthetic appearance as for its flavor. In Thailand, too, food is

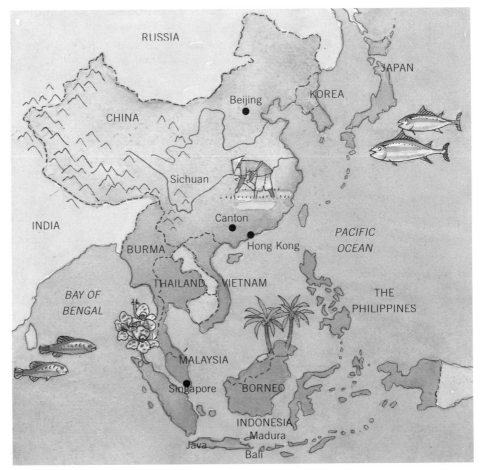

EQUIPMENT AND UTENSILS

The equipment in the average Western kitchen will be perfectly adequate for most of the recipes in this book, particularly now that the wok has become an indispensable item in many households. There are some items, however, that will make cooking Asian food easier and more pleasurable. The fact that many of these simple pieces of equipment also look good, and instantly establish you as an adventurous cook in the eyes of your friends is a bonus.

The best way to build up your store of special items is to start slowly, with a few basics such as a cleaver, bamboo steamer and wok, then gradually add extra pieces as you experiment with the exciting and different styles of cooking that are explored within these pages. If you enjoy making sushi, for instance, you will need a mat for rolling, and molds for shaping the rice; if Thai curries are your current favorite, you'll be glad of a rough mortar and a pestle for grinding wet spice mixtures.

Visit an Asian or Chinese store and you'll be amazed at the array of items on sale at very reasonable prices. The design of many utensils has not changed in centuries, and items made from basic materials are often more effective than modern equivalents.

Cleaver

To Western cooks, a cleaver can seem rather intimidating. In reality, cleavers are among the most useful pieces of equipment ever invented. The blade of a heavy cleaver is powerful enough to cut through bone, yet delicate enough in the hands of a master chef to create paper thin slices of raw fish for sushi. The flat of the broad blade is ideal for crushing garlic or ginger, and the same blade can be used to convey the crushed items to the wok or pan.

Cleavers come in several sizes and weights. Number one is the heaviest. The blade is about 9 inches long and 4 inches wide. It can weigh as much as 2¼ pounds and resembles a chopper more than a knife. At the other end of the scale, number three has a shorter, narrower blade and is only half as heavy as the larger cleaver. It is mainly used for slicing, rather than chopping. Number two is the cook's favourite. This medium-weight cleaver is used for both slicing and chopping. The Chinese name translates

Above: A medium-weight cleaver is a multi-purpose tool.

as "civil and military knife" because the lighter, front half of the blade is used for slicing, shredding, fileting and scoring (civil work), while the heavier rear half is used for chopping with force (military work). The back of the blade is used for pounding and tenderizing, and the flat for crushing and transporting. Even the handle has more than one purpose— the end can be used as a pestle.

Cleavers are made of several types of material. They can be made of carbonized steel with wooden handles, or of stainless steel with metal or wooden handles. Choose the one you are comfortable with. Hold it in your hand and feel the weight; it should be neither too heavy nor too light. One point to remember is that while a stainless steel cleaver may look good, it will require frequent sharpening if it is to stay razor-sharp. To prevent a carbonized steel blade from rusting and getting stained, wipe it dry after every use, then give it a thin coating of vegetable oil. Cleavers should always be sharpened on a fine-grained whetstone, never with a steel sharpener. The cleaver is user-friendly. It is not as

dangerous as it looks, provided you handle it with care. Learn to regard it as just another kitchen knife, and you will be rewarded with a lot of fun and very satisfactory results.

Chopping block

The traditional chopping block in the East is simply a cross-section of a tree trunk, usually hardwood. The ideal size for use in a domestic kitchen is about 12 inches in diameter and about 2 inches thick, but you will see much larger blocks being used in restaurants.

Season a new block with a liberal dose of vegetable oil on both sides to prevent it from splitting. Let it absorb as much oil as it will take, then clean the block with salt and water and dry it thoroughly. After each use, scrape the surface with the back of your cleaver, then wipe it down with a cloth. Never immerse a wooden block in water.

A large rectangular cutting board of hardwood can be used instead, but make sure it is at least 2 inches thick or it may not be able to take a hard blow from a cleaver. Acrylic boards can obviously be used if preferred, but they will not have the same aesthetic appeal as a traditional wooden one.

Left: A traditional Asian grater made of wood.

Above: The rough surface of a stone mortar and pestle helps grip the ingredients that are being pounded.

Grater

Traditional graters, used for preparing ginger, galangal and daikon (mooli), are made from wood or bamboo, but a metal cheese grater makes a satisfactory substitute.

Mortar and pestle

Oriental cooks prefer granite or stone mortars and pestles, since these have rough surfaces that help to grip the ingredients that are being chopped or pounded. Bigger, flat-bowled mortars are good for making spice pastes that contain large amounts of fresh spices, onion, herbs and garlic.

Spice mill

If you are going to grind a lot of spices, a spice mill will prove useful. An electric coffee grinder works very well for this

Right: A double-handled wok is useful for all types of cooking; those with a single handle are particularly good for stir-frying.

purpose, but it is a good idea to reserve it for spices, unless you like to have your coffee flavored with cardamom or cloves.

Wok

It is not surprising that the wok has become a universal favorite, for it is a remarkably versatile utensil. The rounded bottom was originally designed to fit snugly on a traditional Chinese brazier or stove. It conducts and retains heat evenly and, because of its shape, the food always returns to the center where the heat is most intense. This makes it ideally suited for stir-frying, braising, steaming, boiling and even for deep-frying.

Although the wok might not at first glance appear to be the best utensil for deep-frying, it is actually ideal, requiring far less oil than a flat-bottomed deep-fryer. It has more depth and a greater frying surface, so more food can be cooked more quickly. It is also much safer than a saucepan. As a wok has a larger capacity at the top than at the base, there is plenty of room to accommodate the oil, even when extra ingredients are added, and it is not likely to overflow and catch fire.

There are two basic types of wok available in the West. The most common type, the double-handled wok, is suitable for all types of cooking. The single-handled wok is particularly suitable for quick stir-frying, as it can easily be shaken during cooking. Both types are available with flattened bases for use on electric cookers or gas cookers with burners that would not accommodate a round base.

The best woks are made from lightweight carbonized steel. Cast iron woks are too heavy for all but the strongest cooks to handle, and woks made from other materials, such as stainless steel or aluminium, are not as good for Asian cooking. They also tend to be a great deal more expensive than the standard carbonized steel wok.

A new carbonized steel wok must be seasoned before use. The best way to do this is to place the wok over high heat until the surface blackens, then wash it in warm, soapy water. Use a stiff brush to get the wok clean, then rinse it well in clean water and place it over medium heat to dry completely. Finally, wipe the surface with a pad of paper towels soaked in vegetable oil. After each use, wash the wok under the hot water tap, but never use detergent as this would remove the "seasoning" and cause the wok to rust. Any food that sticks to the wok should be scraped off with a stiff brush or with a non-metal scourer, and the wok should then be rinsed and dried over a low heat. Before being put away, a little oil should be rubbed in to the surface of the wok.

Below: A perforated metal scoop and a wire skimmer.

Steamers

The traditional Chinese steamer is made from bamboo and has a tight-fitting lid. Several sizes are available, and you can stack as many tiers as you like over a wok of boiling water. The modern steamer is free-standing and made of aluminium, but the food cooked in a metal steamer lacks the subtle fragrance that a bamboo steamer imparts. If you do not have a steamer, you can improvise with a wok and a trivet. Having placed the trivet in the wok, fill it one-third full of water

Above: Essential wok tools include a dome-shaped lid, wooden or bamboo chopsticks, and a long-handled spatula and a ladle.

Wok tools

Some wok sets come with a spatula and ladle made from cast iron or stainless steel. These are very useful, particularly the ladle. It addition to its obvious purpose as a stirrer, it can be used to measure small quantities of liquid. A standard ladle holds about ¾ cup. A dome-shaped lid is also useful, as is a metal draining rack that fits over the wok. Small items such as deep fried foods can be placed on the rack to keep warm while successive batches are cooked. Other accessories include wooden or bamboo chopsticks. Short ones can be used at the table or in the kitchen—they are ideal for beating eggs —and the long pair are used for deep frying, as stirrers or tongs. Finally, a wok stand is handy for protecting your table when serving.

Strainers

Several types of strainer are available, but the two most useful are the perforated metal scoop or slotted spoon, and the coarse-mesh, wire skimmer, preferably with a long bamboo handle. Wire skimmers can retain strong flavors; do not use them with liquids based on fish or fish sauce.

Below: Bamboo steamers come in several sizes.

Above: An authentic clay pot can be used in the oven or, with care, on top of the stove.

and bring this to a boil. Place the food in a heatproof bowl on the trivet, cover the wok with the dome-shaped lid and steam the food until it is cooked.

Clay pot

Also known as the sand-pot or Chinese casserole, this earthenware cooking utensil must have preceded the cast iron pot by thousands of years. Several shapes and sizes are available, and most are glazed on the inside only. They are not expensive and can be bought in

Below: A large saucepan with a tight-fitting lid is ideal for cooking rice.

Asian or Chinese markets. With care, the pots can be used on top of the stove, where they retain an even heat. They are, however, fairly fragile, and are prone to crack easily.

Rice cooker

Electric rice cookers work extremely well and are worth investing in if you cook a lot of rice. However, a good-sized, deep, heavy-based saucepan with a tight-fitting lid is just as suitable for this purpose.

Mongolian fire pot

Also known as a Chinese hot pot or steamboat (in Singapore), this is not unlike a fondue pot, in that it allows food to be cooked at the table. The design is different from that of a fondue, however, as it consists of a central funnel, which is filled with burning charcoal, surrounded by a moat in which hot stock is placed. The pot is placed in the center of the table and guests cook small pieces of meat and vegetables in the hot stock. Once these are all cooked and eaten, the stock is served as a soup. There are several different models available, the most expensive being made of brass, while the cheaper ones are made of aluminium or stainless steel.

Japanese omelet pan

To make the rolled omelets that are so widely used in Japanese cooking, a rectangular omelet pan or *makiyaki-nabe* is useful, but not essential: a large non-stick, heavy-based skillet or a flat, heavy griddle could be used instead.

Below: A Mongolian fire pot or steamboat is used for cooking at the table. The central funnel is filled with burning charcoal, and this heats the stock in the surrounding moat.

Sushi equipment

If you are going to make sushi properly, you will need a few simple pieces of equipment. A *makisu*, also known as a *sushimaki sudare*, is essential. This is the bamboo mat (shown below), which is about the size of a table mat, that is used for rolling sheets of nori (seaweed) around vinegared rice and other fillings when making *norimaki*.

Sushi chefs spread the rice on the nori with their fingers, but this is a sticky business and can prove tricky for the uninitiated. A rice paddle or *shamoji* makes the job easier. For pressed sushi, shaped molds made from wood or plastic are very useful.

INGREDIENTS

This visual catalogue includes essential information on every type of Asian food, from the daily staples, such as rice and noodles, to unusual fruit and vegetables and exotic fish, and includes preparation, cooking and storing instructions.

RICE

CHINESE: *MI;* THAI: *KHAO*

Rice is the staple grain of the whole of Asia, which is well over half the world's population. It is true that wheat is also grown in northern China and India, but its consumption is rather small in comparison with rice.

Throughout Asia, the importance of rice is underlined by the fact that in Chinese and other Asian languages, there is no single word for rice, but many. The crop, grain, raw rice and cooked rice are all referred to by different terms, and the Chinese character *fan* for cooked rice has acquired a much wider meaning in colloquial speech; it is also synonymous with nourishment and good health. When friends meet, instead of asking "How do you do?" they will often greet each other with the words: "Have you eaten rice?" An affirmative answer indicates that all is well.

Another common Chinese word with more than one meaning is *fan-wan* (rice-bowl). Aside from the obvious, this also means a job or livelihood; so the expression "to lose one's rice bowl" or "to have one's rice bowl broken", suggests that one has been given the sack; similarly, someone described as having an "iron rice-bowl" has probably got a job for life. Paradoxically, the expression *fan-tong,* which means a rice bucket (something that holds a large amount of cooked rice) has become a derogatory expression to describe a person who lacks refinement (a big eater of plain rice).

Rice has been cultivated in southern Asia for over five thousand years. There are more than forty thousand different strains grown in China alone. Since rice requires a wet and warm climate for its cultivation, some 90 per cent of the world production of rice is grown (and consumed) in the monsoon regions of Asia. A small amount of rice is cultivated on dry land in northern China, but because of the cold climate, only one crop can be grown each year, whereas two crops per annum is the norm in the temperate south.

Below: Patna rice is one of the many types of long grain rice.

Above: Thai fragrant rice has a delicate, fragrant scent.

Freshly harvested rice has a special aroma, and is eagerly sought after in China and Japan, the rice from the autumn harvest (usually in November) being reckoned to taste the best.

TYPES OF RICE

Broadly speaking, rice can be classified as being either *Oryza sativa indica* or *Oryza sativa japonica.* Varieties of both types are cultivated in Asia. Long grained indica *(xian)* rices—of which there are many strains—are the most common. Long grain white rice has had its husk, bran and germ removed, taking most of the nutrients with them and leaving a bland-flavored rice that is light and fluffy when cooked. Long grain brown rice has had only its outer husk removed, leaving the bran and germ intact, which gives it a chewy, nutty flavor. It takes longer to cook than white rice but contains more fiber, vitamins and minerals.

Patna rice gets its name from Patna in India. At one time, most of the long grain rice sold in Europe came from Patna, and the term was used loosely to mean any long grain rice. The custom persists in parts of America, but elsewhere Patna is used to describe a variety of long grain rice from the Bihar region of India.

Basmati rice is a slender long grain rice that is grown in northern India, in the Punjab, in parts of Pakistan and in the foothills of the Himalayas. After harvesting it is aged for a year, which gives it a characteristic flavor and a light, fluffy texture. The grains are long and slender, and become even longer during cooking. Widely used in Indian cooking, basmati rice has a cooling effect on hot and spicy curries.

Thai fragrant rice has a delicate but distinctive scent of jasmine, and is particularly highly prized.

Short-grained japonica *(geng)* rices are less fragrant, but tend to taste slightly sweeter than indicas. This type of rice is cultivated in northern China, Japan, Korea and surrounding areas. The rices' are higher in amylopectin than long grains, and are therefore more starchy. The grains cling together when cooked, which makes them ideal for sushi and similar Japanese dishes.

Glutinous rice — also known as sweet or waxy rice—is even more sticky than Japanese short grain rice. This endears it to South-east Asian cooks, as the cooked rice can be shaped or rolled, and is very easy to pick up with chopsticks. White glutinous rice, with its fat, opaque grains, is the most common type, but there is also a black glutinous rice, which retains the husk and has a nutty flavor. A pinkish-red glutinous rice is cultivated on the banks of the Yangtze River, and a purple black variety has recently been developed. Glutinous rice has a high sugar content, and is used in Japan for making *senbei* (rice crackers) and *mochi* (rice cakes), as well as sweet rice wine.

Above: Basmati rice is considered by many people to be the prince of rice. There are various grades of basmati, but it is impossible to differentiate between them except by trying various brands to discover the best fragrance and taste.

Right: Short-grained japonica rice is ideal for sushi because, when cooked, the grains stick together.

Culinary uses

It is impossible to think of Asian food without rice. Rice is served in one form or another at every meal, including breakfast. Although wheat—in the form of dumplings or noodles—is eaten more often than rice in some parts of Asia, such as northern China, Asians everywhere regard rice as their staple food, with wheaten foods as mere supplements. In some languages the phrase for eating rice is the same as that for eating food.

The most common way of serving rice throughout Asia is simply boiled or steamed; fried rice does not normally form part of an everyday meal, but is either served as a snack on its own, or reserved for a special occasion such as a banquet. Unlike the India pilau, the Italian risotto or the Spanish paella, Asian fried rice dishes are never based upon raw rice, but always use ready cooked rice (either boiled or steamed). For the finest results, the rice should be cold and firm, rather than soft.

The universal breakfast in all Asian countries is a creamy, moist rice dish, which is known as congee or rice pudding. Considered to be highly nutritious, it is often given to babies and people with digestive problems as well as the elderly. Coconut milk is used instead of water in many South-east Asian countries, but because it usually takes over an hour to make a smooth, creamy congee, many Japanese cooks (and some Chinese) cheat by simply adding hot water to cold cooked rice.

Below: Black and white glutinous rice

others, and the amount of liquid required varies, too. The general rule is to use double the amount of water by volume to dry rice. However, if the rice has been washed or soaked first, less water will be needed otherwise, when cooked, the rice will be soft and sticky, instead of firm and fluffy.

Asian cooks often add a teaspoon of vegetable oil to the water to prevent the rice from sticking to the bottom of the pan. Whether to add salt or not is a matter of choice. It is usually added when cooking regular long grain rice, but not for Thai fragrant rice. The width, depth and material of the pan used will also make a difference to the result. One of the best ways of cooking perfect boiled rice is in an electric rice-cooker, while some cooks get very good results in the microwave.

Storage

Raw rice should not be kept for too long, or the grains will lose their fragrance. Keep the rice in an airtight container in a dry, cool place, away from strong light, and use it within 3–4 months of purchasing.

Preparation and cooking techniques

There can never be a definitive recipe for cooking plain rice, because each type requires individual treatment.

Some benefit from being rinsed in cold water first, while others should be soaked before use. Some types of rice need to be cooked for longer than

---

Plain boiled rice

Use long grain Patna or basmati rice; or better still, try Thai fragrant rice. Allow a generous ¼ cup raw rice per person.

1 Put the dry rice in a colander and rinse it under cold running water.

2 Tip into a large pan, then pour in enough cold water to come ¾ inch above the surface of rice. (In Asia the traditional way of measuring this is with the help of the index finger. When the tip of the finger is touching the surface of the rice, the water level should just reach the first joint.)

3 Add a pinch of salt, and, if you like, about 1 teaspoon vegetable oil, stir once and bring to a boil.

4 Stir once more, reduce the heat to the lowest possible setting and cover the pan with a tight-fitting lid.

5 Cook for 12–15 minutes, then turn off the heat and leave the rice to stand, tightly covered, for about 10 minutes. Fluff up the rice with a fork before serving.

FLOURS

The most popular thickening agents in Asian cooking are cornstarch, tapioca flour and potato flour. Mung bean flour, water chestnut flour, lotus root and arrowroot are favored for clear sauces. Chick-pea flour is used to make batters. Rice flour is used as a thickener, and for rice papers, dumplings and cakes.

Cornstarch

This fine white powder, made from corn (maize) is a useful thickening agent for sauces, soups and casseroles.

Rice flour

More finely milled than ground rice, this is also known as rice powder. The texture is similar to that of ornstarch. Rice flour is used for thickening sauces, and to make rice papers and the dough for dumplings. It is often used to make sticky Asian cakes and sweets, but because rice flour does not contain gluten, the cakes made with it are rather flat. Rice flour can be combined with wheat flour to make bread, but this produces a crumbly loaf.

Chick-pea flour

This very fine flour is also called gram flour, or besan. Mainly used in India, where it originated, it also plays a role in Malayan cooking, thanks to Indian immigrants who introduced it.

Wheat flour

This is ground from the whole grain and may be whole wheat or white. Hard, or bread wheat flour is high in gluten, which makes it ideal for adding to rice flour to make bread.

Soy flour

This is a finely-ground, high-protein flour made from the soybean. It is used as a thickener in a wide range of sauces and soups, and is often mixed with other flours such as wheat flour to make bread and pastries. It adds a pleasant nutty flavor.

Left: Japanese rice flour

Far left: Japanese wheat flour

Below: Chick-pea flour

Left: Thai rice flour

Right: Cornstarch

Left: Japanese soy flour

NOODLES

MANDARIN: *MIAN (TIAO)*; CANTONESE: *MEIN*;
THAI: *GUEYTEOW*

Whether Marco Polo actually introduced noodles from China to Italy is a debatable point, but we do know that noodles made from wheat flour appeared in China as early as the first century BC, around the time of the Roman Empire. Noodles rapidly became a popular food, not only in China, but throughout the whole of Asia.

Up to the end of the last century, when modern machinery was first imported from Europe, noodles were always made by hand, and even today, certain types of noodle are still hand-made, most notably, the "hand-pulled" or "drawn" noodles made by chefs in northern China. It takes more than ten years to master the technique, so is beyond the reach of ordinary mortals.

Noodles form an important part of the daily diet in the Far East, ranking second only to rice as a staple food. Unlike rice and steamed buns, however, which are usually served plain to be eaten with cooked dishes, noodles are

Left: Four types of Japanese Udon noodles

usually cooked with other ingredients. For this reason, noodle dishes are seldom served as accompaniments, but are eaten on their own as light meals or snacks. In Vietnam, rice noodle soup is the standard breakfast. In Japan there are restaurants that specialize in noodle dishes such as noodles served solo with dipping sauces; bowls of steaming noodle soup; and noodles cooked with slivered vegetables and seaweed.

Below: Bundles of thin, white, Japanese Somen noodles

Below: Plain Chinese (top) and Thai noodles (bottom)

Thailand has its noodle stalls, noodle boats and even noodle meals on wheels available from vendors with ingenious mobile shops mounted on their bicycles. In Asia, you need never be far from a noodle seller.

WHEAT NOODLES

Asian noodles are made from a variety of flour pastes, including wheat, rice, mung bean, buckwheat, seaweed, corn and even devil's tongue, which is a plant related to the arum lily. Some noodles are plain, others are enriched with egg. Dried wheat noodles, with or without eggs, are often called "longevity noodles" because of their association with long life.

Right: Fresh egg noodles

Plain noodles
Made from white bread flour and water, these can be flat or round and come in various thicknesses. In Japan, they are known as **Udon** and are available fresh, pre-cooked or dried. **Somen** are thin, delicate, white Japanese noodles. They are sold in bundles, held in place by a paper band.

Egg noodles These are far more common than plain wheat noodles. In China they come in various thicknesses and are sold fresh or dried. **Ramen** are the Japanese equivalent and are usually sold in coils or blocks. Very fine egg noodles, which resemble vermicelli, are called **Yi noodles** in China, after the family that originally made them. They are popular in Hakka-style cooking.

Shrimp noodles These seasoned egg noodles are flavored with fresh shrimp and/or shrimp roe. They are usually sold dried, in coils of various widths.

Instant noodles Packages of pre-cooked egg noodles are a familiar sight in the West. They come in various flavorings, such as chicken, prawn and beef.

Preparation and cooking techniques

Noodles are very easy to prepare. Some types benefit from being soaked before being cooked, so see individual recipes for advice, read the instructions on the package or seek advice from someone in the store where you bought them. Both dried and fresh noodles have to be cooked in boiling water before use. How long for depends on the type of noodle, the thickness of the strips, and whether (as is usual) the noodles will be cooked again in a soup or sauce. Dried noodles generally require about 3 minutes' cooking, while fresh ones will often be ready in less than a minute, and may need to be rinsed under cold water to prevent them from overcooking. After the initial cooking, noodles are then usually prepared and served in one of the following ways:

Noodles in soup
Most popular in China, Korea, Japan, Vietnam, Burma and Singapore, this usually consists of noodles served in bowls of clear broth with cooked meat, poultry, seafood and/or vegetables, sometimes with a sharp sauce on the side.

Braised noodles *(lao mein)* The difference between this and noodles in soup is that braised noodles are first cooked in a broth, then served with a thickened sauce.

Fried noodles
(chow mein) This has to be one of the most popular Chinese dishes in the West (and in South-east Asia, but not so much in north China or Japan). The two basic types of fried noodles are dry-fried (crisp) or soft-fried. Generally speaking, only the fine vermicelli-type of noodles are used for dry-frying; the thicker round or flat noodles are more suitable for soft-frying.

Left: Blocks of dried Japanese Ramen noodles

Above: Instant noodles come in a variety of flavorings.

RICE NOODLES

CHINESE: *MIFEN*; VIETNAMESE: *LAI FAN*

Wheat noodles must have preceded rice noodles by several centuries, since there were no written records of their existence until well into the Han Dynasty in the third century AD. Not surprisingly, rice noodles are very popular in southern China and South-east Asia where not much wheat is grown.

Unlike most other noodles, which are made from flour of one type or another, rice noodles are made from whole grains of rice, which are soaked and then ground with water into a paste. This paste is drained through a strainer to form a dough, which is divided into two. One half is cooked in boiling water

Below: Thin and thick Chinese rice noodles or sticks

Above: Fine Thai rice noodles are sometimes referred to as vermicelli.

for 15 minutes, before it is kneaded with the raw half to make a firm dough. The dough is then put through a press, which cuts it into various shapes and sizes. The finished strands are blanched in water, drained and rinsed before being sold as fresh noodles, or dried in the sun before packaging.

Types of rice noodles

Although they are known by different names, the rice noodles sold in southern China, Thailand and Vietnam are all similar. Like wheat noodles, they come in various widths, from the very thin strands known as rice vermicelli or *lai fan* (*sen mee* in Thailand) to rice sticks, which start at around $\frac{1}{16}$ inch and can be as wide as $\frac{1}{2}$ inch, as in the case of *ho fun*, a special variety from south China reputedly made with river water rather than tap water. In Thailand it is possible to buy a rice noodle enriched with egg. Called *ba mee,* it is sold in nests. A wide range of dried rice noodles is available in Asian or Chinese markets, and fresh ones can occasionally be found in the chiller cabinets.

Preparation and cooking techniques

Because all rice noodles are pre-cooked, they need only be soaked in hot water for a few minutes to soften them before use. If they are soaked for too long, they will go soggy and lose the texture that is part of their appeal.

Below: Japanese rice noodles

Preparing rice noodles

Rice noodles need only to be soaked in hot water for a few minutes to soften them.

Add the noodles to a large bowl of water that has been recently boiled and leave for 5–10 minutes, or until softened, stirring occasionally to separate the strands as they soften.

Left: Cellophane noodles

MUNG BEAN (CELLOPHANE) NOODLES

CHINESE: *FENSI;* VIETNAMESE: *BUN;*
JAPANESE: *HARUSAME*

Also known as transparent noodles, bean thread vermicelli or glass noodles, these very fine, rather brittle strands are made from green mung beans, which are the same beans as those used for sprouting. Although very thin, the strands are firm and resilient, and they stay that way when cooked, never becoming soggy, which doubtless contributes to their popularity.

Preparing cellophane noodles
Cellophane noodles are never served on their own, but always used as an ingredient in a dish. Soak them in hot or warm water for 10–15 minutes to soften them.

When they are soft, use a pair of scissors or a sharp knife to chop the noodles into shorter strands for easier handling.

Cellophane noodles are almost tasteless unless cooked with other strongly flavored foods and seasonings, but they have a fantastic texture. They are not served solo, but are always used as an ingredient in a dish, most notably in vegetarian cooking and in hot pots, as well as in Vietnamese spring rolls. They are only available dried. In Japan, cellophane noodles are called *harusame,* which means "spring rain".

BUCKWHEAT NOODLES

JAPANESE: *SOBA*

The best-known buckwheat noodles are the Japanese soba, which are usually sold dried in bundles of fine strands. Soba are much darker in color than wheat noodles. There is also a dark green variety called cha-soba (tea soba), which is made of buckwheat and green tea. Korean cooks use buckwheat noodles, too, preferring a very thin variety.

Unusual noodles

Shirataki This popular Japanese noodle (*above left*) is made from a starch derived from the tubers of the devil's tongue plant, which is related to the arum lily.
Bijon Made from corn, these noodles (*above right*) are produced in South-east Asia.
Canton These Chinese wheat noodes are sometimes enriched with eggs (*above top*).

Storage

Packages of fresh noodles normally carry a use-by date, and must, of course, be stored in the refrigerator. Dried noodles will keep for many months if kept sealed in the original package, or in airtight containers in a cool, dry place, but again, the packages have an expiry date.

Below: Soba noodles

PANCAKES AND WRAPPERS

PANCAKES

CHINESE: *BING*

The pancakes of Asia are quite different from their counterparts in the West. For a start, they are almost always made from plain dough, rather than a batter, and they are more often than not served with savory fillings rather than sweet.

There are two types of pancakes in China, either thin or thick. Thin pancakes *(bobing)* are also known as mandarin or duck pancakes, because they are used as wrappers for serving the famous Peking duck. They are also served with other savory dishes, most notably, the very popular *mu-shu* or *moo-soo* pork, which consists of scrambled egg with pork and wood ears

(dried black fungus). Making pancakes demands considerable dexterity, so many cooks prefer to buy them frozen from the Chinese supermarket.

Thick pancakes are made with lard and flavored with savory ingredients such as scallions and rock salt. In northern China, they are eaten as a snack, or as part of a main meal, rather like the Indian paratha. Both thin and thick pancakes are sometimes served as a dessert, with a filling of sweetened bean paste.

NONYA SPRING ROLL PANCAKES

These are the exception to the rule that most pancakes in the East are made from dough. Typical of the Singaporean style of cooking known as Nonya, they

are made from an egg, flour and cornstarch batter and are traditionally served with a wide selection of fillings.

Reheating Chinese pancakes

1 Stack the pancakes, interleaving them with squares of non-stick baking paper.

2 Carefully wrap the stacked pancakes in foil, folding over the sides of the foil so that the pancakes are completely sealed.

3 Put the foil parcel in a steamer and cover. Place the steamer on a trivet in a wok of simmering water. Steam for 3–5 minutes until the pancakes are hot.

Above: Thick pancakes are eaten as a savory snack, or filled with sweet bean paste and served as a dessert.

Below: Thin pancakes are used as wrappers, notably for Peking duck, or served with savory dishes.

SPRING ROLL WRAPPERS

MANDARIN: *CHUNJUAN PI*; CANTONESE: *SHUEN GUEN PIE*

Spring rolls are called egg rolls in the US, and pancake rolls in many other parts of the world. They must be one of the most popular Chinese snacks everywhere, including China itself. While the fillings may vary from region to region, or even between different restaurants and fast food stalls, the wrappers are always more or less the same. They are made from a simple flour and water dough, except in Vietnam, where they are made from rice flour, water and salt.

There are three different sizes of ready-made spring roll wrappers available from the freezers of Asian markets: small, medium and large. They are all wafer-thin. The smallest wrappers, which are about 4½ inches square, are used for making dainty, cocktail-style rolls. The standard-size wrappers measure 8½–9 inches square, and usually come in packages of 20 sheets. The largest, 12-inch square, are too big for general use, so they are usually cut in half or into strips for making samosas and similar snacks.

Above: Small and medium-size spring roll wrappers. Any unused wrappers can be returned to the freezer.

Preparing spring rolls

Use medium-size spring roll wrappers, which you will find in the freezer cabinet in Asian or Chinese markets. They should be thawed before use. For the filling, use ingredients such as bean sprouts, bamboo shoots, water chestnuts and dried mushrooms, with chopped shrimp or finely ground pork. When you have prepared the rolls, deep-fry them a few at a time in hot oil for 2–3 minutes, or until crisp.

2 Spoon the spring roll filling diagonally across the wrapper.

4 Brush the edges of the wrapper with a little cornstarch paste.

1 Carefully peel off the top spring roll wrapper and place on a board.

3 Fold over the nearest corner of the wrapper to cover the filling.

5 Fold the edges towards the middle, then roll up in to a neat parcel.

WONTON SKINS

MANDARIN: *HUNTUN PI*;
CANTONESE: *WANTON PIE*

Wonton skins or wrappers are made from a flour and egg dough, which is rolled out to a smooth, flat thin sheet, as when making egg noodles. The sheet is usually cut into small squares, although round wonton wrappers are also available. Ready-made wonton skins are stacked in piles of 25 or 50, wrapped and sold fresh or frozen in Asian or Chinese markets.

Unlike spring roll wrappers, which have to be carefully peeled off sheet by sheet before use, fresh wonton skins are dusted with flour before being packed, This keeps each one separate from the others and so they are very easy to use. Frozen wrappers must, however, be thawed thoroughly before use, or they will tend to stick together. Any unused skins can be re-frozen, but should be carefully wrapped in foil so that they do not dry out in the freezer.

There are several ways of using wonton skins. They can be deep-fried and served with a dip, filled and boiled, steamed or deep-fried, or simply poached in a clear broth. On most Chinese restaurant menus in the West, this last option is listed under soups, which is misleading, as in China and South-east Asia, wonton soup is always served solo as a snack, never as a separate soup course as part of a meal.

Above: Large spring roll wrappers can be cut into strips for making samosas.

Below: Wonton skins can be square or round and come in a variety of sizes.

Preparing Wontons

Place the filling in the center of the wonton skin and dampen the edges. Press the edges of the wonton skin together to create a little purse shape, sealing the filling completely.

RICE PAPERS

VIETNAMESE: *BANH TRANG*

The rice paper used in Vietnamese (and Thai) cooking is quite different from the rice paper that is used for writing and painting in China and Japan, nor does it bear any resemblance to the sheets of rice paper cooks use as pan liners when baking macaroons. Made from rice flour, water and salt, it is a round, tissue-thin "crepe", dried on bamboo mats in the sun, which results in the familiar crosshatch pattern being embedded on each sheet.

Rice paper is used for wrapping Vietnamese spring rolls and small pieces of meat and fish to be eaten in the hand. The sheets are rather dry and brittle, so must be softened by soaking in warm water for a few seconds before use. Alternatively, they can be placed on damp dish towels and brushed with water until they are sufficiently pliable to be used. Spring rolls are usually deep-fried, but this is not always the case. Vietnamese cooks also make a fresh version. Cooked pork, shrimp, bean sprouts and vermicelli are wrapped in rice paper, which has been dipped in cold water until it is pliable and transparent. The filling can clearly be seen through the wrappers, and the rolls look very pretty.

Storage

Packaged and sold in 6-inch, 10-inch and 12-inch rounds, rice papers will keep for months in a cool, dry place, provided the packages are tightly sealed. When buying, look for sheets that are of an even thickness, with a clear, whitish color. Broken pieces are a sign of bad handling, and are quite useless for wrapping, so avoid any packages that look as if they have been knocked about.

Below: Rice papers are dried on bamboo mats, which give them their familiar cross-hatch pattern.

DUMPLINGS

MANDARIN: *JIAO ZI/BAO ZI*; CANTONESE: *DIM SUM*

Dumplings are very popular in China, and there is a wide variety of different shapes and sizes, with fillings ranging from pork and vegetables to mushrooms and bamboo shoots. Some enclose the filling in a very thin dough skin *(jiao zi)* while others use a dough made from a glutinous rice flour. There are also steamed buns *(bao zi)* filled with meat or a sweet bean paste.

The best way to experience the diversity and delicious flavors of dumplings is to indulge in dim sum, that wonderful procession of tasty morsels that the Cantonese have elevated to an art form. Although dumplings originated in northern China, it was in Canton that the practice developed of enjoying these snacks with tea at breakfast or lunch time.

Dim sum literally means "dot on the heart" and indicates a snack or refreshment, not a full blown meal. Although the range of dishes available on a dim sum menu now embraces other specialties (spring rolls, wontons and spareribs, for instance), dumplings remain the essential items.

Below: Broiled dumplings or "pot stickers" and chili sauce.

What is more, unlike the majority of dim sum, which are so complicated to make that they can only be prepared by a highly skilled chef, dumplings are comparatively simple to make at home. Both *jiao zi* and *bao zi* are available ready-made from Asian or Chinese markets—the former are sold uncooked and frozen, and the latter are ready-cooked and sold chilled.

Preparation and cooking techniques

Frozen *jiao zi* dumplings should be cooked straight from the freezer. There are three different ways of cooking and serving them.

Poaching

The most common way of cooking dumplings in China is to poach them in boiling water for 4–5 minutes—longer if cooking from frozen.

The dumplings are added to boiling water. When the water boils again, a cupful of cold water is added to the pan and the water is brought to a boil again. This is repeated twice more, by which time the dumplings will be ready. They are traditionally served hot with a vinegar and soy sauce dip, chili sauce or chili oil.

Cooking Dumplings

1 To poach dumplings, drop them into boiling water. When the water boils again, add a cupful of cold water. Repeat twice more, cooking the dumplings for 4–5 minutes.

2 To steam dumplings, place them on a bed of lettuce or spinach leaves on the base of a bamboo steamer, cover with the lid and cook for 8–10 minutes.

3 To "broil" dumplings, fry in a shallow skillet until they are brown, then add a little water, cover with a bamboo steamer lid, and cook until the water has completely evaporated.

Above: Plain steamed buns and sweet buns filled with bean paste.

Steaming

The best way to do this is by using a bamboo basket as a steamer. The dumplings are placed on a bed of lettuce or spinach leaves on the rack of the steamer, which is then covered. The dumplings are served hot with a dip.

Broiling

This description is a bit misleading, because the dumplings are not broiled in the conventional sense but are cooked in a flat skillet. The dumplings are fried, then a small amount of boiling water is added to the pan and they are steamed under cover until all the liquid has evaporated. When cooked by this method, the dumplings are crispy on the base, soft on top and juicy inside. The popular name is "pot-stickers".

PEKING DUMPLINGS

These crescent-shaped dumplings are filled with ground pork, greens and scallions and seasoned with salt, sugar, soy sauce, rice wine and sesame oil. In northern China they are eaten for breakfast on New Year's Day, but are available all year round, and are often served as snacks or as part of a meal.

STEAMED BUNS

Steamed buns are to Asia what baked bread is to the West, and *bao* (filled buns) are the Chinese fast food equivalent of hot dogs, hamburgers and sandwiches. There are two main types of steamed buns, either plain or filled. The plain, unfilled buns made from leavened dough are treated in much the same way as plain boiled rice and are intended to be eaten with cooked food. Then there are filled buns *(bao zi)*. The name literally means "wraps" and these can be savory or sweet. The sweet ones usually contain either a lotus seed paste or a sweet bean paste filling and are usually eaten cold. Savory *bao zi* come with a wide range of fillings, the most common being pork, and a very popular type is filled with Cantonese *char siu* (honey-roasted pork). Available ready-made, they are best eaten hot.

Also available ready-made, but uncooked, are what are known as Shanghai dumplings. These are little round dumplings, much smaller than *char siu bao*, and each consisting of ground pork wrapped in a thin skin of unleavened dough.

Shrimp chips

Also called prawn crackers, these are made from fresh shrimp, starch, salt and sugar. They are very popular as cocktail snacks, and some restaurants serve them while you wait for your order to arrive. The raw chips are grey in color. The small Chinese ones are not much bigger than a thumbnail, while those used in Indonesia are much larger, about 6 inches long and 2 inches wide. Indonesian shrimp chips are more difficult to find in the West. Once deep-fried, both types puff up to four or five times the original size, and become almost snow white. Ready-cooked chips are also available. They are sold in sealed packages, but do not keep well once exposed to the air, so should be eaten as soon as possible after opening.

VEGETABLES

CHINESE LEAVES

MANDARIN: *DA BAICAI; HUANG YA BAI;*
CANTONESE: *SHAO CHOI; WONG NGA BAK*

There are almost as many names for this member of the brassica family as there are ways of cooking it. In the West, it is generally called Chinese leaves, but it is also sometimes known as Chinese cabbage, Napa cabbage or celery cabbage. The alternative Chinese name translates as "yellow-sprouting-white", a description of the crinkled leaves, and the Cantonese call it Peking or Tianjin cabbage in honor of its northern origin.

It is a cool season vegetable, most abundant from November through to April, but available all year round. There are three common varieties which all look similar, but differ in length, width and tightness of leaf.

Aroma and flavor

Chinese leaves have a delicate sweet aroma with a mild cabbage flavor that disappears completely when the vegetable is cooked. The white stalk has a crunchy texture, and it remains succulent even after long cooking.

Culinary uses

This is a very versatile vegetable and it can be used in stir-fries, stews, soups or salads. It will absorb the flavors of any other ingredients with which it is cooked—be they fish or shellfish, poultry, meat or vegetables—and yet retain its own characteristic flavor and texture. In Asian or Chinese restaurants, braised Chinese leaves are often served as a flavorsome base for roasted meats or duck.

Preparation and cooking techniques

Discard the outer layer of leaves and trim off the root, then slice off as much you need. Should you wish to wash the leaves (and this is not strictly necessary unless you are using them in a salad), do so before cutting them, otherwise you will wash away much of the vitamins. If you stir-fry Chinese leaves in hot oil, the stems often develop dark scorch marks. Restaurant chefs blanch the vegetable in boiling stock, which enhances the flavor, before frying.

Storage

Chinese leaves can be stored for a long time without losing their resilience. Keep them in the salad compartment of the refrigerator and they will stay fresh for 10–12 days. Don't worry if there are tiny black specks on the leaves as this is normal and will not do any harm.

Left: Chinese leaves have a crunchy texture and a delicate aroma. The mild cabbage flavor disappears when the vegetable is cooked.

Preparing Chinese leaves

1 Discard any damaged outer leaves and trim off the root.

2 It is not usually necessary to wash the leaves, simply cut the head of Chinese leaves crossways into thin shreds.

3 You may prefer to wash the leaves, before using in a salad, for instance. Separate the leaves, then wash under cold running water. Shake off any excess water before shredding.

Right: Dark green bok choy tastes similar to spinach. The white stems can be cooked and eaten separately.

BOK CHOY/PAK-CHOI

MANDARIN: *XIAO BAICAI;*
CANTONESE: *BOK CHOI*

Another member of the brassica family, bok choy goes by lots of different names. In the West it is sometimes known as *pak-choi,* horse's ear (from the shape of the leaves) or Chinese celery cabbage. It is also called Chinese white cabbage, which is a bit of a misnomer, as the glossy leaves that are a distinctive feature of this vegetable are dark green. The stems, however, are pale, and range from light green to ivory white. Bok choy is a perennial, and several varieties are available throughout the year.

Aroma and flavor

Although bok choy is less delicate and does not taste as sweet as Chinese leaves, it has a distinctive flavor, which is a sort of cross between a mild cabbage and spinach.

Culinary uses

Bok choy and Chinese leaves are interchangeable in most dishes, even though their color and flavor are different. Bok choy can be used in soups and stir-fries, and is delicious when quickly braised, but should not be subjected to prolonged stewing.

Preparation and cooking techniques

Bok choy is prepared in much the same way as Chinese leaves, except that the stems are as important (some would say more important) than the leaves. It is a good idea to separate leaves and stems for cooking, as the latter take slightly longer. Baby bok choy can be cooked whole or in halves or quarters. Only when very young and tender can bok choy be eaten raw.

Storage

Bok choy is completely different from Chinese leaves when it comes to storage. Try to use it as soon as you buy it, because the leaves will start to wilt, and the outer leaves will turn yellow, after 2–3 days, much sooner than lettuce and spinach.

Below: Bright green choi sum is easy to prepare.

CHOI SUM

MANDARIN: *YOU CAIXIN;*
CANTONESE: *CHOI SUM*

Choi sum is a Cantonese word, meaning "cabbage heart". A member of the brassica family, it is related to oilseed rape. It has bright green leaves and thin, pale green stems that are slightly grooved. The bright yellow flowers at the center are responsible for its common name of Chinese flowering cabbage.

Aroma and flavor

Choi sum has a pleasant aroma with a mild taste, and remains crisp and tender if correctly cooked.

Culinary uses

A very popular green vegetable, choi sum can be used for soups or stir-fries, either solo or with other ingredients.

Preparation and cooking techniques

Little preparation is required, just wash and shake off excess water before cutting the leaves to the required size. Most restaurant chefs leave the stems whole, simply blanching them in stock for a minute or two before draining them and serving with oyster sauce.

Preparing choi sum

Choi sum is easy to prepare. You can chop leaves and stems into large pieces before cooking, but they are more often left whole.

Wash choi sum under cold running water, then shake off the excess water and separate the stems before use.

Storage

Choi sum can be kept in the salad compartment of a refrigerator for 3–4 days if bought fresh, but should ideally be used as quickly as possible.

Right: Every part of Chinese broccoli is edible.

MUSTARD GREENS

MANDARIN: *GAICAI;* CANTONESE: *GAI CHOI*

Although this vegetable is related to choi sum it looks and tastes completely different. In shape, it resembles a romaine lettuce. Unlike many oriental vegetables, which were relatively unknown outside their country of origin until recently, mustard greens have long been cultivated in Europe. However, the dark green, slightly puckered leaves were always thrown away; only the seeds were prized. It took the Chinese to introduce people in the West to their delicious flavor. Mustard greens are most abundant during the winter and spring, especially from Asian markets, but also from farmer's markets.

Aroma and flavor

Although mustard greens look a bit like lettuces, there the resemblance ends. The leaves have a robust, often fiery flavor. They can taste quite bitter.

Culinary uses

Very young leaves can be eaten raw in salads; mature leaves are best stir-fried or simmered in soups. In China, most of the crop is salted and preserved.

Preparation and cooking techniques

Before being stir-fried, mustard greens benefit from being blanched in lightly salted boiling water or stock; this preserves the green color of the leaves and also gets rid of some of the bitter taste.

Storage

Provided that they are fresh when you buy them, mustard greens will keep for a few days if stored in the salad compartment of a refrigerator.

CHINESE BROCCOLI

CHINESE: *GAILAN*

Chinese broccoli has more in common with purple sprouting broccoli than the plump, tight heads of Calabrese broccoli familiar to Western shoppers. The Chinese version has long, slender stems, loose leaves and can be recognized by the tiny white or yellow flowers in the center.

Aroma and flavor

As its Chinese name *gailan* (mustard orchid) implies, Chinese broccoli belongs to the same family as mustard greens, but is more robust, both in terms of texture and of taste. There is a definite cabbage flavor.

Culinary uses

Every part of this beautiful vegetable is edible—the flower, leaves and stalk —and each has its own individual flavor and texture. Chinese broccoli is often served on its own as a side dish, but it can also be combined with other ingredients that have contrasting colors, flavors and textures.

Preparation and cooking techniques

Discard the tough outer leaves, then peel off any tough skin from the stems. Leave each stalk whole if it is to be served on its own, or cut into two to three short sections if it is to be cooked with other ingredients. Before stir-frying it is usual to blanch the vegetable briefly in salted boiling water or in stock, which will enhance the flavor.

Storage

Chinese broccoli will keep for only 2–3 days even if it is very fresh when bought; after that the leaves will start to wilt and go yellow, and the stems are liable to become tough.

EGGPLANT

MANDARIN: *QIEZI*; CANTONESE: *NGAI GWA*

There are numerous varieties of this wonderfully versatile vegetable, which is technically a fruit. Although it belongs to the same family as peppers and tomatoes, which originated in America, the eggplant is actually native to tropical Asia, where it has been cultivated for more than 2,000 years.

The most common type in Asia—the Asian or Japanese eggplant—is tubular rather than ovoid in shape and is usually straight or slightly curved. As a rule, Asian eggplant tend to be much smaller and more slender than western varieties, and some are tiny. In

Below: Purple and green eggplant from Thailand

Right: Thai baby eggplant

Thailand, there are eggplant that are not much bigger than peas. Eggplant comes in a wide range of colors, from black through purple, orange and green to the white egg-shaped vegetables that inspired the vegetable's American name of eggplant.

Aroma and flavor

Whatever its shape, size or color, the eggplant has a unique flavor that is almost impossible to describe. Some object to its smoky, subtly bitter taste, others prize it for the same reason.

Culinary uses

Eggplant absorbs the flavors of other ingredients like a sponge, and therefore benefits from being cooked with strongly flavored foods and seasonings. It can be stir-fried, deep-fried, stuffed and baked, braised, steamed, or served cold, but seldom eaten raw except in Thailand, where strips of very young eggplant are served like crudités, with spicy dips.

Preparation and cooking techniques

Wash and remove the stalk, then cut into slices, strips or chunks. It is seldom necessary to peel an eggplant, and the smooth skin not only adds a beautiful color, but also provides the dish with an interesting texture and flavor.

Some recipes advise layering eggplant slices with salt before cooking. This is not essential if the vegetables are young and tender, but in older specimens this is done to reduce bitterness and to prevent the slices from absorbing excessive amounts of oil during cooking. If you do salt an eggplant, be sure to rinse and dry it thoroughly afterwards.

Another method that stops the eggplant from drawing up too much oil, but which has the advantage of retaining the succulent texture, is to dry-fry the strips or slices over a medium heat for 4–5 minutes before cooking them in hot oil.

Storage

Eggplants from various parts of the world are available all year round. Select small- to medium-size firm eggplant with a uniformly smooth skin that is free from blemishes. Large specimens with a shrivelled skin are overmature and are likely to be bitter and rather tough.

When bought in prime condition, eggplant will keep for 3–4 days in the salad compartment of the refrigerator.

CHAYOTE

CANTONESE: *FAT SAU GWA*

There are several names for this pear-shaped marrow, vegetable pear being one, and patty pan squash being another. In the Caribbean they know it as christophine, but in other parts of the world it is *choko, shu-shu* or *chinchayote.* The Chinese call it "Buddha's fist", because it resembles hands clasped in prayer, with the fingers folded inside.

Aroma and flavor

Chayote has a smooth, pale green skin with a subtle aroma. The taste is delicate, and the texture is fairly firm, not unlike that of zucchini.

Culinary uses

Because of the religious connotations of its shape, chayote is often used as an offering during Buddhist festivals. It can be eaten raw or cooked, and in Asia is usually stir-fried or simmered in soups.

Preparation and cooking techniques

Wash but do not peel the vegetable, cut it open and remove the stone from the center, then cut into thin slices or strips. Since chayote has a mild taste, Asian cooks often cook it with strong seasonings such as garlic, ginger, onion and/or chiles.

Above: Chayote can be eaten raw, stir-fried or cooked in soups.

Storage

Chayote is a quite good keeper. If it is hard and smooth, it will stay fresh for up to a week if stored in the salad compartment of the refrigerator.

MOOLI/DAIKON

MANDARIN: *LUOBO;* CANTONESE: *LOH BAK;* VIETNAMESE: *LOBAC;* MALAY: *LAPHUG*

This large, thin cylindrical vegetable looks rather like a carrot, but with a smooth, white skin. A member of the radish family, it is sometimes known as the oriental radish.

Left: Raw mooli has a delicious, crisp and crunchy texture.

Believed to be a native of China, the mooli is now widely cultivated in many parts of the world.

Aroma and flavor

Mooli has an unmistakable, pungent smell of radish. The texture is crisp and crunchy and it tastes quite mild, with a juicy, sweet flavor similar to turnip.

Culinary uses

Mooli can be eaten raw or cooked. Both the Chinese and the Japanese also pickle it. Cantonese cooks use it to make a stiff pudding with rice flour, which is often served as part of the dim sum selection in a restaurant. At home, mooli is usually braised with meat such as pork or beef, but it is also delicious in a stir-fry. Add it for the last few minutes of cooking so that the slices stay crisp and juicy.

Preparation and cooking techniques

Like carrots, mooli should be scraped or peeled, then cut into slices or chunks before cooking. The beauty of this vegetable is that it withstands long cooking without disintegrating, and absorbs the flavors of other ingredients, but also tastes good raw.

Storage

Buy mooli with firm, unblemished skin. Stored in a cool, dark place or in the salad compartment of the refrigerator, it should keep for 3–4 days.

BITTER MELON

MANDARIN: *KUGUA;* CANTONESE: *FOO GWA*

Also called "bitter gourd", this warty-skinned vegetable originated in South-east Asia, and is popular in Indonesia, the Philippines and Thailand, where it is used as the basis for a delicious curry. The plant resembles a wild grape vine, and is grown in the West mainly as an ornament, for its attractive foliage and strange-looking fruit.

Aroma and flavor

As the name implies, the flesh of this vegetable tastes quite bitter, especially when it is green and immature, but it has a rather sweet and fragrant smell. The flavor mellows somewhat as the vegetable ripens and turns first pale green and then yellow orange (when it is past its prime).

Culinary uses

Bitterness may be an acquired taste, but it has a cooling effect in a hot climate, and is highly regarded in Asia. The flesh readily absorbs other flavors and its bitter tang can provide a wonderful accent in a dish.

Preparation and cooking

Since the odd-looking skin is a special feature of this vegetable, it is never peeled. Just wash it, slice it in half lengthwise, remove and discard the seeds, then cut into slices or chunks. Blanch these in lightly salted boiling water for about 2 minutes to remove excess bitterness, then drain before stir-frying or adding to soups.

Right: In China and Thailand winter melon is made into a soup and served in the shell.

Storage

Firm, green bitter melon will keep for 3–4 days (and should be allowed to ripen a little before use), but a soft yellowish one should be used within a day or two.

WINTER MELON

CHINESE: *DONG GUA*

This is one of the largest vegetables grown in Asia, or anywhere else. They can grow to 10 inches in diameter, and weigh more than 55 pounds. Thankfully for the cook, there are small ones, and the larger melons are normally sliced and sold in sections.

Above: Despite its name, bitter melon has a sweet smell.

Aroma and flavor

Winter melon has a subtle, delicate smell. It tastes rather like zucchini.

Culinary uses

Despite its name, winter melon is really a warm season vegetable, and since more than 90 per cent of it is water, it is popular in hot weather as it is juicy yet not too filling. It is always cooked before being eaten.

Preparation and cooking

Winter melon is prepared in much the same way as pumpkin. The rind must be cut off and the seeds and coarse fibers at the center scooped out before the flesh is cut into thin strips or wedges. It tastes good in stir-fries or soups. Winter melon readily absorbs other flavors, and is often cooked with strongly-flavored ingredients such as dried shrimp, ham and dried mushrooms.

Storage

A whole winter melon will keep for days if not weeks, but if it has been sliced open, it should be eaten as soon as possible as the exposed surface will deteriorate rapidly.

ONIONS

MANDARIN: *YANG CONG;* CANTONESE: *YUN TS'UNG*

The common onion so widely used in the West is known as "foreign onion" in Asia, where shallots and scallions are generally preferred. They come in a wide variety of sizes and colors from huge golden-skinned globes to smaller, milder red and white onions.

Aroma and flavor

There is no mistaking the strong aroma and flavor of the onion. It is used as a flavoring ingredient throughout Asia, but is seldom served on its own as a side vegetable.

Culinary uses

The onion is a very versatile vegetable. It can be eaten fried, boiled, steamed or raw, and it is an essential component of a great number of sauces and dishes, such as curries and stews. Fried onions are a popular garnish, especially in South-east Asia.

Preparation and cooking techniques

Peel the onions and remove the papery skin, then slice and chop as required. A good tip for avoiding irritation to the eyes when cutting an onion is to leave the root in place until the last minute, and, when the root is exposed, to press it down on the surface of the chopping board rather than expose it to the air.

Storage

If you buy firm onions with smooth, unmarked skins, and store them in a cool, dry place, they will keep for several weeks. If any show signs of sprouting, use them immediately.

SHALLOTS

MANDARIN: *FEN CONG;* CANTONESE: *TS'UNG TAU;* THAI: *HOM DAENG*

Although they belong to the same family as garlic, leeks, chives and onions— and look suspiciously like baby onions —shallots are very much their own vegetable. Sometimes called bunching onions, they have bulbs that multiply to produce clusters joined at the root end.

Aroma and flavor

Shallots tend to be sweeter and much milder than large onions. Some Thai varieties are sweet enough to be used in desserts.

Above: Small red onions

Culinary uses

Indispensable in South-east Asian kitchens, shallots are far more popular than both regular onions and scallions for everyday use. Ground with garlic, ginger and other aromatics, shallots form the standard marinade and are also an essential ingredient in curry pastes and satay sauce. Dried shallots *(hanh huong)* are a popular alternative in Vietnam.

Preparation and cooking techniques

Top and tail the shallots, peel off the skin, then prize the bulbs apart. Leave these whole for braising, or chop as required. Thinly-sliced shallot rings are sometimes dry-fried until crisp, then used as a garnish.

Storage

Shallots will keep for several months in a cool, dry place.

SCALLIONS

MANDARIN: *QING CONG;* CANTONESE: *TS'UNG;* JAPANESE: *NEGI*

Also known as green onions or spring onions in the West, this vegetable has been cultivated in China and Japan since time immemorial. The leaves are tubular, and are always sold with the small white onion bulb attached. Japanese scallions are larger than the Western variety and have blue-green stems.

Above: Small and large onions

Left: scallions

Aroma and flavor

Scallions have a more subtle smell than onions and the taste can vary from fairly mild to really pungent. Smaller bulbs generally have a milder flavor.

How to make scallion curls

1 Trim off most of the green leaves from the scallion bulbs to leave a 3-inch length.

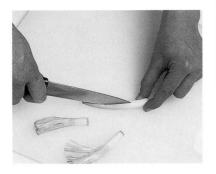

2 Finely shred the scallions using a sharp knife to within about ½ inch of the root end.

3 Place the shredded scallions in a bowl of iced water and chill for 15–20 minutes or until the shredded ends have curled.

Culinary uses

In Asia, scallions are served as a vegetable as well as being used as a flavoring agent. The vegetable forms a yin-yang pair when used in combination with ginger. Scallions are yin, and ginger is yang.

Preparation and cooking techniques

Trim off the roots from the bulbs and discard any wilted outer leaves, then separate the green and white parts, and cut these into short lengths or shreds. Recipes sometimes stipulate that only the white parts are used. If scallion green is used in a recipe, it is usually added at the last moment (the white part takes longer to cook) or is simply used raw, as a garnish.

Storage

It is best not to keep scallions in a plastic bag, but instead to store them loose in the salad drawer of the refrigerator to allow them to "breathe". They should stay fresh for up to 4–5 days if bought in prime condition.

CHINESE CHIVES

MANDARIN: *JIUCAI*; CANTONESE: *GAU CHOI*

Although they belong to the same family, Chinese chives are quite different from the Western variety, both in their appearance and taste. Two species are available: one has long, flat green leaves like a small, thin leek, the other has long, tubular stems with a single bud at the tip.

Aroma and flavor

Chinese chives have a much stronger aroma

Right: Chinese chives

than the ones grown in the West. They don't really taste of onions, but have a flavor that resembles a cross between garlic and leek.

Culinary uses

Chinese chives are seldom used as a garnish, but are either served as a vegetable in their own right, or used as an ingredient in cooked dishes, especially with seafood or meat. A very popular Chinese vegetarian dish features chopped chives cooked with scrambled eggs and beancurd. This is not only colorful, but tastes delicious.

Preparation and cooking techniques

Chinese chives are always sold as leaves only, without the bulb. Uniformly dark green leaves are good, and any that are turning yellow should be discarded. Wash well, drain, then chop or slice into short sections. Cantonese cooks often blanch chives in boiling water or stock for a minute or two before stir-frying.

Storage

Fresh chives stored in an airtight box in the refrigerator should keep for about 4–5 days.

POTATOES AND SWEET POTATOES

MANDARIN: *PENSHU;* CANTONESE: *FAN SHUE*

Although potatoes and sweet potatoes are unrelated, this was not appreciated when they first reached Asia, and they were both given the same Chinese name. In northern China white potatoes are a staple food, although not as important as noodles; in southern China they are far less significant. Sweet potatoes are popular in the Philippines.

Aroma and flavor

Several varieties of both regular potatoes and sweet potatoes are grown in the East, so tubers vary in size, shape and color, as well as in taste and texture. The sweet potatoes have a red skin and flesh that varies from pale white to yellow-orange in color.

Culinary uses

Where potatoes are used, they generally form part of a braised dish, or are served as a side dish or snack. Potato flour is a popular thickener.

Preparation and cooking techniques

Both regular potatoes and sweet potatoes are prepared in the same way: after peeling, they are sliced or diced, then stir-fried or braised with seasonings or spices. Thai cooks make a very sweet dessert based on deep-fried sweet potatoes.

Above: Potatoes and sweet potatoes

Storage

Potatoes should always be stored in a cool, dark, dry place. Because of their high sugar content, sweet potatoes do not keep well.

TAROES

MANDARIN: *YUTOU;* CANTONESE: *WOO TAU*

These tubers grow in tropical areas and are widely used throughout South-east Asia. There are two basic varieties: the big, barrel-shaped one with the hairy brown skin is the most common, but there is also a smaller variety which is known in the West as eddo or dasheen. The flesh is white, with purple flecks.

Aroma and flavor

Cooked taro has a subtle flavor that has been described as resembling floury water chestnuts.

Culinary uses

Taroes can be substituted for potatoes in most dishes. They take up a great deal of liquid, so are good in stews. Asian cooks often include taro when cooking belly pork or duck as it absorbs the excess fat.

Above: A barrel-shaped taro

Preparation and cooking techniques

It is essential to cook taroes as there are toxins just below the skin. These are eliminated when the vegetable is boiled. Peel the vegetables thickly, wearing gloves, or cook them in their jackets.

Storage

Store in a cool, dark, dry place. Taroes have a thick skin, so they keep well.

YAMS

MANDARIN: *SHANYAO;* CANTONESE: *SA GOT*

Yams are believed to have originated in China, but are now grown in all tropical regions. The Chinese yam has fine whiskers and the flesh is creamy white.

Aroma and flavor

Yams do not have a pronounced flavor, but are mildly sweet and quite juicy.

Culinary uses

Like taroes, yams can be used instead of potatoes. Asian cooks often use them as a substitute for bamboo shoots.

Preparation and cooking techniques

Peel yams thickly, removing both the outer skin and the layer underneath. Like taroes, they contain a toxin that is eliminated when boiled. Slice or dice the flesh and put into salted water.

Storage

As for taroes.

LOTUS ROOT

MANDARIN: *LIAN OU;* CANTONESE: *LEEN NGAU*

Lotus root, also known as *renkon,* is used throughout Asia and is particularly popular in China and Japan. Raw lotus root looks like a string of fat sausages covered in black mud. Clean, peel and slice it, however, and a beautiful pattern emerges in each cross-section, the result of narrow channels that run through the root. Fresh lotus roots can sometimes be purchased from Asian markets. Canned lotus root is readily available, and dried slices are popular for serving in soups.

Aroma and flavor

The root has very little aroma, but the flavor is mild and subtly sweet. It has a wonderful crunchy texture.

Culinary uses

Apart from the root being used as a vegetable, the seeds of the lotus are eaten as a delicate fruit when fresh, or used as a dessert in dried form. They can also be puréed and blended with sugar to make a filling for cakes and buns. Dried lotus leaves are used for wrapping food in a number of famous Asian dishes.

Preparation and cooking techniques

Fresh lotus roots must be scrubbed. Chop them into sections, discarding the tough "necks" between, then peel off the outer skin. The sliced flesh is usually

Above: Lotus root and seeds

sliced or cut into large chunks, but whole roots can also be stuffed. Japanese cooks often soak the slices in water acidulated with rice vinegar for 5 minutes before boiling them. They cook quickly and make a pretty garnish. Dried lotus roots are sold sliced, and should be soaked in water for 1–2 hours before using in soups or stews. Canned lotus roots are ready for use.

Storage

Fresh lotus roots should keep for about 4 days if bought in good condition. Select firm and unblemished roots. If the surface is punctured, dirt will have penetrated inside, which makes the roots difficult to clean. Dried roots will keep almost indefinitely if stored in a dry, cool place.

DRIED LILY BUDS

MANDARIN: *HUANG HUA; JINZHEN*
CANTONESE: *GUM JUM*

Also known in Chinese as "yellow flower" or "golden needles", these dried buds of the tiger lily are popular throughout China and South-east Asia.

Aroma and flavor

Tiger lily has a unique fragrance, which intensifies when the buds are dried. They have a mild sweet taste and a pleasant crunchy texture.

Culinary uses

In Chinese cooking, dried lily buds are often combined with dried black fungus to create an interesting contrast in color, flavor and texture. The buds are also a popular ingredient in Buddhist vegetarian cooking.

Preparation and cooking techniques

Dried lily buds must be soaked in warm water for 30 minutes or so, then drained and rinsed in cold water until clean. Once the hard ends have been snipped off, the buds can be used whole, or cut in half.

Storage

Dried lily buds keep almost indefinitely if stored in an airtight jar, away from strong light, heat or moisture.

Below: Lily buds are never used fresh, but always dried.

BAMBOO SHOOTS

MANDARIN: *ZHUSUN*; CANTONESE: *CHUK SUN*;
JAPANESE: *TAKENOKO*

Bamboo is one of the most important plants of eastern Asia, and several species are grown, of varying sizes. The shoots used as a vegetable are dug just before they come above ground. Fresh bamboo shoots are difficult to come by outside Asia, but canned shoots are readily available. Vietnamese cooks are fond of pickled bamboo shoots.

Aroma and flavor

The aroma of bamboo shoots is quite delicate. Lovers of this vegetable—and they are legion—claim that the mild sweet flavor changes subtly with the seasons. Therefore winter bamboo shoots are more highly prized.

Culinary uses

In China, where bamboo shoots have been eaten for well over a thousand years, they are regarded as the queen of all vegetables. The shoots not only taste delicious of themselves, but also complement the flavors of other ingredients with which they are cooked.

Above: Chunks of raw bamboo shoot and canned slices

Preparation and cooking techniques

If you are lucky enough to locate fresh bamboo shoots, it is vital to parboil them before cooking, as they contain an acid that is highly toxic. Remove the base and the hard outer leaves, then cut the core into large chunks. Boil these in salted water for 20–30 minutes, then drain, rinse in clean water and drain again. Cut into slices, shreds or cubes for further cooking. Canned bamboo shoots are ready cooked, so they just need to be rinsed and drained before using them. Dried bamboo shoots have been dried in the sun, so they are tastier than

Right: Mung bean (in bowl) and soy-bean sprouts

the canned ones, but need more preparation. They must be soaked in water for 2–3 hours before use.

Storage

Fresh shoots will keep for up to a week in winter, but only 2–3 days in summer. Unused shoots from a can will keep in the refrigerator for several days if stored in a jar of fresh water that is changed daily. Dried shoots will keep almost indefinitely in a cool, dry place.

BEAN SPROUTS

MANDARIN: *DOUYA*;
CANTONESE: *DAU NGA CHOI*

Several types of bean can be sprouted, but the ones most often used in Asian cooking are the small "green" sprouts from mung beans and the larger "yellow" or soybean sprouts. The fresh sprouts are widely available in supermarkets, health food shops and markets, or you can sprout the beans at home. Avoid canned bean sprouts, which are limp and tasteless.

Aroma and flavor

soybean sprouts have a stronger flavor than mung bean sprouts, but both are relatively delicate, with a pleasant crunchy texture.

Culinary uses

Stir-frying, with or without meat, is the most popular way of cooking bean sprouts. Mung bean sprouts can be eaten raw in salads, while soybean sprouts are often used in soups.

Preparation and cooking techniques

Wash the bean sprouts in cold water to remove the husks and tiny roots. Some restaurants actually top and tail each individual shoot, which turns this humble vegetable into a luxury dish. Since the sprouts are largely composed of water, overcooking will render them limp and fibrous, and the characteristic crisp texture will be lost.

Storage

To preserve their lily-white translucence, keep bean sprouts in water in a covered box in the refrigerator. They will stay fresh for 2–3 days.

WATER CHESTNUTS

MANDARIN: *BIQI;* CANTONESE: *MA TAI*

Water chestnuts are popular throughout Asia, cropping up in Chinese, Japanese, Korean and South-east Asian recipes. The name is slightly misleading as they do grow in water (and are actually cultivated in paddy fields) but they certainly aren't nuts. Instead, they are corms, which are about the size of walnuts. There are several varieties, but the Chinese type, which are dark brown and look a bit like small daffodil bulbs, are the most widely available outside Asia. They have a soft skin which, because they grow in water, tends to be covered in dried dirt. Fresh water chestnuts are superior to canned.

Aroma and flavor

The best thing about water chestnuts is their texture. The snow-white flesh is crunchy and juicy, and stays that way,

no matter how long they are cooked for. This, coupled with their pleasantly sweet taste, makes them irresistible.

Culinary uses

Water chestnuts can be eaten raw in both savory and fruit salads. In many Asian countries they are eaten as a snack food, in much the same way as peanuts are eaten in the West. Cooked water chestnuts taste wonderful in stir-fries or braised dishes. The flesh is also made into a flour, which is used both as a thickening agent and in cakes.

Preparation and cooking techniques

Fresh water chestnuts are not very appealing, especially as they are usually covered in dried mud, but once they are washed and peeled, they do not look very different from the canned variety. Water chestnuts can be left whole, sliced or diced, and are sometimes ground up with fish or meat.

Storage

Fresh, unpeeled water chestnuts will keep well if stored in a paper bag in the refrigerator. Once peeled, however, fresh water chestnuts must be kept in water in a covered container in the refrigerator and should be used within a week.

Horned water chestnuts

This nut is often confused with the vegetable of the same name, but they look entirely different. Horned water chestnuts (*ling gok*), which have been eaten in China for hundreds of years, have a hard, shiny black shell with two distinctive, sharp horns. The nuts measure about 2 inches from tip to tip, and the shells, which are extremely difficult to crack, enclose ivory colored flesh that is starchy and sweet tasting. The nuts are never eaten raw, but can be steamed or boiled and served like a vegetable, added to soups or braised in stews.

Horned water chestnuts can be bought in Asian markets and will keep fresh for several weeks in the refrigerator. However, once shelled the flesh, which should be white and unblemished, needs to be used within a day or two as it quickly becomes rancid.

Below: Canned water chestnuts (in bowl) and fresh water chestnut corms, which look a little like small daffodil bulbs.

SNOW PEAS

MANDARIN: *XUEDOU*; CANTONESE: *HOH LAN DAU*

Also known as mangetouts, these must be one of the best known and best loved of all oriental vegetables, yet its Cantonese name, meaning Dutch bean, suggests that at some point in its long history it was perceived as being of Western origin. The French name—*mangetout*—means "eat all" and is an apt description, for the vegetable is valued for its pods, not the peas, which never mature. Sugar snap peas are similar, but have slightly plumper pods.

Aroma and flavor

Freshly picked snow peas have a fresh aroma, but this vanishes quite quickly. The flavor is slightly sweet. The best way to appreciate these delicate, tender pods is to stir-fry them, when they will prove perfect partners for shrimp, scallops and other shellfish.

Preparation and cooking techniques

Snow peas need very little by way of preparation. Simply wash, then top and tail the pods. It should not be necessary to string them if the pods are young and tender. Leave whole if small; snap in half if large. Stir-fry on their own, or with other vegetables such as carrots, scallions and baby corn cobs, in hot oil over high heat for a short time, and do not use too much seasoning.

Storage

Young, crisp and unblemished snow peas with thin skins will keep fresh for up to 4–5 days in the salad compartment of the refrigerator.

SNAKE BEANS/GREEN BEANS

MANDARIN: *DOUJIAO* CANTONESE: *DAU GOK*

Also called yard-long beans, asparagus beans or Thai beans, these resemble green beans but are much longer and even thinner. There are two varieties: a pale green type,

Above: Snake beans are also known as yard-long beans.

and a darker green one that is considered to be better. Thinner beans with underdeveloped seeds are best.

Aroma and flavor

These exceptionally long beans smell and taste rather like their smaller cousins, but the flavor is not identical. When young they are slightly sweeter and more tender, but the mature beans can be tough, and may need slightly longer cooking than green beans.

Culinary uses

Snake beans are usually stir-fried, either on their own or with other ingredients, or blanched and served cold as a salad. They are also delicious blanched and tossed in sesame oil.

Preparation and cooking techniques

Having washed the beans, cut them into 2-inch lengths. They go particularly well with shredded pork, chicken or shrimp, and should only be lightly seasoned. In Sichuan, they are used for a dish called *kan shao* (dry-frying), with strongly flavored seasonings such as garlic, ginger or chiles.

Storage

Try to use snake beans within about 3 days of purchase before they turn yellow and become stringy.

Right: Snow peas (top) and sugar snap peas

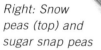

LUFFA

MANDARIN: *SIGUA;*
CANTONESE: *SZE GWA*

Also known as angled luffa, silk gourd, silk squash or Chinese okra, this vegetable looks like a long, skinny zucchini or a very large okra pod. The most common variety is ridged down its length and is dark green in color. Although not so common, smooth luffa is larger and the shape is more cylindrical, with a slightly thicker base. It is much heavier than ridged luffa, and is lighter in color.

Aroma and flavor

Luffa has a mild, delicate taste, very similar to that of cucumber and the two are interchangeable in most cooked dishes.

Culinary uses

Used mostly in stir-fries and soups, luffa goes well with foods that will not overwhelm its delicate flavor, such as chicken breast, fish and seafood. It is also a popular ingredient in all kinds of vegetable dishes.

Preparation and cooking techniques

If the luffa is young, all you need to do is wash and slice it. Luffas seldom need peeling, but sometimes the ridges toughen as the vegetable ripens, in which case remove the ridges but leave

Above: A whole luffa and slices

the skin between, so that the luffa is striped green and white. If the skin is very tough, it is best to peel it completely. Like cucumber, luffa should not be overcooked, but unlike cucumber, it is never eaten raw.

Above: Crunchy-textured baby corn makes a colorful addition to stir-fries.

Storage

Keep fresh luffa in the vegetable compartment of the refrigerator, but do not store it for too long as within two or three days of purchase it will start to go limp.

BABY CORN

MANDARIN: *YUMI SUN;*
CANTONESE: *YOOK MY SON*

Baby corn is available both fresh and canned. The canned ones can be quite large, and are not as tender and delicate as the smaller, fresh corn.

Aroma and flavor

Baby corn has a lovely sweet fragrance and flavor, as well as an irresistible crunchy texture.

Culinary uses

The baby cobs can be used in salads, stir-fries and soups. In stir-fries, they add color as well as flavor, and are good combined with carrots, peppers, broccoli and snow peas.

Preparation and cooking techniques

Wash the cobs. Large ones can be halved lengthwise or sliced in thick diagonal chunks, but small ones are best left whole. Asian cooks blanch them in lightly salted water for 1 minute before stir-frying. Drain and rinse canned baby corn before use. Do not overcook them.

Storage

Fresh baby corn will keep for up to a week in the salad compartment of the refrigerator, but they are best eaten soon after purchase.

FRESH AND DRIED MUSHROOMS

SHIITAKE

MANDARIN: *XIANG GU*; CANTONESE: *HUNG GWO*; JAPANESE: *SHIITAKE*

Fresh shiitake mushrooms used to be a rarity in the West, but are now cultivated and are freely available in supermarkets. They resemble large, brown button mushrooms in appearance, but are actually a type of fungus that grows on hardwood logs in their native Japan. Shiitake mushrooms are frequently dried (see Dried Black Mushrooms, overleaf) and are also available in cans.

Aroma and flavor

These meaty mushrooms taste slightly acidic, and have a decidedly slippery texture. They contain twice as much protein as button mushrooms. When shiitake are dried the flavor intensifies.

Culinary uses

Although small mushrooms can be eaten raw, cooking brings out their flavor. They are used in soups, stir-fries and braised dishes. They are a popular ingredient in vegetarian dishes, and go well with noodles and rice. They are good combined with less strongly flavored food.

Below: Fresh and dried shiitake mushrooms

Preparation and cooking techniques

The stems of fresh shiitake mushrooms are usually removed before cooking. Whole or sliced caps can be sautéed, used in stir-fries, cooked in braised dishes or added to soups. Because of their robust texture, shiitake need a slightly longer cooking time than button mushrooms, but they should not be cooked for too long or they may begin to toughen. To serve shiitake mushrooms in a salad, boil

Left: Oyster mushrooms

them briefly in water or stock, then cool them slightly and toss in a French dressing before serving.

Storage

Store fresh shiitake mushrooms in a paper bag in the refrigerator. Eat within three days of purchase.

OYSTER MUSHROOMS

MANDARIN: *BAOYU GU*; CANTONESE: *HOWYOO GWO*; JAPANESE: *SHIMEJI*

In the wild, oyster mushrooms grow in clumps on rotting wood. The caps, gills and stems are all the same color, which can be pearl grey, pink or yellow. Once thought of exclusively as wild mushrooms, they are now grown commercially and are widely available in Western supermarkets.

Aroma and flavor

The flavor is fairly mild, with a slight suggestion of seafood.

Culinary uses

Oyster mushrooms are popular in soups and stir-fries, and they are also used in noodle and rice dishes.

Preparation and cooking techniques

Oyster mushrooms seldom need trimming. Large ones should be torn, rather than cut into pieces. The soft texture becomes rubbery if they are overcooked, so always add them to cooked dishes at the last moment.

Storage

Buy mushrooms that smell and look fresh, avoiding any with damp, slimy patches and those that have discolored. Store in a paper bag in the refrigerator, and use as soon as possible after purchase. They do not keep well for more than 2–3 days.

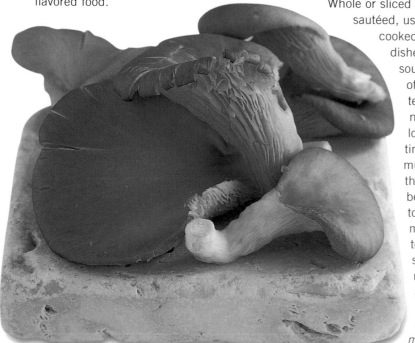

ENOKI MUSHROOMS

MANDARIN: *JINZHEN GU;* CANTONESE: *GUM JUM GWO;* JAPANESE: *ENO ITAKE*

Also called *enokitaki,* these are slender and exceedingly delicate mushrooms with long thin stems and tiny white caps. The Chinese name—"golden needle mushrooms"—is the same as that given to the dried tiger lily buds which they resemble. Fresh enoki mushrooms are popular in both China and Japan. Avoid canned ones.

Aroma and flavor

Enoki mushrooms have a delicate sweet and almost fruity flavor, and a deliciously crisp texture.

Culinary uses

The delicate flavor of enoki mushrooms is best appreciated if they are added raw to salads or lightly cooked and used as a garnish for soups or hot dishes.

Preparation and cooking techniques

The mushrooms are harvested in clumps, attached to a spongy root base which is cut off before use. The mushrooms are then ready for use.

Below: Sliced straw mushrooms, showing their attractive "umbrella" pattern.

Above: Enoki mushrooms have pretty, tiny caps on elegant long stems.

Enoki mushrooms rapidly toughen if overcooked, so are usually added to soups or braised dishes shortly before serving. They are good in stir-fried dishes, too, but should not be cooked for longer than 1 minute.

Storage

If bought fresh, enoki mushrooms will keep for 4–5 days in the salad compartment of a refrigerator. Avoid any that have damp, slimy patches and those that have discolored.

STRAW MUSHROOMS

MANDARIN: *CAOGU;* CANTONESE: *TSO GWO*

These small, grey-brown mushrooms are grown on beds of rice straw, hence the name. A native of China, they were introduced to South-east Asia by Chinese immigrants.

Aroma and flavor

Fresh straw mushrooms are not readily available in the West, but dried ones can sometimes be found in Chinese markets. Straw mushrooms have an even stronger aroma than Chinese dried black mushrooms. Canned straw mushrooms are widely available in Asian markets; they have a delicate, silky surface with a subtle, sweet taste and an unusual slippery texture.

Culinary uses

Because they have an almost neutral flavor, straw mushrooms can be combined with all sorts of ingredients in stir-fries, braised dishes and soups. They are an essential ingredient in many Chinese dishes, and they are also used for making mushroom soy sauce.

Preparation and cooking techniques

Canned straw mushrooms must be drained and thoroughly rinsed before use. They are usually cut in half lengthwise. This not only reveals the rather attractive "umbrella" pattern, but it also makes them much easier to pick up with chopsticks. Like all mushrooms, straw mushrooms must not be overcooked, especially the canned ones, as they have been cooked already.

Storage

Fresh straw mushrooms are difficult to store, which explains why they are not often seen outside Asia. Dried ones can be stored almost indefinitely, though they may lose some of their flavor.

DRIED BLACK MUSHROOMS/ FRAGRANT MUSHROOMS

Dried black mushrooms are widely used throughout Asia, and are exported around the world. Although they are frequently labeled as "Chinese", to distinguish them from other dried mushrooms, and have come to be widely known as such, the majority of dried black mushrooms sold in Asian markets actually come from Japan, which produces and exports more dried black mushrooms than does China.

Aroma and flavor

There are generally three different grades of dried black mushrooms, with caps that range in color from dark grey, to brown-black or tan. The cheapest of these has quite thin caps, may be sold with or without stems, and may well be labelled "fragrant mushrooms", which is the generic term for shiitake mushrooms. Next come the "winter mushrooms" which have thicker caps and taste more fleshy. The most expensive type are called "flower mushrooms". These are the best of the winter mushrooms. The caps are so thick that they crack, revealing the flower pattern that earned them their name. All three have a dusky aroma with a fragrant flavor, which is much intensified by the drying process.

Above: Dried black mushrooms, also known as fragrant mushrooms, are the dried form of shiitake mushrooms.

Culinary uses

These mushrooms are wonderfully versatile as they can be stir-fried, braised, steamed and used in soups. They form an important part of the vegetarians' diet, and are an ideal partner for bamboo shoots, as they offer a harmonious contrast in color, aroma, flavor and texture. For non-vegetarians, they can be cooked with seafood, poultry and meat, and, of course, other vegetables.

Preparation and cooking techniques

Dried mushrooms must be soaked in water under cover until supple, before use. The best way is to soak the mushrooms in cold water for several hours or overnight, depending on the thickness of the caps. When time is short, they can be soaked in warm water for 30 minutes, but should not be soaked in hot water, as much of the fragrance will be lost. Do not discard the soaking water; it will enrich the flavor of the dish.

After soaking the mushrooms squeeze them dry and discard the stems, if any. Small mushrooms can be left whole, but larger ones should be halved, quartered or coarsely chopped. The thinner dried mushrooms are usually either sliced or shredded, but thicker ones, particularly the pretty "flower mushrooms" are generally left whole to show off their attractive shape.

Storage

Dried black mushrooms should keep for a very long time (over a year) if stored in their package or in an airtight jar in a dry, dark and cool place.

Using dried mushrooms

Dried mushrooms have a rich, intense flavor and are a useful pantry stand-by for adding to Asian dishes. Once they have been reconstituted they can be stir-fried, braised, steamed and used in soups. Dried mushrooms often require longer cooking than fresh ones.

To reconstitute dried mushrooms, soak them in boiling water for 20–30 minutes, depending on the variety and size of mushroom, until tender. Drain and rinse well to remove any grit and dirt.

WOOD EARS

MANDARIN: *MU'ER;* CANTONESE: *WAN YEE;*
VIETNAMESE: *MOC NHI*

Also known as cloud ears, tree
mushrooms or simply dried black
fungus, these are widely used in
China, Thailand and Vietnam. The
dried fungi are thin and brittle, and
look like pieces of charred paper.

Aroma and flavor

There is a slightly smoky smell when
wood ears are first removed from the
bag, but this disappears once they
have been soaked. They are almost
tasteless, but have an intriguing
texture, which is slippery yet crisp.

Culinary Uses

Wood ears are used in stir-frying,
braising and soups; the fungus is
traditionally paired with dried tiger lily in
several Chinese dishes, including the
popular hot-and-sour soup.

Preparation and cooking techniques

The fungus expands to six or eight
times its volume after soaking, so
use plenty of water in a

*Right: Wood ears are
also known as cloud
ears, tree mushrooms or
dried black fungus*

large bowl. As a guide, a piece of
dried fungus that would fit in a
tablespoon would require at least 1 cup
water. Cover the bowl and leave the
fungus to soak for about 30 minutes,
then drain, rinse well and drain again.
Discard any hard roots and sandy bits.
Do not cut the fungus into small pieces,
just separate the larger clumps into
individual "ears" in order to
preserve the pretty
wavy shape.

Storage

Dried fungus will
keep almost
indefinitely if
stored in a dry,
cool place; once
soaked, it should
be stored in clean,
cold water in a
covered bowl
in the
refrigerator.
It will keep
for 2–3
days.

*Left: Silver ears,
or dried white
fungus*

SILVER EARS

MANDARIN: *YINER;* CANTONESE: *PAK
MOOK YEE*

Also known as dried white fungus, this
earned its Chinese name of "silver ear"
partly because of its rarity, and partly
because of the high price it fetches on
account of its medicinal value. It is
regarded as being an excellent tonic,
and is also used for the relief of
insomnia and lung and liver diseases.

Aroma and flavor

Silver ears do not belong to the same
genus as wood ears. Although the
texture is similar, white fungus has a
sweeter flavor.

Culinary uses

While wood ears are regarded as
everyday ingredients, silver ears are
reserved for special occasions. Besides
being cooked with other vegetables in
vegetarian dishes, silver ears are often
cooked and then served on their own,
as one of the many dishes that
comprise a banquet.

Preparation, cooking techniques
and storage

Dried silver ears should be prepared,
cooked and stored in the same way as
dried wood ears.

SEAWEED

KOMBU

CHINESE: *HAIDAI*; JAPANESE: *KOMBU*

Several types of seaweed are used in Asian cooking, especially in Japan and Korea. The most common variety is the giant seaweed known as kelp in English. It is only available in dried form in the West, usually labelled with the Japanese name of kombu or konbu.

Aroma and flavor

Kombu is full of vitamins and minerals, and is particularly rich in iodine. It has a strong "sea" flavor and a crunchy texture.

Culinary uses

This type of seaweed is mainly used in soups in China, but is served poached or stewed as a vegetable in Japan, as well as being used to flavor the fish stock known as dashi.

Left: Kombu has a strong sea flavor

Dashi

This stock, based on kombu and dried bonito flakes, is the basis of most Japanese soups; it can also be used instead of water in any dish that requires a delicately flavored stock.

MAKES 3½ CUPS

> 4-inch square of kombu
> 3¾ cups water
> 1½ ounces katsuobushi (dried bonito flakes)

2 Place the pan over medium heat. Just before the water boils, lift out the seaweed (shred and use for soup).

1 Wipe the kombu with a damp cloth; cut it into 3–4 strips and put in a pan. Pour over the water, making sure that the seaweed is submerged, and soak for an hour.

3 Stir in the bonito flakes, bring to a boil, remove from heat and leave to stand until the flakes have sunk to the bottom of the pan. Strain through a muslin-lined strainer.

Preparation and cooking techniques

Kombu has a pale powdery covering that contributes to its flavor, so do not wash it off; just wipe the seaweed with a damp cloth, then cut it into pieces of the required size. Soak these in cold water for 45–50 minutes. Both the seaweed and soaking water are used.

Storage

Kombu keeps for a long time if stored in a dry, cool place away from strong light.

NORI

JAPANESE: *NORI*

This is the wafer-thin, dried seaweed that is mainly used as a wrapping for sushi. It is sold in sheets that are dark green to black in color, and almost transparent in places. The sheet should be broiled lightly on one side for making sushi, or on both sides until crisp if it is to be crumbled and used as a topping. Ready-toasted sheets known as yaki-nori are available from Asian markets. These are seasoned with ingredients such as soy sauce, salt and sesame oil. Ao-nori is dried seaweed that is crumbled so finely it looks like powder.

WAKAME

JAPANESE: *WAKAME*

This young dark-colored seaweed has a delicate flavor and soft but crisp texture. It is available shredded, fresh (vacuum-packed) or dried, and is used in soups and salads. Dried wakame should be soaked in lukewarm water for 10–15 minutes until it softens and the fronds turn green. At this stage it should be drained, blanched in boiling water for about 1 minute, then refreshed under cold water and drained again. Use as directed in recipes or cool and chop to use in a salad.

HIJIK

JAPANESE: *HIJIK*

This Japanese seaweed—sometimes called hijiki—is similar to wakame. It is available dried and finely shredded, and should be reconstituted as for wakame.

AGAR-AGAR

CHINESE: *DONGFEN; YANGCAI;*
JAPANESE: *KANTEN*

This is the gelatinous substance obtained from the seaweed known as "rock-flower vegetable" in Chinese. Available from Thai or oriental markets as long dried strips or as a fine white powder sold in tubs, it is a very popular setting agent, especially for vegetarians seeking an alternative to gelatin.

Aroma and flavor

Agar-agar has no aroma and is entirely flavorless, but will absorb the seasonings with which it is prepared for serving.

Culinary uses

Asian cooks sometimes use soaked strips of agar-agar in a salad, just as they would any other form of seaweed, but it is more often used as a setting agent, usually to make sweet jellies.

Right: Agar-agar is sold in thick and thin strips and as a powder that is used as a setting agent.

Above : Wakame (in bowl), hijik (on top) and nori seaweeds

Preparation and cooking techniques

To use agar-agar in a salad, soften the strips in lukewarm water for about 20–25 minutes, then drain and dry them on some paper towels. Separate the strips and cut them into short lengths. Combine the agar-agar with the other salad ingredients, add a dressing and toss to mix.

To use agar-agar to set a jelly, dissolve it slowly in water over a very low heat, which may take up to 10 minutes. Heat some milk and sugar, with a flavoring such as almond essence, in a separate pan, then mix with the agar-agar solution. Leave the mixture to cool, then chill in the refrigerator for 3–4 hours until set. Agar-agar varies in strength, so check the packaging to see how much you should use. As a guide, 1 teaspoon powder will set about 1¼ cups of liquid.

Storage

Agar-agar will keep almost indefinitely if stored in a cool, dry place.

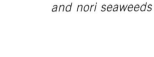

FRUIT

DURIAN

CHINESE: *LIU LIAN*; THAI: *THURIAN*

This tropical fruit originated in Malaysia or Borneo, and is very popular in South-east Asia. Round or oval, it has a dull green shell-like skin covered with pointed spines that turn yellow as the fruit ripens. A typical durian weighs about 4½ pounds, but they can grow even larger, up to 10 pounds.

Aroma and flavor

Durian has a very unpleasant smell, often likened to the stench of raw sewage. The ripe flesh, however, is as delicious as the odor is awful: sweet and creamy, with a hint of strawberries.

Culinary uses

The fruit is eaten raw, and the seeds are often roasted and eaten like nuts.

Preparation

Each fruit consists of three, four or five segments. Using a sharp knife, slit the hard shell of the durian at the segment

Below: A durian and its large seeds

Right: Mangosteen can be eaten on its own or added to a fruit salad.

joints, then press the segments out. Take care not to let the juice drip on to your clothes, as it stains. The soft, creamy flesh can be eaten with a spoon, or puréed, either for serving as a dessert or as an accompaniment to a curry. Some Asian cooks soak the durian segments in coconut milk for 10–12 hours before eating them, as they claim this eliminates the unpleasant smell.

Storage

This is not recommended, as the smell will soon pervade your home, however carefully you store the fruit. When buying, look for perfect, undamaged specimens, and get them home as quickly as possible. Don't attempt to take them on public transport; most carriers ban them!

MANGOSTEEN

CHINESE: *SANZHU GUO*; THAI: *MANG KHUT*

The only thing mangosteens and mangoes share in common, aside from being tropical fruits, is the first five letters of their names. Mangosteens are small, apple-shaped fruits with leathery brown skin that turns purple as they ripen. The flesh looks similar to that of a lychee, but tastes completely different. They are native to South-east Asia and are cultivated in Thailand.

Aroma and flavor

The tough skin surrounds delicious white flesh, which is divided into segments, each with a large seed. The pearly white flesh is fresh and fragrant. Some say it tastes like grapefruit.

Culinary uses

Mangosteens are always eaten raw, but the related kokum, which has a pleasant sour taste, is used as a souring agent in Indian cooking.

Preparation

Cut the fruit in half and remove the segments, taking care not to include any of the dark pink pith. Serve the segments solo or in a fruit salad.

Storage

Mangosteens keep well. If not over-ripe when bought, they should remain in good condition for up to 8–10 days.

LYCHEES

MANDARIN: *LIZHI;* CANTONESE: *LA-EE-TZEE;*
THAI: *LIN-CHI*

Indigenous to subtropical areas of
southern China and Thailand, lychees
grow in clusters on small trees. The ripe
fruit is about the size of a small plum,
with a beautiful, scaly red skin or
"shell". Once this is removed, the
pearly white fruit, which surrounds a
large inedible seed, is revealed. Fresh
lychees are seasonal. When they are not
available, canned fruit can be used
instead, but it lacks the subtlety of the
fresh fruit. Choose the ones in natural
juice rather than syrup.

Aroma and flavor

Peeled lychees have a delicious
perfume. The flesh has a wonderful,
clean taste, somewhat like a grape, but
much more scented.

Culinary uses

Lychees and their close relatives,
longans, "dragon's eyes", are said to
boost fertility. In some parts of
China it is traditional,
when a young
person

reaches puberty, to celebrate the
event with a meal composed of a
young cockerel cooked with
dried lychees or longans. On
most occasions, however,
lychees are eaten fresh, and
are good for cleansing the
palate after a rich meal. They
are also used in fruit salads
and for making sherbets.

Preparation

Lychees are very easy to prepare.
The brittle skin parts readily, and you
can either eat the fruit as is, nibbling
the flesh off the pits, or the fruit can
be pitted and sliced before
being added to a fruit salad.

Storage

Store lychees in the
refrigerator, as they taste
best chilled. They will stay
fresh for up
to a week.

RAMBUTANS

CANTONESE: *HONG MAO TANG;* THAI: *NGO*

These small tropical fruits
originated in Malaysia, but
they are also grown in
the Philippines
and Thailand.
Rambutans
belong to the
same family
as lychees and
longans, and
they have a
similar taste and
texture, but look

*Above: Canned and
fresh rambutans*

very different. The reddish-brown skins
are covered with fine green-tipped
hairs. Inside, the flesh is white, and
hides an oblong seed.

Aroma and flavor

Rambutans are not as strongly scented
as lychees. The delicate flesh tastes a
little sharper.

Culinary uses

Rambutans are usually eaten in the
hand, served on the bottom half of the
shell, with the top half cut off to expose
the flesh. They are used in fruit salads,
but are seldom cooked.

Preparation

Make a cut around the equator of the
rambutan, then remove half or all
the skin. The flesh tends to stick to the
seed, so they are more difficult to pit
than lychees.

Storage

Like lychees, rambutans are best stored
in the refrigerator, where they will keep
for at least a week.

Right: Canned and fresh lychees

Above: A selection of some of the many different varieties of mangoes

MANGOES

CHINESE: *MANG GUO;* THAI: *MA-MUANG*

One of the world's favorite fruits, mangoes originated in India and are now widely cultivated throughout South-east Asia, as well as in other tropical and sub-tropical countries. There are thousands of different varieties. Most are oval in shape, with green, gold or red skin and succulent orange flesh, which can be quite fibrous, although modern varieties are usually smooth and velvety. Canned and dried mangoes are also available.

Aroma and flavor

The aroma of a ripe mango is quite unique. Some people say it reminds them of a pine wood in springtime. The juicy flesh is highly scented and tastes deliciously sweet.

Culinary uses

Apart from being eaten fresh as a fruit, mangoes are used extensively for making chutneys and pickles. Asian cooks also use them in savory dishes, and when stir-frying a rich meat such as duck, will often add mango instead of pineapple. Mango ice cream is legendary, and Thai cooks make a wonderful dessert from glutinous rice, coconut milk and mangoes.

Preparation

To prepare a mango for eating, first cut off both sides of the fruit, on either side of the pit, then scoop the flesh out of the skin with a spoon. After that, strip the skin off the remaining central part and suck the pit clean. This may sound rather messy, but in Asia it is the traditional way of eating a mango. If you are fastidious, you can always peel the mango first, slice the fruit off the pit and then slice it neatly. Finally—and this appeals to children—you can cut two large slices on either side of the pit, cross hatch the flesh on the skin, then press the skin down so that the pieces of mango pop up to make a mango "hedgehog".

Storage

Mangoes are usually picked just before they are ripe, and then they are packed in straw and shipped by air to the West. Fruit that is bought when it is still firm can be ripened at home. One of the easiest ways of doing this is to wrap the mango in newspaper, lay it in a box and cover with more newspaper. Color is not necessarily an indication of ripeness, but touch is. Ripe fruit will just yield when lightly pressed. Eat mangoes as soon as they are ripe.

Preparing mangoes

Mangoes can be difficult to prepare because they have a large, flat stone that is slighty off-center, and they are very juicy.

1 Cut off both sides of the fruit in thick slices, keeping as close to the central pit as possible.

2 Scoop the flesh out of the skin using a small spoon. Peel the skin off the remaining central part and slice the fruit off the pit.

PAPAYAS

MANDARIN: *FAN MUGUA;* CANTONESE: *MUK GWA;* THAI: *MALAKO*

Papayas—or paw paws as they are sometimes known—are native to tropical America. It was not until 1600 that they were introduced into Asia, but they rapidly became extremely popular so that today they are one of the most common and most important fruits in all tropical and sub-tropical countries.

Papayas can be small and round, but are more often pear-shaped. When ripe, the skin turns from green to yellow, and the flesh, which can be deep salmon pink or glorious orange, becomes soft and juicy. The small grey seeds are not usually eaten, although Asian cooks use them as a garnish.

Aroma and flavor

The flavor of a ripe papaya is sweet and delicately perfumed. It can be sickly, but this can be counteracted by lemon or lime juice. The flesh of underripe papaya is pale green, and nowhere near as sweet.

Culinary uses

In South-east Asia, papaya is eaten both as a fruit and a vegetable. When ripe, the flesh is usually eaten as it is, sometimes with a squeeze of citrus, but it is also used in fruit salads and other desserts. Papayas that are not too ripe can be added to soups, curries or seafood dishes. Unripe green papayas are served raw in vegetable salads, especially in Thailand, and can also be made into pickles. Papaya contains an enzyme called papain, which is an excellent tenderizer. Both the juice and skins are used to tenderize meat.

Preparation and cooking techniques

Slice lengthwise in half and scoop out the seeds. To serve papayas raw as a table fruit, slice in wedges, sprinkle with lemon or lime juice, and either cut the flesh off the skin, slicing it into bite-size chunks,

Right: Papayas are one of the most popular tropical fruits.

or provide spoons for scooping. To serve papaya raw in a salad, peel slightly unripe fruit, shred the flesh and combine it with carrots and lettuce or cucumber, then toss with a spicy dressing. Thai cooks often add dried shrimp, which give a salty tang.

Storage

Green papayas are not often available outside their country of origin but, if located, can be kept in a refrigerator for up to a week. In the West, ripe fruit is much easier to come by. Look for fruit that is yellow all over, and which has a delicate perfume. If the fruit is not quite ripe, check the skin around the stem end and only buy if this is yellow. If it is green, the fruit will never ripen. Fruit that is almost ripe will soften if kept at room temperature for a few days, but should not be left for too long.

Dragon fruit

These brightly colored fruits are widely grown in Vietnam. They come in pink and yellow varieties. The pink ones are about 4 inches long, and are covered with pointed, green-tipped scales. The yellow ones are smaller and look more like prickly pears. The flesh is sweet and refreshing, and is best eaten chilled, sprinkled with a little lemon juice.

NUTS AND SEEDS

PEANUTS

CHINESE: *HUASHENG MI*

Also known as groundnuts or monkey nuts, peanuts are thought to have originated in South America, and were introduced into Asia in the 16th century. Today, peanuts are an important world crop, being rich both in oil (40–50 per cent) and protein (about 30 per cent).

Aroma and flavor

Raw peanuts don't have much of a smell, but once cooked—they are usually roasted—they have a powerful, unmistakable aroma, a crunchy texture and a distinctive flavor.

Culinary uses

Peanuts play an important role in Asian cuisine. The smaller ones are used for making oil, while the larger, less oily nuts are widely eaten, both as a snack food and as ingredients in salads and main courses. In Indonesian and Malayan cooking, roasted peanuts, pounded to a paste, are the basis for satay sauce, as well as for a salad dressing in the classic gado-gado salad.

Preparation and cooking techniques

Strictly speaking, the peanut is not a nut, but a legume. Its outer shell is the dried fibrous pod of the plant, and contains the seeds or "nuts", which in turn are coated with a thin layer of reddish skin. This skin has to be removed before the nut can be used as a food, and the easiest way to do that is to roast or fry the peanuts, then, when they are cool enough to handle, rub off the brittle skins with your fingers. When the nuts are processed commercially, a fan is used for winnowing, or the nuts are left outside to allow the wind to do the job.

Storage

Raw peanuts in their shells will keep for many months if stored properly. Shelled peanuts will only keep for 7–10 days, even if stored in an airtight container.

GINKGO NUTS

CHINESE: *BAIGUO;* JAPANESE: *GINGKO BILOBA*

The ginkgo tree is native to China, and has been grown for many centuries in Japan, where it is called the maidenhair tree.

Aroma and flavor

Ginkgo nuts resemble lotus seeds in appearance and taste, but have a smoother and firmer texture and are somewhat less sweet.

Culinary uses

Ginkgo nuts play an important role in vegetarian cooking in Asia, particularly in China and Japan. They feature in the popular Buddha's delight (a vegetarian casserole) and are used in several Japanese vegetable and rice dishes. When cooked, ginkgo nuts have a viscous texture.

Above: Raw and shelled peanuts

Left: Canned ginkgo nuts

Preparation and cooking techniques

These nuts do not travel well. The flesh inside the shells tends to dry up or rot after a time, so only dried and canned ginkgo nuts are available in the West. Dried nuts need soaking in water for several hours. Drain before adding to stir-fries, casseroles and soups.

Storage

Any unused soaked or canned ginkgo nuts can be stored in fresh water in the refrigerator for 2–3 days.

ALMONDS

MANDARIN: *XINGREN;*
CANTONESE: *HANG YAHN*

These nuts come from the kernel of a fruit closely related to the apricot, but the fruit of the ripe almond is leathery, dusky green and quite inedible.

Aroma and flavor

Almonds have a unique aroma quite unlike that of any other nut. There are bitter and sweet varieties, both with a pleasant, crunchy texture.

Culinary uses

In Asia, sweet almonds are mostly used as garnishes and in desserts and cakes. Bitter almonds contain prussic acid. They must not be eaten raw, but their essence is distilled and used as a flavoring for sweet dishes.

Above: Shelled almonds

Preparation and cooking techniques

Whole kernels should be soaked to remove the thin red skin. This is seldom necessary in the West, however, as shelled almonds are readily available, whole, sliced, as thin slivers or ground.

Storage

Almonds have a high fat content, so they become rancid if stored for too long. Keep unopened packages in a sealed container in a cool, dry place, and use within 2–3 months. Nuts bought loose, or in packages that have been opened, should be used as soon as possible.

SESAME SEEDS

CHINESE: *ZHIMA*

The sesame plant probably originated in Africa, but has been cultivated in India and China since ancient times. Today, it is grown all over the world in tropical and sub-tropical countries. Sesame seeds are small, flat and pear-shaped. They are usually white, but can be cream to brown, red or black.

Aroma and flavor

Raw sesame seeds have little aroma and are almost tasteless until they have been roasted or dry-fried, when their nutty aroma becomes very pronounced and their flavor is heightened.

Culinary uses

Sesame seeds are about 50 per cent oil, and processed sesame oil is used in oriental cooking for flavoring. The seeds are used in a number of popular Chinese dishes, most notably in Chinese honeyed apples and bang-bang chicken. They also feature in Singaporean, Malayan, Indonesian and Japanese cooking, and are often toasted then sprinkled over salads and other dishes just before serving.

Preparation and cooking techniques

Sesame seeds are frequently roasted before being used. Place them in a wok or pan over medium heat. They burn readily, so shake the pan constantly to keep them moving and do not leave them unattended at any time. If ground seeds are required, this can be done in a mortar with a pestle, or, as in Korea, between two flat plates. Japanese cooks use a device rather like a pepper mill, which grinds the roasted sesame seeds as finely or as coarsely as needed. The finely ground seeds are called *irigoma*.

Storage

The high oil content means that sesame seeds do not keep well. Store in a cool, dry place and observe the "use by" dates on packages.

Above: White and black sesame seeds

Other nuts

Candlenuts Native to Indonesia, these nuts are similar to macadamia nuts, which can be used as a substitute. In Asia, the pounded nuts are used as a thickener. They are slightly toxic when raw, and should always be cooked.

Cashew nuts Both raw and roasted cashews are used in Asian cooking.

Chestnuts These have a robust flavor and meaty texture, which makes them a popular addition to a variety of vegetarian dishes. They are particularly delicious stir-fried with bok choy or other leafy vegetables.

Above: From left, cashew nuts, candlenuts and chestnuts

BEANCURD/TOFU AND GLUTEN

BEANCURD/TOFU

MANDARIN: *DOUFU*; CANTONESE: *DAU FOO*; JAPANESE: *TOFU*

Made from soybeans, beancurd (more commonly known in the West by its Japanese name tofu) is one of China's major contributions to the world as a cheap source of protein. Highly nutritious and low in fat and sugar, it is a much healthier food than either meat or fish, at a fraction of the cost.

The soybean plant is a legume that has been cultivated in China for thousands of years. A number of bean by-products constitute an important element in the Chinese diet. Soy sauce is one of them, and beancurd is another, as well as miso, the fermented soybean paste that is essential to Japanese cooking. Written records indicate that fermented bean sauces were in use well over 2,000 years ago, but no one knows precisely when beancurd was invented. All we know for certain is that it was introduced to Japan during the Tang dynasty in the 8th century AD, along with Buddhism.

The process of making beancurd is not unlike making cheese, only much less time-consuming. The soybeans are soaked, husked, then pounded with water to make soya milk. This mixture is then filtered, boiled and finally curdled with gypsum.

There are two basic types of fresh beancurd widely available in the West: soft or silken tofu (called *kinu* in Japan); and a firm type, which Japanese cooks know as *momen*. Both are creamy-white in color and are either packed in water or sold in vacuum packs. The firm type is usually sold in cakes measuring about 3 inches square and 1 inch thick. Also available, but only from oriental stores, are marinated beancurd, deep-fried beancurd and pressed beancurd.

Aroma and flavor

The quality of fresh beancurd is largely dependent upon the water used to make it. Good quality beancurd should smell fresh with a faint, pleasant "beany" aroma. On its own, it is quite bland, but the beauty of beancurd is that its soft, porous texture will absorb the flavor of any other ingredient with which it is cooked.

Culinary uses

The nutritional value of beancurd cannot be stressed too highly. As a vegetable protein, it contains the eight essential amino acids plus vitamins A and B. It is free from cholesterol, and is regarded as an excellent food for anyone with heart disease or high blood pressure. In addition, it is very easy to digest, so is an ideal food for infants, invalids and the elderly.

Beancurd is very versatile and, depending upon the texture, it can be cooked by almost every conceivable method, and used with a vast array of ingredients, both sweet and savory.

Preparation and cooking techniques

Soft or silken tofu is mainly steamed or added to soups, since its light and delicate texture means that it will disintegrate if handled roughly. It makes a refreshing sweet dessert and is also used to make "ice cream".

Firm beancurd is the most common type, and also the most popular for everyday use. Although it has been lightly pressed, and is more robust than silken tofu, it still needs to be handled with care. Having been cut to the required size and shape—cubes, strips, slices or triangles—the pieces are usually blanched in boiling water or briefly shallow-fried in oil. This hardens them and prevents them from disintegrating when stir-fried or braised. Yaki tofu is beancurd that has been lightly broiled on both sides.

Because beancurd is bland, it is important to cook it with strongly flavored seasonings such as garlic, ginger, scallions, chiles, soy sauce, oyster sauce, shrimp paste (blachan), fermented black beans,

Above: Clockwise from top, deep-fried beancurd, silken tofu, and cubes of fresh beancurd. All these types of tofu absorb the flavors of the other ingredients with which they are cooked.

salted yellow beans, or sesame oil. Although its primary purpose is as a vegetarian ingredient, beancurd also tastes very good with meat. It is often cooked with pork or beef, but seldom with chicken. It goes well with fish and shellfish, too. One of the most popular beancurd dishes is *ma po doufu* from Sichuan, in which cubed beancurd is first blanched, then braised with ground beef, garlic, scallions, leeks, salt, Sichuan pepper, rice wine, chili bean paste, fermented black beans and sesame oil.

Left: Pressed beancurd

Storage

Buy beancurd from an oriental store, if possible. Fresh beancurd submerged in water in a plastic box will keep for several days in the refrigerator. Vacuum-packed fresh beancurd bought from health food stores and supermarkets will keep for slightly longer, but is unlikely to taste quite as good. Beancurd is also available as a powder mix. This has a long shelf life, so is a useful pantry item.

DEEP-FRIED BEANCURD

MANDARIN: *YOUZHA DOUFU;* CANTONESE: *DAU FOO POK;* JAPANESE: *ABURAGE*

This is fresh, firm beancurd that has been cut into cubes, squares or triangles, then deep-fried until light brown. Deep-fried beancurd has an interesting texture. It puffs up during cooking, and underneath the crispy brown skin the flesh is white and soft. It sucks up seasonings and the flavors of other ingredients like a sponge.

Culinary uses

Deep-fried beancurd can be used in the same way as fresh beancurd in soups, stir-fries, braised dishes or casseroles. As it has been fried in vegetable oil, it is suitable for vegetarian cooking. Non-vegetarians stuff the larger squares or triangles of beancurd with ground pork, chicken, fish and

shrimp, then braise them in a sauce. The Japanese version of deep-fried beancurd, known as *aburage,* is a popular addition to a wonderful hotpot called *oden,* which is sold from street stalls during the winter.

Preparation and cooking techniques

Unlike fresh beancurd, which is very delicate, deep-fried beancurd can be handled fairly roughly without disintegrating. Even though the crisp crust is porous, it is best to chop up the larger pieces a little to allow the seasonings to penetrate more easily.

Storage

Cakes of deep-fried beancurd are sold in plastic bags from the chiller or freezer in oriental markets. They usually have a "use by" date stamped on them, and will keep for much longer than uncooked fresh beancurd. They can be frozen for up to a year or more.

PRESSED BEANCURD

MANDARIN: *DOUFU GAN;* CANTONESE: *DAU FOO GONN*

Pressed beancurd is fresh beancurd that has been compressed until almost all the liquid has been squeezed out, leaving a solid block with a smooth texture. It is usually marinated in soy

sauce and seasoned with five-spice powder, so is pale brown on the surface, but white inside.

Culinary uses

Pressed beancurd is cut into thin slices, cubes or fine shreds, then stir-fried with meat and vegetables. It offers a contrast in both texture and flavor when it is combined with other ingredients.

Storage

Pressed beancurd is sold in vacuum-packs in oriental markets, and will normally keep for several weeks in the refrigerator. Check the "use-by" date on the packaging. Do not freeze, as this would alter the texture of the beancurd.

DRIED BEANCURD SKINS

MANDARIN: *FUZHU;* CANTONESE: *FOO PI;* JAPANESE: *YUBA*

Dried beancurd skins are made from soya milk. The process is simple, but requires considerable skill: a large pan of soya milk is gently brought to a boil, the thin layer of skin that forms on the surface is skimmed off with a stick in a single swoop, and this is hung up. When it dries, it forms a flat sheet. Dried beancurd sticks are made by rolling the skin up while still warm, then leaving the sticks to dry.

Above: Dried beancurd skins have no discernible flavor or aroma.

Aroma and flavor

Like fresh beancurd, dried beancurd skins have neither aroma nor flavor until they are cooked, when they will absorb the flavor of seasonings and other ingredients.

Culinary uses

The flat skins are used in soups, stir-fries and casseroles, and are sometimes used as wrappers for spring rolls. The sticks are used in vegetarian dishes, and are also cooked with meat in braised dishes and casseroles.

Preparation

Dried beancurd skins need soaking before use: the sheets only require an hour or two, but the sticks need to be soaked for several hours or overnight.

Storage

Dried beancurd sheets and beancurd sticks will keep for a very long time. Store them in their package or in a sealed plastic bag in a cool, dry place.

FERMENTED BEANCURD

MANDARIN: *DOUFU NAI*; CANTONESE: *FOO YU*; THAI: *TAO-HOO-YEE*

This is made by fermenting fresh beancurd on beds of rice straw, then drying the curd in the sun before marinating with salt, alcohol and spices. Finally, it is stored in brine in sealed earthenware urns and left to mature for at least six months before being packaged and sold.

Aroma and flavor

Fermented beancurd is definitely an acquired taste. It is no coincidence that it is sometimes referred to as Chinese cheese, because it smells very strong indeed, and the flavor is pretty powerful, too. There are two types of fermented beancurd available in the West: the red type is colored on the surface only, and the white one can be quite hot and spicy.

Culinary uses

Fermented beancurd is either served on its own with rice congee at breakfast, or used as a seasoning in marinating and cooking.

Storage

Fermented beancurd is available from oriental markets. Once opened, store the contents in the refrigerator.

Below: Fermented beancurd

Above: Tempeh has a firmer texture than tofu.

TEMPEH

INDONESIAN: *TEMPEH*

This Indonesian specialty is made by fermenting cooked soybeans with a cultured starter.

Aroma and flavor

Tempeh is similar to tofu but has a nuttier, more savory flavor.

Culinary uses

It can be used in the same way as firm tofu and also benefits from marinating. Its firm texture means that it can be used as a meat replacement.

Storage

Tempeh is available chilled or frozen. Chilled tempeh can be stored in the refrigerator for up to a week. Frozen tempeh can be left in the freezer for 1 month. Defrost before use.

MISO

JAPANESE: *KOME MISO, MUGO MISO AND HACHO MISO*

This thick paste is made from a mixture of cooked soybeans, rice, wheat or barley, salt and water. Miso is left to ferment for up to 3 years.

Aroma and flavor

There are three main types: kome, or white miso, is the lightest and sweetest; medium-strength mugi miso, which has a mellow flavor and is preferred for everyday use; and hacho miso, which is a dark chocolate color, and has a thick texture and a strong flavor.

Culinary uses

Miso can be used to add a savory flavor to soups, stocks, stir-fries and noodle dishes, and is a staple food in Asia.

Storage

Miso keeps very well and can be stored for several months, but it should be kept in the refrigerator once it has been opened.

Left: Mugi miso

Gluten

MANDARIN: *MIANJIN;* CANTONESE: *MING GUN;* JAPANESE: *FU*

Also known as "mock meat", gluten is another source of vegetarian protein. It is made from a mixture of wheat flour, salt and water, from which all the starch has been washed out. What remains is a sponge-like gluten. Its Chinese name literally means "muscle or sinew of flour".

Like beancurd, gluten has no aroma nor flavor of its own, but it has a much firmer texture, and can be shaped, colored and flavored to resemble meat, poultry or fish.

Unlike beancurd, which is often cooked with meat and fish, gluten is regarded as a pure Buddhist ingredient, and as such, no non-vegetarian item may be mixed with it. This does not prevent accomplished Asian cooks from using a bit of sleight of hand, however, and gluten is often used with beancurd to produce dishes such as "mock chicken", "mock abalone", "vegetarian duck" or "Buddhist pork"—which are all said to look and taste very much like the real thing.

Although gluten can be made at home, the task is too time-consuming to contemplate. Flavored and cooked gluten is available in cans from oriental markets. It only needs to be reheated before being served.

Once opened, it will keep in the refrigerator for up to a week.

DRIED FISH AND SHELLFISH

SALTED FISH

MANDARIN: *YAN YU*; CANTONESE: *GON HAHM YU*

Many different types of fish, both freshwater and saltwater, are salted and cured for general use in South-east Asia. They range from tiny whitebait to large croakers, and they are generally preserved in salt or brine, although some are dried in the sun. In Japan, sun-dried young sardines, known as *niboshi*, are eaten as snacks, and are also used for making stock.

Aroma and flavor

To say that salted fish is an acquired taste is an understatement. It smells so pungent and has such a strong flavor that some people may find it positively disagreeable. It is, however, very popular throughout South-east Asia.

Culinary use

Like fermented beancurd, salted fish has two basic functions. It is either eaten on its own with rice, or used as a seasoning for vegetables and meat in steamed dishes or soups.

Preparation and cooking techniques

Soak the salted fish in water before use, to remove the excess salt. Large fish are usually sold without the heads.

Storage

Preserved fish in brine is seldom seen in the West, but salted and dried fish are both available from Asian markets. They will keep almost indefinitely if stored in a cool and dry place.

Left: Dried anchovies

DRIED ANCHOVIES

MALAY: *IKAN BILIS*

Dried anchovies, which are known as *ikan bilis*, are a Malayan specialty. For some unknown reason, anchovies are seldom eaten fresh in South-east Asia, they are either used for making fish sauce, or are salted and dried. Fishing for anchovies is a huge industry in Malaysia. Having located the schools of fish with the aid of electronic fish finders and echo sounding equipment, the fishermen haul in their catch and immediately boil the fish in salted water for about 5 minutes. Back on shore, the fish are dried, graded and packed.

Aroma and flavor

Dried anchovies have an overpowering aroma and a very strong flavor.

Culinary uses

Dried anchovies can be used as a flavoring, as an ingredient in a composite dish, or as a snack food. A favorite Malayan recipe involves steaming and filleting the fish, then serving them with a sauce made from preserved black beans that is flavored with fresh chiles, lime juice and sweetened to taste with sugar. Dried anchovies are also often deep fried until they are crunchy and served either at parties as a snack to eat with drinks, or as a starter. They also make a tasty accompaniment to spicy curries and chicken rendang.

Storage

Dried anchovies will keep for a very long time if stored in a dry and cool place, but make sure that their container is airtight, or you will attract all the neighborhood cats.

Above: Bonito flakes or shavings (top) and powder

BONITO FLAKES

JAPANESE: *KATSUOBUSHI*

Bonito is the name given to several different kinds of fish in different parts of the world. For instance, the Atlantic bonito is a relative of mackerel, and is known as Spanish mackerel in Europe, while the Pacific bonito is a small tuna, much used in Japanese cooking.

Aroma and flavor

The Pacific bonito has a much stronger flavor than regular tuna, particularly when it is dried.

Culinary uses

In Japan, where dried bonito is widely used, the flakes come in various thicknesses. Fine shavings are one of the main ingredients in the basic stock known as *dashi,* and are also used as a topping or garnish. Powdered bonito flakes are used as a seasoning.

Storage

Dried bonito flakes will keep almost indefinitely if stored in an airtight jar in a dark and cool place.

DRIED SHRIMP

MANDARIN: *XIAMI;* CANTONESE: *HA MY;* THAI: *GUNG HAENG*

Dried shrimp are popular throughout Asia, especially in China and Thailand.

Left: Dried shrimp

They are pale pink in color, having been boiled before being spread out in the sun to dry. There are several different sizes, from tiny shrimp not much bigger than grains of rice (hence the Chinese name, "sea rice") to large ones, which are still less than ½ inch long. The larger ones are usually sold shelled and headless, while the tiny ones are sold whole, heads and all.

Aroma and flavor

Dried shrimp have a very strong smell, so strong that it can be detected through the cellophane bags in which they are sold. The smell dissipates with cooking. The flavor is sharp and salty.

Culinary uses

Because of their strong taste, dried shrimp are usually used as a seasoning rather than as an independent ingredient. They are often used as a garnish in salads and also feature in the popular "eight-treasure stuffing", when they are combined with dried mushrooms, bamboo shoots, glutinous rice and other ingredients.

Preparation and cooking techniques

Dried shrimp must be soaked for an hour or so before use, either in water or rice wine. The soaking liquid is saved and often added to the dish during cooking.

Storage

Dried shrimp keep well in airtight containers if they are stored in a dry, cool place. Their color is a good indication of freshness as older shrimp tend to fade. Any shrimp that look grey, or

Above: Dried scallops

start to turn grey while being stored, will be past their prime. Stored dried shrimp may become a bit moist. If this happens, spread them on baking sheets and dry them briefly in a hot oven.

DRIED SCALLOPS

MANDARIN: *GANBEI;* CANTONESE: *GONG YU CHU*

Another oriental delicacy, dried scallops are very expensive because the most sought-after varieties are so scarce. The Chinese variety known as *conpoy,* for instance, is only found in the inland sea called Po Hai, and then only during a short summer season. The best scallops are round and golden, with a delicate, sweet flavor. Japan produces fine dried scallops, including the variety *aomori.*

Aroma and flavor

Before being dried, scallops are cooked in their shells in boiling water. The flesh is then removed and cleaned. Dried scallops have quite a distinct aroma with a highly concentrated flavor.

Culinary uses

Dried scallops are seldom used on their own, but are combined with other ingredients in soups and stuffings.

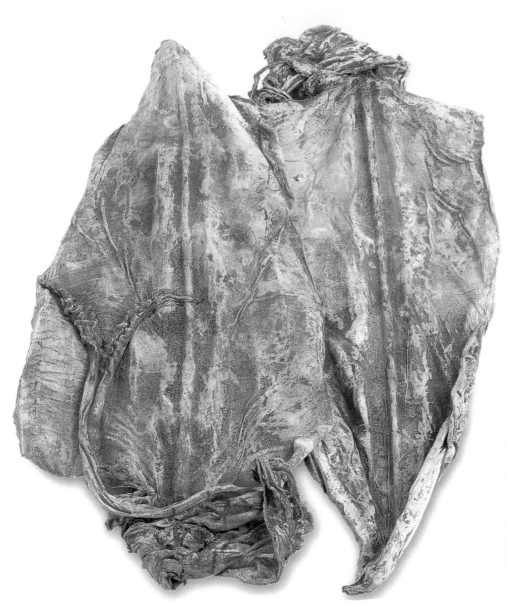

Above: Dried squid has a subtle fishy aroma, but a strong flavor.

1 Soak the dried squid in warm water for 30 minutes or so, then drain and wash in fresh water.

2 Score the squid on the inside in a criss-cross fashion, then cut it into small pieces.

Dried and fresh scallops are sometimes used in the same dish. Dried scallops are the classic garnish for crispy seaweed, but when this dish is served in Chinese restaurants overseas, ground fried fish is often used as a substitute.

Preparation and cooking techniques

The dried scallops must be soaked in boiling water for at least an hour, then drained.

Storage

For some inexplicable reason, dried scallops seem to be available only in large boxes in the West. Should you acquire any, transfer them to jars, close the lids tightly and store them in a cool, dry place. They will keep indefinitely.

DRIED SQUID

MANDARIN: *YOUYU*; CANTONESE: *YOW YU*

In inland China and other parts of Asia that are far from the coast, where fresh seafood was for a long time unobtainable, dried squid and cuttlefish have always been regarded as delicacies.

Aroma and flavor

Dried squid is pale brown in color and has a subtle fishy aroma, but a very strong taste. Some people find the texture rather tough when compared to fresh squid, but others like the chewiness of the dried version.

Culinary uses

Dried squid is mainly used in soups or meat stews. The stronger texture and flavor provides an interesting contrast to fresh squid, and the two are often stir-fried together in a popular dish that is known as "two-colored squid-flowers".

Preparation and cooking techiques

Before using them for cooking, dried squid must be soaked in warm water for at least 30 minutes, then drained and cleaned in fresh water. If the dried squid is to be stir-fried, it is the normal practice to score the inside of the flesh in a crisscross pattern, then cut it into small pieces. Cooking causes the cuts to open up so that each piece of squid resembles an ear of corn, which is how they came to be called "squid flowers".

Storage

Dried squid will keep almost indefinitely if they are wrapped tightly and stored in a dry, cool place.

FISH MAW

CHINESE: *Yu Du*

Fish maw is the swim bladders or stomachs of certain types of large fish and eels, which have been dried in the sun for several days, then deep-fried. It is considered a delicacy in both China and Thailand.

Aroma and flavor

Fish maw has little aroma, nor does it have a distinctive flavor.

Culinary uses

Fish maw is mainly valued for its texture, which is slippery.

Preparation and cooking techniques

The maws must be soaked in a large bowl of cold water for 24 hours before use. They will float at first, so will need to be kept submerged with the aid of a plate or dish. As they absorb the water, the maws will swell to four times the original size and slowly sink to the bottom of the bowl. Before use, drain but do not dry the maws, then slice or cube them as required.

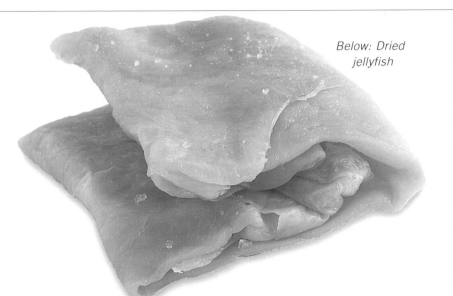

Below: Dried jellyfish

Dried jellyfish
Sheets of dried edible jellyfish are sold in plastic bags in some Chinese markets. This Chinese delicacy is valued for its crunchy yet elastic texture. To prepare, soak the sheets in cold water for several hours, changing the water frequently, and squeezing the jellyfish each time to get rid of as much of the fishy smell as possible. Drain, give the jellyfish sheets a final squeeze to remove the excess water, then cut them into strips. Strips of dried jellyfish are often added to a stir-fry, but they must be tossed in at the last moment; if they are over-cooked, they will become rubbery.

Left: Dried sea cucumber, which is actually a type of sea slug and not a vegetable at all.

Dried sea cucumber Sold as *iriko*, *trepang* or *bêche-de-mer*, this is not a vegetable, but a marine animal, also known as a sea slug. Before use, dried sea cucumber must be soaked in cold water for at least 24 hours, during which time it will double in bulk and become quite gelatinous. It is mainly used in soups and stocks.

Above: Fish maw

PRESERVED MEATS AND EGGS

CHINESE SAUSAGES/ WIND-DRIED SAUSAGES

MANDARIN: *XIANG CHANG*; CANTONESE: *LOP CHONG*

Although these are always described as Chinese sausages, wind-dried sausages are made throughout South-east Asia, and are widely available in the West. There are basically two types: a pink and white sausage, which is made from pork and pork fat, and a darker sausage, in which the pork is mixed with duck liver. The sausages are about 6 inches long and about ¾ inch wide, and are sold in pairs, tied together with string.

Aroma and flavor

The dried sausages do not have any aroma, but as soon as they are cooked, they become really fragrant and taste deliciously sweet.

Culinary uses

Chinese sausages are very versatile. They can be eaten on their own, combined with milder meats such as chicken, or used as the main ingredient in a vegetable dish.

Preparation and cooking techniques

Unlike salami, Chinese sausages must be cooked before eating them. The best way of cooking them is to cut them diagonally into thin slices, then steam them on top of rice for 10 minutes or so. Alternatively, the whole sausage can be steamed for 10 minutes, then skinned and sliced before adding to dishes such as fried rice.

Storage

As the sausages are cured and contain preservatives, they will keep for several months in the refrigerator, and almost indefinitely in the freezer.

Right: Chinese sausages are popular throughout South-east Asia.

Above: Pork crackling

PORK CRACKLING

MANDARIN: *SAI YUDU*; CANTONESE: *JA YUHK PEI*

Also known as chicaron, pork crackling is made from pork rind that has been deep-fried, forming crisp puffy crackers. It is served as a crunchy contrast alongside curries, or sliced in salads.

Aroma and flavor

The deep-fried rind has a meaty aroma with a subtle flavor. It has a very interesting, firm yet spongy texture that absorbs other strongly flavored ingredients.

Wind-dried belly pork

This is a Chinese specialty, found principally in Hunan province but available all over China. It must be cooked before eating. Wind-dried belly pork can be bought in oriental markets.

Culinary uses

Pork crackling is used in soups, stews, hotpots and casseroles.

Preparation

Pork crackling is simply sliced if it is to be used as a crunchy topping for salads, otherwise it needs to be soaked before use, partly to soften it and partly to rid it of excess fat. It is usually soaked in hot water for about 35 minutes before being drained and chopped.

Storage

Pork crackling should keep for several months if well wrapped and stored in a cool, dry place. It will become rancid if kept for too long.

PRESERVED EGGS

MANDARIN: *YANDAN; PIDAN;* CANTONESE: *HAHAM DON; PEI DON*

In China, and among the Chinese communities throughout South-east Asia, preserved eggs are a very popular delicacy. There are two main types, and both use duck eggs. This is partly because duck eggs are bigger and have a stronger flavor than hen's eggs, but also because the yolk of a duck egg contains more fat than a hen's egg. The more common type, much favored in southern China, is the salted duck egg. The other, which has more universal appeal, is the famous thousand-year-old egg.

Both types of preserved egg are made by a similar method; it is the materials used in the process that are different. Basically, salted eggs are made by coating raw duck eggs in a salt and mud paste, then rolling them in rice husks until they are completely covered. At this stage the eggs are packed into an earthenware urn, which is tightly sealed and stored in a cool, dark place for 30–40 days. Thousand-year-old eggs are nothing like as old as their name suggests. They are raw duck eggs that have been covered with a mixture of wood ash and slaked lime and left for up to a hundred days. By the time they are used, the egg whites will have turned to pale brown jelly and the yolks will be creamy and tinged green.

Aroma and flavor

The two types of preserved egg smell and taste quite different. As might be expected, the former are quite salty. Thousand-year-old eggs taste milder, but still have a definite aroma and flavor.

Above: The solid whites and yolks of thousand-year-old eggs are eaten raw. The eggs only require peeling.

Culinary uses

Salted eggs must be cooked. They are often eaten on their own, or used as part of the filling in cakes for festivals. Thousand-year-old eggs need no cooking. Sliced and seasoned with soy sauce and sesame oil, they are often served as a starter, or chopped and added to congee and eaten at breakfast time. They can also be used in a delicious omelet, with pork and fresh hen's eggs.

Preparation and cooking techniques

Both types of egg must have their outer coating removed and then they should be thoroughly washed. Salted eggs can then be boiled or steamed before removing the shells. The whites and yolks of thousand-year-old eggs will have solidified, so all that is required is to carefully remove the shell before cutting the eggs into quarters or eighths for serving.

Storage

Since these eggs are preserved, they should keep for a long time in the refrigerator. The salted eggs will keep for about a month, and the thousand-year-old eggs will keep for 4–6 months.

Left: Throughout Asia thousand-year-old eggs (front) and salted duck eggs (back) are a very popular delicacy.

POULTRY

CHICKEN

The chicken is a descendant of a South-east Asian jungle fowl that was domesticated over 4,500 years ago. Today chicken features in almost every cuisine. Its universal popularity is due to the fact that the flesh combines happily with a huge variety of different ingredients. Nowhere is this more amply illustrated than in Asia, where it is used in soups, salads, stir-fries, curries, roasts and braised dishes. Every part of the bird is utilized, including the liver, gizzard, heart and even the feet, which are used to make a delicious stew.

Preparation and cooking techniques

Chicken can be cooked whole, jointed, or taken off the bone and chopped or cut into thin strips—this is the usual practice if the meat is to be stir-fried. In China, chicken breasts on the bone are sometimes cut into as many as 20 pieces before being stir-fried. The ability of theChinese to pick up these tiny pieces of chicken with chopsticks

Game birds
Small game birds are eaten in China and South-east Asia, but most are caught in the wild. Only quail and pigeon are farmed.

and to remove the meat from the bone in the mouth is a marvel of dexterity.

Serving meats and other foods in manageable morsels is the norm in Asia, where knives are viewed as weapons, and therefore inappropriate for such enjoyable communal activities as meals. Chopsticks are widely used, except in Thailand, where it is more common to find a spoon and fork at each table setting.

In Japan, chicken is the most important meat on the menu, second only to fish in terms of popularity. Chicken breast is the favorite cut, largely because it cooks so quickly and remains beautifully tender in dishes such as the famous *yakitori* or *teriyaki*. Skinless, boneless chicken breasts are readily available in Japan, unlike in the rest of Asia, where it is more usual for cooks to buy chickens whole as portions are regarded as wasteful, or simply as too expensive.

Throughout the East, frugality is a virtue, so one chicken might be used in three dishes: the breasts sliced in strips for a stir-fry; the rest of the meat or joints braised in a red-cooked dish or a curry; and the carcass used to make a flavorsome stock.

The skill that is exhibited by oriental cooks with the simplest equipment is testament to their creative love of food. Using a stout chopping board a cleaver, and a small sharp knife, a chicken can be chopped into appropriate portions in no time at all.

DUCK

Ducks symbolize happiness and fidelity, which doubtless contributes to their popularity in the Chinese cuisine. Duck is central to celebratory meals, and is served in countless imaginative ways. At Chinese New Year, for instance, duck is an essential part of every banquet.

How to joint a chicken
This method will give you eight good-sized portions of chicken.

1 Place the chicken breast side up on a chopping board. Ease one of the legs away from the body, and using a sharp knife make an incision to reveal the ball of the thighbone as you pull the leg further away from the body. When the thigh socket is visible, cut through the bone to release the drumstick and thigh in one piece. Repeat with the other leg.

2 Trim off the end of the leg bone, then locate the knee joint and cut the leg portion in half at this joint. Repeat with the other chicken leg.

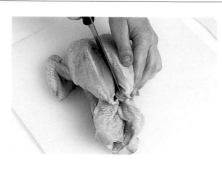

3 Cut through the breastbone so that the carcass is in two halves. Cut and separate each breast and wing from the backbone.

4 Cut both of the wing and breast pieces into two portions.

COOK'S TIPS
• Use the backbone to make stock, adding onion, celery and a piece of bruised root ginger if appropriate.
• If more pieces of chicken are required, say for stir-fries, the portions can be further divided. Deft oriental cooks will cut the breast and wing portions into as many as ten pieces, the legs into four pieces and the thighs into six pieces.

Right: In Asia, every part of the chicken is used—even the feet.

Duck is also popular in Vietnam, Thailand and Indonesia, but is seldom served in Japan.

Preparation and cooking techniques

The most famous duck dish has to be Peking duck. The classic way of making this universally popular restaurant dish involves hanging the prepared birds in a windy place to dry before roasting them in a special oven. At one time only the skin was eaten, but it is now more usual to eat the succulent meat as well. This is wrapped in a Mandarin pancake that has been spread with a little plum sauce and sprinkled with a few pieces of shredded scallion and slivers of cucumber. This dish is so popular that is now possible to buy packages of Peking duck, with all the trimmings, in the West.

The Chinese technique for preparing duck for roasting involves pricking the skin lightly all over with a fork, placing the bird on a trivet in the sink, then pouring a kettle of freshly boiled water over the top. The bird is then drained well, and the cavity wiped with paper towels, before being suspended from duck hooks or butcher's hooks and left to dry overnight. Once the bird is dry, the skin is sprinkled with a little salt. The bird is then placed on a trivet in a roasting pan and roasted in a hot oven until the skin is quite crisp and golden brown and the bird is fully cooked.

If the duck is to be jointed the same procedure can be used as for chicken.

COOK'S TIP

To make duck sauce to serve with Peking duck, heat 2 tablespoons sesame oil in a small pan. Add 6 tablespoons yellow bean sauce and 2 tablespoons soft light brown sugar and stir until smooth. Leave to cool before serving.

Right: An oven-ready duck

MEAT

PORK

This is as popular as chicken in China and in other parts of Asia with large Chinese communities. Like chicken, it blends happily with a wide range of ingredients, from vegetables to shellfish, and is equally at home with salted and pickled foods.

Wherever there are Muslim communities, however, pork is off limits and either beef or lamb is served instead. This is the case throughout Malaysia, the only exception being the Nonya style of cooking. This came about because of the intermarriage of Chinese merchant men with Malayan women who then started to cook pork dishes for their husbands. Nonya cooking is popular in Singapore, the west coast of Malaysia around Malacca and on the island of Penang.

Pork seldom features in Indonesian cuisine, except where cooked by members of the Chinese communities on the thousands of islands of the archipelago. Bali is an exception. The population of this island are mainly Hindu and therefore pork is permissible and widely used. A barbecued suckling pig is often served at the festivals that are such a feature of Balinese life.

Throughout Asia, therefore, the choice of meat is greatly influenced by religious beliefs and habits. Almost all Chinese except those who have converted to Islam love pork. Thais find the smell of lamb and mutton offensive; and Indians would never touch beef, because for them the cow is sacred. Poultry has none of these taboos.

Preparation and cooking techniques

For stir-frying, tenderloin, lean leg or belly are the preferred cuts, along with the meaty parts of chops or spareribs. The meat is cut into thin shreds so that it responds to really quick cooking over high heat, which is economical in the use of fuel.

For casseroles and braised dishes shoulder, spareribs or belly pork might be used, and the meat is often cooked for so long that it forms a luscious jelly-like mixture.

OTHER MEATS

Beef has only relatively recently been eaten in China and Asia, because cattle were considered beasts of burden and highly valued as such. The buffalo, too, has always been used widely, mainly in the paddy fields to plough the land prior to planting by hand. Beef and lamb are traditionally eaten only in the north of China and in places such as Malaysia where there are Muslim communities.

However, because of the proximity of Beijing to the northern provinces and the number of Chinese Muslim restaurants in the capital, lamb and beef are becoming increasingly popular there, too.

Lamb is cooked in the famous Mongolian hotpot, while beef is used in many different types of recipes, mainly as a substitute for pork. It is generally thinly sliced and used for dishes where a quick method of cooking such as stir-frying is required. Because it has a stronger flavor than pork, it works best in dishes that contain aromatic flavoring ingredients, such as garlic and onions.

Above: Lean leg steaks, tenderloin and spare ribs are the preferred cuts of pork.

FISH

There is an old Thai saying that suggests that all is well when "there is fish in the water and rice in the field". The main source of protein in the Thai diet is fish, which is hardly surprising when you take a look at the map and see the immense coastline in addition to the rivers, canals, lakes and flooded paddy fields. Along these waterways local people catch their daily supply of fish using simple fishing poles or nets. The fish is steamed, broiled with local spices or herbs, served in soups or curries, or added to salads or omelets.

The Cantonese word for fish is "yu" which sounds the same as the word for abundance or bounty. A whole fish is traditionally served at the Chinese New Year banquet as a symbol of hope that the family will enjoy a plentiful supply of food during the coming year. Serving a fish whole, as opposed to cutting it into portions, has great appeal in Asia, as the fish is aesthetically pleasing and complete. Also, by cooking the fish whole the juices are retained and the prized morsel that is the fish cheek can be served to the guest of honour.

Fish—nature's bounty—is exploited and enjoyed all over the East. With a coastline of over three thousand miles China has an abundant and varied supply of saltwater fish, some of which are familiar to Westerners, such as bass and sea bass, halibut, mackerel, sea bream, sole, plaice, tuna, cod, salmon, sardines and herring. China also has majestic rivers and lakes, which are a source of freshwater fish, including the ubiquitous carp.

Indonesia, the Philippines and Japan are all island nations, so it is not surprising that fish plays an important role in their cuisines. This is especially so in Japan, where an early moratorium on meat eating was one of the factors

Above: Freshwater carp, mackerel and grey mullet

that led to the Japanese expertise in preparing this popular food. Sashimi—very fresh fish that is finely sliced and served raw—is a delectable treat that is now appreciated well beyond the shores of the country that invented it. Trout, mackerel, tuna, salmon and herring are popular in Japan, as well as more exotic varieties, such as parrot fish or pomfret.

The most important requirement when buying and preparing is that it be as fresh as possible. This goes for all of Asia, but particularly Japan.

Buying fish

When buying fresh fish, the following indicators should be considered:
• The eyes of the fish should be bright and clear, not sunken.
• Gills should be clean and bright red/coral in color.
• The skin should be firm and fresh with a sheen and, when held, the fish should feel almost springy, as if it could swim away at any moment.
• Freshness can also be detected in the smell. It is difficult to disguise the odor of a fish that is past its prime.

Cooking fish

Steaming and simmering in clear stock are typical Asian cooking methods, along with deep-frying, pan-frying, stir-frying and braising.
Steaming Choose a very fresh whole fish. It should not be too large (about 1½ pounds). Rub the skin with salt and scatter the fish with shredded fresh

ginger root. Pour over a mixture of Chinese rice wine, soy sauce and sugar, then steam immediately over rapidly boiling water. For the best results remove the fish from the steamer when the fish is almost, but not absolutely cooked. The flesh should have just begun to flake when tested with the tip of a sharp knife, but should still be beautifully moist. Serve with the cooking juices poured over.

Clear simmering This method is usually reserved for larger fish (about 3 pounds). Use a fish kettle, if you have one. Pour in 7½ cups water and add salt to taste. Slice a 1½-inch piece of ginger root and add the slices to the kettle. Bring the water to a boil. Meanwhile slip a wide strip of foil under the fish to act as a strap. Lift the fish into the kettle, placing it on the trivet. Allow the water to return to a boil, then lower the heat and simmer for about 4 minutes. Lower the heat again, until the water barely bubbles, and cook the fish for 6–8 minutes. Lift the fish out of the fish kettle and let it drain before transferring it to a heatproof serving dish. Heat 5 tablespoons peanut oil and pour this over the hot fish to complete the cooking. This is a finish also used in Vietnamese cuisine, but they would scatter the fish with shredded scallion before pouring over the hot oil.

Frying Fish can be stir-fried, deep-fried or pan-fried, and whichever method is used, the fish is always cooked quickly to retain its shape and flavor.

Braising Used for whole fish, which is first fried in garlic and ginger oil. Soy sauce, Chinese mushrooms and other flavorings are added, then the pan is covered tightly and the fish is cooked very briefly.

Right: Snapper, parrot fish and pomfret

TYPES OF FISH

Carp A freshwater fish that is believed to have originated in Asia thousands of years ago. It is extensively farmed and thrives in ponds, lakes and flooded paddy fields. There are several varieties. Ask the fishmonger to remove the large scales and strong dorsal fins. The flesh is meaty and moist. Bake carp whole. Like grey mullet, it needs a stuffing with a distinctive flavor.

Cod A handsome fish with greenish bronze skin dappled with yellow, cod can vary in size from 2¼ pounds to 66 pounds. When properly cooked the flesh is moist and will break into large flakes. It is ideal for broiling, baking or frying, and is excellent in fish curries, but only add the cubes of pearly white fish at the very end of cooking so that they keep their shape.

Grey mullet This fish has dark stripes along the back, lots of thick scales and a heavy head. The flesh is soft and rather coarse but responds well to distinctive flavors. Try it baked, with a stuffing of ground pork and shrimp with ginger and scallion or chopped Chinese mushrooms, or moisten it with fish sauce and steam it.

Halibut This is a rather chunky flatfish and can reach an enormous size. It has a brownish skin on one side and is pearly white underneath with two eyes on the bridge of the snout. The smaller type, called a chicken halibut, weighs under 3 pounds and is ideal for poaching or baking.

Mackerel Mackerel and bonito are from the same family. The fish is easy to recognize, thanks to the wavy dark blue markings which run part of the way down to a silvery green side and pale underbelly. The inside of the mouth is black. Mackerel is an oily fish, with soft, pinkish flesh, and is ideal for broiling or poaching with miso. Serve mackerel with wedges of lemon or lime. It is also excellent in a *laksa* or a Thai fish soup.

Parrot fish Either blue or brightly colored, these are striking to look at and delicious to eat.

Plaice Easy to recognize, this flatfish has dark brown skin with orange spots and a white underside. The flesh is soft and moist. Cook plaice whole, either deep-fried or poached. If filleted, make a stock from the bones with bruised ginger, onion and seasoning.

Pomfret Held in high regard by Malayan and Thai cooks, the pomfret is a fisherman's dream as it is very easy to net. So easy that at one stage these fish were almost fished out. A type of flatfish, pomfret is silver grey with a pearly white underside. The ideal way to preserve the delicate flavor of this fish is to steam it with a few simple flavorings, such as ginger, scallion, light soy sauce and seasoning. It is good broiled and fried, too.

Salmon Often called the king of fish, the finest wild salmon makes delicious sashimi. Farmed salmon makes a very reasonable and good buy for a vast array of cooked dishes. The skin on a salmon's back is steely blue going down to a silver body. The flesh is oily, an attractive shade of pink, and firm. It is best either clear simmered or poached in a fish kettle or wrapped in foil and baked. Cutlets can be barbecued and served with Thai salad or used to make the Filipino dish, escabeche.

Sea bass The family of sea bass also includes the groupers (sometimes called garoupas). Sea bass is silver in color with a dark back and white underbelly. The flesh is delicate in flavor and holds its shape when cooked. The fish can be broiled, steamed, baked or barbecued whole, or cut into fillets or steaks before being cooked. It is expensive but worth it.

Sea bream Look for the gilt head with a gold spot on each cheek and squat compact body. Sea bream must be scaled before being cooked. The flesh is rather coarse but remains moist if not overcooked. Slash each side two or three times so that the thicker part of the fish will cook more evenly. Sea bream is best baked whole in an oiled or buttered foil parcel with ginger, scallion and seasoning. It is good served with a sweet and sour sauce.

Above: Tuna steaks and and salmon cutlets

Snapper The red snapper is perhaps the best known but there other colors, too, such as grey, silver and even a silver-spotted grey. The red color is quite distinctive. The fish has large eyes and very strong dorsal fins, which should be removed before cooking. The flesh is moist and well flavored. Small to medium snappers are good for steaming or baking whole.

Sole Another member of the flatfish family, sole has rough brown skin on top and a long lozenge-shaped body. The flesh has superb texture and a delicate flavor. Sole is best broiled or fried whole. It can be sold filleted, in which case ask for the bones to make stock for a fish soup.

Squid Asian cooks are fond of squid. In the West, this cephalopod usually comes ready cleaned, but if you should you come across squid in the unprepared state here is what to do: Pull the tentacles out from the body sac. Squeeze the tentacle in the center gently to remove the hard central bone or "beak". Trim the tentacles from the head and set aside. Using fingers pull the quill and innards from the body cavity and discard. Pull off the mottled outer skin, it should come away quite easily. Wash the squid well inside and out. It is now ready for stuffing. When it is two-thirds full, pop the tentacles back into the top of the sac. Secure the tentacles and the top of the squid body with a tooth pick.

If the squid are to be stir-fried, further preparation will be necessary: Slit the sac from top to bottom and turn it inside out. Flatten it on a board and score the inside surface lightly with a knife, pressing just hard enough to make a crisscross pattern. Cut lengthwise into ribbons. These will curl when cooked.

Tuna These enormous fish are the big brothers of the mackerel family. Tuna swim enormous distances at speed and this causes the muscles to fill with blood, which explains the deep red color of the fresh fish. The skipjack and the albacore are much sought after by the Japanese for making **sashimi** and **sushi.** When broiling or barbecuing tuna, marinate the fish first and then baste it to keep it moist throughout the cooking. It is also good pan-fried.

SHELLFISH

Asian cooks have access to a wonderful assortment of shellfish, not only from the ocean, but also—in the case of crabs and shrimp—from freshwater lakes, rivers and canals. In Asia it is considered essential that shellfish be as fresh as possible when cooked. This isn't always possible for the Western cook, who often has no option but to resort to using good quality frozen shellfish. In this case, the shellfish should be thawed slowly, and dried before being cooked. The cooking period should be kept to a minimum to preserve the delicate flavor and texture of the shellfish. In Asia, favored cooking methods for shellfish are steaming, deep-frying and stir-frying, but they are also used in soups, and made into dishes such as crab cakes.

Abalone This large shellfish has a particularly pretty shell, lined with what looks like mother-of-pearl. The flesh of abalone can be tough, and it is usually beaten to tenderize it before cooking. Frozen abalone is available from some oriental markets, and it is also possible to buy canned abalone. This is yellow-brown in color and has a savory flavor. The texture tends to be rubbery, so canned abalone is seldom served solo, but is usually combined

Above: Mussels and clams

with other ingredients. The can juices can be used in soups and sauces. Dried abalone is an expensive and much sought-after delicacy.

Clams There are many different types of clam. In Japan, the giant clam and the round clam are both used for making sushi, and in China clams with black bean sauce are a favorite treat. When buying clams, check that none of the shells are broken. Wash them well in running water, then leave in salt water before steaming for 7–8 minutes or until the shells open. Serve clams simply, with a dipping sauce

Above: Canned abalone

Mussels and Clams in Coconut Cream

Mussels and clams can be steamed, but here they are cooked Thai-style in coconut cream and flavored with lemongrass, kaffir lime leaves and Thai green curry paste.

SERVES 4–6

4 – 4 1/2 pounds mussels
1 pound baby clams
1/2 cup dry white wine
1 bunch scallions, chopped
2 lemongrass stalks, chopped
6 kaffir lime leaves, chopped
2 teaspoons Thai green curry paste
scant 1 cup coconut cream
2 tablespoons chopped
 fresh cilantro
salt and ground black pepper

1 Scrub the mussels, pull off the beards and remove any barnacles. Discard any mussels that are broken or which do not close when tapped sharply. Wash the clams thoroughly.

2 Put the wine in a large heavy pan with the scallions, lemongrass, kaffir lime leaves and curry paste. Bring to a boil, then simmer gently until the wine has almost evaporated. Add the mussels and clams to the pan, cover tightly with a lid and steam the shellfish over high heat for about 6 minutes, until they open.

3 Using a slotted spoon, transfer the mussels and clams to a heated serving bowl and keep hot. Discard any shellfish that remain closed. Strain the cooking liquid into a clean pan and simmer to reduce to about 1 cup.

4 Stir in the coconut cream and cilantro, with salt and pepper to taste. Heat through. Pour the sauce over the mussels and clams.

crab can be eaten whole. The meat is often pan-fried or cooked in a pot of rice where it releases a delicious, delicate flavor.

Lobster This luxury shellfish is usually served as a restaurant dish. To cook a live lobster, put it in a pan of ice cold water, cover the pan tightly and bring the water to a boil. The shell will turn bright red and the flesh will be tender and succulent when the lobster is cooked. If you buy a ready-cooked lobster, the tail should spring back into a curl when pulled out straight. One of the best ways of eating lobster is with a simple dip of soy sauce with grated ginger root.

Scallops Prized for their tender, sweet flesh, scallops are popular throughout Asia. The delicate flesh needs the briefest possible cooking. An excellent way of cooking scallops is to marinate them in a mixture of Chinese rice wine, sugar and soy sauce for 30 minutes, then steam them with the marinade and some slivers of ginger and scallion.

Above: Lobster and scallops

based on hoisin sauce, plum sauce or soy sauce with ginger. Clams are also very good in soups.

Mussels Another shellfish that is widely used in oriental cooking. Farmed mussels are now readily available and have the advantage that they are usually relatively free of barnacles. They are generally sold in quantities of 2 pounds, sufficient for a main course for two or three people. Look for good-size specimens with glossy shells. Discard any that are not closed, or which fail to shut when tapped. Use the back of a short stout knife to scrape away any barnacles, pull away the hairy "beards", then wash the shellfish thoroughly. The best way to cook mussels is to steam them in a small amount of flavored liquid in a large lidded pan for 3–4 minutes until the shells open. Use finely chopped ginger root, lemongrass, a few torn lime leaves and some fish sauce to add flavoring to the mussels.

Crabs are eaten with great relish all over the East. There are many different species which are exclusive to Asia.

Travelers to Thailand and Hong Kong will doubtless have seen—and enjoyed—blue swimming crabs. This species obligingly moults its shell so that the

Below: Blue swimming crabs

Fantail or phoenix shrimp

This way of serving shrimp comes from China. The cooked shrimp, with their bright red tails, are supposed to resemble the legendary phoenix, which is a symbol of dignity and good luck. Jumbo shrimp are used.

1 Remove the heads from the shrimp and peel away most of the body shell. Leave a little of the shell to keep the tail intact.

2 Make a tiny incision in the back of each shrimp and remove the black intestinal cord.

3 Hold the prepared shrimp by the tails and dip them lightly in seasoned cornstarch, and then in a frothy batter before cooking in hot oil until the tails, which are free from batter, turn red.

Left: Cooked shrimp

Shrimp and prawns Both shrimp and prawns can be caught in either fresh water or the sea. The names tend to be used indiscriminately in Asia. Shrimp can be small or large and the same holds good for prawns. Buy fresh raw shellfish where possible, choosing specimens that are a translucent grey colour tinged with blue. If using frozen shrimp, it is preferable to buy raw shellfish, thaw them slowly and dry them well before using. Further preparation will depend upon the chosen recipe. The shells may be left on or removed, or the shrimp may be shelled, with the tails left intact.

Left: Raw shrimp

Butterfly shrimp

Shrimp prepared this way cook quickly and curl attractively.

1 Remove the heads and body shells of the shrimp, but leave the tails intact. Pull out the intestinal cords with tweezers.

2 Make a cut through the belly of each shrimp.

3 Gently open out the two halves of the shrimp so that they will look like butterfly wings.

HERBS, SPICES AND AROMATICS

Above: Garlic

GARLIC

MANDARIN: *SUAN*; CANTONESE: *SUEN*;
THAI: *KRATIAM*

Garlic is a member of the lily family, which is the same genus as leeks and onions. It is believed to have originated in Asia, and is mentioned in Chinese texts that date back over 3,000 years. The ancient Egyptians valued it for food and also accorded it a ceremonial significance. Garlic's curative qualities are well documented, and in many cultures it is used to ward off evil.

Aroma and flavor

There are several varieties of garlic, from tiny heads to the aptly named elephant garlic. The color of the skin varies from white through to pink and purple, and the flavor can be anywhere from mild to extremely pungent. The most common variety in the Far East has a purple skin, a distinctive aroma and a fairly strong flavor with a hint of sweetness. In South-east Asia, cooks use a miniature variety of garlic. There are only four to six cloves in each bulb, and both the aroma and the flavor are much more concentrated. Thai cooks favour small garlic bulbs whose cloves have such thin skins that it is seldom necessary to remove them for cooking. The cloves are simply smashed with a cleaver, then added to the pan, where the skins dissolve to become part of the dish.

Culinary uses

Garlic forms a trinity of flavors with scallion and ginger in thousands of dishes in Chinese cooking, particuarly in Beijing and Sichuan. It is a basic ingredient in much of Asia, including Korea, but is less popular in Japan, where it is used mainly for medicinal purposes. Vietnamese cooks use a great deal of garlic, and in Thailand a mixture of crushed garlic, cilantro root and pepper is the foundation of many dishes. Garlic is an essential ingredient in the famous Thai curry pastes, too. Throughout Asia, garlic is also used to flavor oil for frying, partly because of the aromatic flavor it imparts, and also because it cuts down on the "oiliness".

Raw garlic is often used in dips, marinades and dressings.

Preparation and cooking techniques

Except in a few rare instances, when whole cloves of garlic are roasted or packed inside a chicken, garlic is always peeled before use. One of the easiest ways of doing this is to place it on a chopping board and crush it with the flat blade of a Chinese cleaver. The skin will separate from the flesh, and can easily be removed before the garlic is crushed completely, again with the flat of the blade. Although both cleaver and board will need to be washed afterwards, this is a lot easier than using a garlic press.

For whole cloves of garlic, or slices, just cut off the root end of the clove and remove the peel with your fingers.

If the garlic is to be used in a spice mix, as is often the case in South-east Asia, put the whole clove in a mortar and give it a blow with a pestle to release the skin. This can then be removed and the garlic crushed with the other ingredients. Recipes indicate whether garlic is to be sliced, chopped or crushed, but as a general rule, crushed garlic is used for overall flavor, the amount determining the intensity. Slices of garlic are used for accent, and are sometimes added early in the

cooking process, and then removed once they have imparted a subtle flavor to the dish.

Apart from buying whole cloves of garlic, Asian cooks appreciate the convenience of ground garlic in jars. Dried garlic is also available, either as granules or flakes. Flakes need to be reconstituted in water before stir-frying, but can be added directly to braised dishes with plenty of liquid. Garlic paste is available in tubes in the West but is not widely used in Asia.

Storage

Look for firm, plump garlic bulbs with clear, papery skins. Avoid any beginning to sprout. Garlic bulbs (also called heads) keep if stored in a cool, dry place. If it is too warm, the cloves will dry and become powdery.

Making garlic oil

1 Heat ½ cup sunflower oil in a small pan. Add 2 tablespoons crushed garlic.

2 Cook gently for about 5 minutes until the garlic is pale gold, stirring occasionally. Do not let it burn or the oil will taste bitter. Cool, strain and use as required.

GINGER

MANDARIN: *JIANG*; CANTONESE: *GEUNG*; THAI: *KHING*; JAPANESE: *SHOGA*

Ginger is believed to be indigenous to the tropical jungles of South-east Asia, and was introduced into China by way of India more than two thousand years ago. The portion of the plant popularly called ginger root is actually a rhizome or underground stem. The color ranges from pale pink (when very young) to a golden beige, with a dry, papery skin. Ginger is highly valued throughout Asia, not only as an aromatic, but also for its medicinal properties. It is believed to aid digestion, check coughs and quell nausea.

Aroma and flavor

Fresh ginger root (green ginger) has a refreshing scent, reminiscent of citrus, and a pleasant, sharp flavor. Young ginger is tender and mild enough to be stir-fried as a vegetable, while older roots become fibrous and more pungent. Ginger root is available dried, but tastes quite different from fresh. It is used mainly as a pickling spice and Asian cooks would not consider it an acceptable substitute for the fresh root. Ground ginger tastes different again; in Asia its use is limited to mixing with other ground spices such as when making curry powder.

Culinary uses

Ginger root is an indispensable ingredient in Eastern cooking. In China, it is usually paired with scallions to create a harmonious yin-yang balance in a wide variety of dishes; the cool scallion providing the yin and the hot ginger the yang. Together they complement (and sometimes tame) the dominant flavors of certain meats and

Above: Fresh ginger root, ground ginger and bottled ginger paste

seafood. Ginger is also used on its own to cut the oily flavor of some cooking oils and marinades. In Thailand, sticks of young ginger are often served as dippers with a spicy sauce, while Indonesians make a wonderful sambal by grinding chiles, shallots and garlic with ginger, and stirring in sugar, salt and rice vinegar. Pickled ginger also plays an important role in oriental cooking. It can be served solo as a side dish, or combined with other ingredients such as beef or duck. One of the most popular items on a Chinese restaurant menu is duck with pineapple and pickled ginger. Chinese pickled ginger is packed in sweetened rice vinegar, and is quite hot. Japanese pickled ginger has a more delicate flavor. The pale pink type called gari is always served with sushi or sashimi to refresh the palate between mouthfuls.

Preparation and cooking techniques

Ginger root is usually peeled before being used. The thin, tough skin is quite easy to scrape or cut away, and the flesh is then thinly sliced, grated, shredded or finely chopped. When the ginger is intended purely for use as a flavoring, and is discarded after cooking, it should be bruised using the flat blade of a knife or cleaver.

Storage

It used to be difficult to get really fresh, juicy ginger root in the shops, but it is now readily available. Look for firm pieces with smooth skin. If bought really fresh, ginger root will keep well for up to two weeks in a cool, dry place, away from strong light. Ginger root can also be frozen. It can be grated straight from the freezer and will thaw on contact with hot food.

Below: Japanese pink, pickled ginger is also known as gari.

Preparing ginger root

1 Thinly peel the skin using a sharp knife or vegetable peeler.

2 Grate the peeled root finely.

3 Alternatively, cut thin slices of ginger into matchstick strips, or coarsely chop the strips.

4 Bruise the root for use in dishes where the ginger will be removed.

GALANGAL

CHINESE: *LIANG JIANG;* THAI: *KHAA;* VIETNAMESE: *CU GIENG*

Like ginger root, galangal is a rhizome that grows underneath the ground. The finger-like protruberances of galangal tend to be thinner and paler in color, but the two look similar and are used in much the same way. Fresh galangal used to be virtually unobtainable in the West (although it was widely used in medieval Europe), but is now almost as easy to come by as ginger. There are two types. Greater galangal, also known as *lengkuas,* is a native of Indonesia, while lesser galangal originated in southern China. It is not as widely used as its larger relation, but is popular in Thailand, where it is known as *krachai.*

Laos powder is dried galangal that has been ground. Although it does not taste the same as fresh galangal, South-east Asian cooks appreciate its convenience and you will find it in many South-east Asian recipes. As a guide, 1 teaspoon of laos powder is equivalent to ½ inch fresh galangal, which has been peeled and chopped.

Aroma and flavor

Greater galangal has a pine-like aroma with a correspondingly sharp flavor; lesser galangal is more pungent and the flavor has been likened to a cross between ginger and black pepper. The rhizome is usually used fresh, but is also dried and powdered.

Culinary uses

Galangal is an essential flavoring in South-east Asian cooking, particularly in seafood and meat dishes. It is often pounded with shallots, garlic and chiles to make a spice paste for dips or curries. In Thailand, slices of galangal are added to soups, with shreds of lemongrass and lime leaves, while Vietnamese cooks add it to a peanut and lime sauce used to dress meat and vegetable salads.

Preparation and cooking techniques

Fresh galangal should always be peeled. It is usually thinly sliced or cut into matchsticks for cooking. Because it is harder than ginger, you will need to slice it before attempting to crush it, and slices or shreds need to be cooked for somewhat longer than ginger if they are to be tender.

Storage

Fresh galangal will keep for up to 2 weeks if stored in a cool, dry place. It can be stored in the refrigerator, but it must be well wrapped in waxed paper to keep it moist.

Right: Fresh and dried galangal

CHILES

MANDARIN: *LAJIAO;* CANTONESE: *LAT JIU;*
THAI: *PRIK*

Chiles are native to tropical America.
Christopher Columbus
introduced them to
Europe, having
come across them
in Mexico while
searching for peppercorns.
Their fame spread rapidly,
and soon they were
being cultivated in
Africa, India and the
Far East, where they rapidly
became an integral part of
the cuisine. There is,
however, a wild variety grown in China's
Sichuan province known as "Towards
Sky Cannon" or "Peacock's Eye Chile"
(*Capsicum sinense*) which appears to
be native to China. Hot chiles and sweet
peppers belong to the same genus,
capsicum. There are scores of varieties,
but the ones most commonly used in
Asia are the Indian *kalyanpur, kovilpatt*
and *kesanakurru* chiles, the
Japanese *honka* or *hontaka,* the
Korean chilli and the family of Thai
chiles, which includes the fiery bird's
eye. Like sweet peppers, many chiles
start out green and ripen to red, while
others change from yellow to

*Below: Green
chiles*

*Below: The same
type of chile can
come in various
colors.*

Chile paste

Ready-made chile
paste is sold in
jars, however, it is
easy to make at home.
Simply halve and
seed fresh chiles,
then place them in the bowl of a
food processor and purée to make
a smooth paste. A coarsely
chopped onion can be added
to the processor to add bulk to the
paste. Store small amounts of
the paste in the refrigerator for up
to 1 week, or spoon into small
containers, cover and freeze for
up to 6 months. *Sambal oelek,* an
Indonesian chile sauce, is made
in a similar way, but first the
chiles are blanched.

*Right: Red
chiles*

red and finally to brown or even black,
so what might appear to be a basket of
assorted chiles could turn out to be the
same type of chile in varying degrees of
ripeness. In size, they range from tiny
pods not much bigger than a pea to
12-inch monsters. Although Asian cooks
tend to use them fresh, chiles are also
available dried.

Aroma and flavor

Although heat is the quality most closely
associated with chiles, flavor is
important too, and aficionados use
terms such as sweet, smoky and
piquant to describe their favorite types.
The degree of heat varies from very

Left: Medium red chiles

blisteringly hot. Chiles grown in hot climes also tend to be hotter than those grown in cooler conditions.

mild to positively explosive, but can be moderated somewhat if the seeds and pithy membrane (where most of the heat resides) are removed. The shape and color give no sure indication of the hotness, for instance, some large green chiles are very mild, while others are

Culinary uses

That chiles and other spicy foods are perfect for hot climates is a bit of a paradox, but because they encourage blood to rush to the surface of the skin, they actually promote cooling. In many Asian countries, they are eaten out of hand, as snacks, and cooks seeking to determine the strength of a chile before buying will often do so by nibbling a sample from a market stall. Chiles are used fresh, in sauces and salads, and are essential ingredients in Indonesian sambals. They also find their way into a huge variety of cooked dishes, including stocks, soups, braised dishes and stir-fries, either with

Above: Neither the color nor the size of chiles gives a sure indication of their hotness as some green chiles are hotter than red ones, and some large chiles are hotter than small ones.

or without the seeds. Where just a hint of heat is required, chiles are sometimes added whole to a dish, then removed again just before serving.

Thailand is one of the world's major producers of fresh chiles, so it is not surprising that Thai cooks have developed some of the most exciting and innovative chile recipes. A favorite way of serving whole chiles is with a pork and shrimp stuffing. The chiles are steamed, then fried.

In Chinese cooking, hot chiles are used not to paralyse the tongue but to stimulate the palate. The regional cuisines of Hunan, Jiangxi, Guizhou and Yunnan all feature chiles, although not as strongly as does the province of Sichuan, which is famous for its spicy food. Even in Sichuan, however, chiles are used with discretion and at least a third of Sichuan dishes do not contain any chiles at all. Even the Cantonese use chiles in some of their dishes, and chili sauce and chili oil are popular condiments on Cantonese tables.

Preparing fresh chiles

1 Remove the stalks, then slice the chiles lengthwise.

2 Scrape out the pith and seeds from the chiles, then slice, shred or chop the flesh as required. The seeds can be either discarded or added to the dish, depending on the amount of heat that is required.

Preparing dried chiles

1 Remove the stems and seeds and snap each chile into 2–3 pieces.

2 Put these in a deep bowl, pour over hot water to cover and leave to stand for 30 minutes. Drain, reserving the soaking water if it can usefully be added to the dish, and use the pieces of chile as they are, or chop them more finely.

Making chile flowers

Thai cooks are famous for their beautiful presentation, and often garnish platters with chile flowers. These are quite simple to make.

1 Holding each chile in turn by the stem, slit it in half lengthwise.

2 Keeping the stem end of the chile intact, cut it lengthwise into fine strips.

3 Put the prepared chiles in a large bowl of iced water, cover and chill for several hours.

4 The cut chile strips will curl back to resemble the petals of a flower. Drain well on paper towels and use as a garnish. Small chiles may be very hot, so don't be tempted to eat the flowers.

Right: Dried chiles

Using dried chiles

Dry roasting heightens the flavor of whole dried chiles. Heat a heavy-based frying pan without adding oil. Press the chiles on to the surface of the pan to roast them, but don't allow them to burn, or their flavor will become bitter. Once the chiles are roasted, remove them from the pan and leave to cool completely, then crush or grind them in a mortar with a pestle before adding to dishes.

Preparation and cooking techniques

Chiles must be handled with care. They contain capsaicin, an oily substance which causes intense irritation to sensitive skin. Get capsaicin on your hands, or worse, transfer it to your eyes by rubbing, and you will experience considerable pain. It is therefore very important to wash your hands immediately after handling chiles, and to use plenty of soap, as the oil does not dissolve in water alone. Some cooks prefer to wear latex gloves when preparing chiles, and some become extremely adept at using a knife and fork, and avoid touching the chiles at all, but whichever method you use, remember that it is also essential to wash cutting boards and implements.

Storage

Look for firm, unblemished fruit, avoiding any chiles that are soft or bruised. Some types look wrinkled even in their prime, so do not let this put you off fruit that otherwise appears to be in good condition. The best way to store chiles is to wrap them in paper towels, place them in a plastic bag and keep them in the refrigerator. They will keep well for a week or more, but it is a good idea to check them occasionally and discard any that begin to show signs of softening. If you intend to use them

solely for cooking, they can be frozen. There is no need to blanch them if you plan to use them fairly quickly. To dry your own chiles, thread them on a string, hang them in a warm place for a week or two until they are dry and crumbly, then put them in a mortar and crush them with a pestle.

Below: Pickled chiles are available in jars. They are mainly used as a relish.

LEMONGRASS

MANDARIN: *NINGMENG CAO;*
CANTONESE: *XIANG MAO;*
MALAY: *SERAI;* THAI: *TAKRAI;*
VIETNAMESE: *XA*

Few ingredients have seized the Western imagination quite so dramatically as has lemongrass in recent years. At one time this scented grass was little known outside Southeast Asia; today it is to be found in nearly every supermarket. Lemongrass is a perennial tufted plant with a bulbous base. It grows in dense clumps in tropical and subtropical countries and is commercially cultivated on a grand scale. The cut stems are about 8 inches long, and look a little like fat scallions or very skinny leeks.

Aroma and flavor

It is only when the stems are cut that the distinctive citrus aroma can be fully appreciated. This is matched by the clean, intense lemon flavor, which has a hint of ginger but none of the acidity associated with lemon or grapefruit.

Below: Dried lemongrass

Left: lemongrass

Lemon rind is sometimes suggested as a substitute, but it lacks the intensity and liveliness of fresh lemongrass, and will give disappointing results. Ground dried lemongrass, also known as serai powder, can be used instead of fresh. As a guide, about 1 teaspoon powder is equivalent to 1 fresh stem. Whole and dried chopped stems are also available in jars from oriental markets, and larger supermarkets as are jars of lemongrass paste.

Culinary uses

Lemongrass is widely used throughout Southeast Asia, in soups, sauces, stir-fries, curries, salads, pickles and marinades. It is a perfect partner for coconut milk, especially in fish, seafood and chicken dishes. Thai cooks often start a stir-fry by adding a few rings of lemongrass and perhaps a little grated or chopped fresh ginger root or galangal to the oil. This not only flavors the oil, but also fills the room with a glorious aroma. A favourite Vietnamese dish consists of sea bream coated in a lemongrass paste. It is left to stand until the flavor penetrates the fish, and then fried.

Preparation and cooking techniques

There are two main ways of using lemongrass. The stem can be bruised, then cooked slowly in a soup or stew until it releases all its flavor and is removed, or the tender portions of the lemongrass (usually the lower 2 inches of the stem) can be

Above: Lemongrass paste

sliced or finely chopped, then stir-fried or used in a salad or braised dish. Often one stem will serve both purposes, the tougher top end is used for background flavoring while the tender portion forms the focal point of a dish. For basting food that is to be broiled or barbecued, the upper portion of the lemongrass stem can be used. The fibrous end is flattened to make a brush.

Storage

Store lemongrass stems in a paper bag in the refrigerator. They will keep for 2–3 weeks.

Making a lemongrass brush

Instead of discarding the dry stalk, make it into a basting brush.

Trim off the bottom 2 inches of the lemongrass stalk to use in a recipe, then flatten the cut end of the remaining stalk using a cleaver or pestle to produce a fibrous brush.

KAFFIR LIMES

THAI: *BAI MAKRUT;* INDONESIAN: *DAUN JERAK;*
VIETNAMESE: *CHANH SAC;* MALAYSIAN: *LIMAU
PURUT;* BURMESE: *SHAUK-NU*

These fruit are not true limes, but
belong to a subspecies of the citrus
family. Native to South-east Asia, they
have dark green knobbly skins, quite
unlike those of their cousins, the
smooth-skinned limes or lemons.
The fruit is not edible. The rind is
sometimes used in cooking, but it is the
leaves that are most highly prized. Kaffir
limes yield very little juice, and what
there is is very sour. Thai and Malayan
cooks occasionally use it to heighten
the flavor of dishes with a citrus base.
Vietnamese women use the juice as a
hair rinse.

Japanese citron peel
In Japan, very thin slices of
citron peel *(yuzu)* are used
to garnish soups. The
ground peel is used to
flavor miso.

Aroma and flavor

The scented bouquet
is unmistakably
citrus, and the full
lemon flavor is
released when the
leaves are torn
or shredded.

Culinary uses

Kaffir lime leaves are
synonymous with Thai cooking,
and are also used in Indonesia,
Malaysia, Burma and Vietnam. The
leaves are torn or finely shredded
and used in soups (especially hot and
sour soups) and curries. The
finely grated rind
is sometimes
added to fish or
chicken dishes.

Storage

Fresh kaffir limes and leaves are
obtainable in oriental markets. They will
keep for several days, or can be frozen.
Freeze-dried kaffir lime leaves are also
available. These are used in much the
same way as bay leaves, and do not
need to be soaked in water first.
Stored in a sealed container in a
cool, dry place, the dried leaves
will keep their flavor for only
a few months.

*Above: Kaffir
limes and kaffir
lime leaves*

ORANGE OR TANGERINE PEEL

MANDARIN: *CHEN PI;*
CANTONESE: *CHAN PEI*

Both oranges and tangerines
originated in China, where they
were held in high regard for
centuries before traders
introduced them to the West.
The sun-dried peel of
both these citrus fruits
is used as a spice,
particularly in
the cooking
of Sichuan
and Hunan.

Left: Dried orange peel

Aroma and flavor

The dried peel is dark brown and brittle,
but retains a strong citrus fragrance.
When it is used in cooking, it imparts a
tangy flavor to the food.

Culinary uses

Originally, dried citrus peels were mainly
used medicinally. Today, they are a
popular seasoning and are often
combined with star anise and cinnamon
when braising meat or poultry.

Preparation and cooking techniques

In braised dishes, pieces of dried peel
are used in much the same way as star
anise, and are discarded after cooking.
When peel is used in a stir-fry, however,
it is first soaked in water until soft, and
the pith is scraped off before the peel is
shredded or sliced.

Storage

Orange and tangerine peel are sold in
plastic bags in oriental markets. Once
opened, the bags should be resealed
and kept in a cool, dry, dark place. The
peel will keep for many months.

Left: Dried curry leaves

CURRY LEAVES

INDONESIAN: *DAUN KARI;* THAI: *BAI KAREE;*
BURMESE: *PINDOSIN*

These are the shiny green leaves of a hardwood tree that is indigenous to India. They are widely used in Indian cooking, especially in South India and Sri Lanka, and were introduced into Malaysia by Tamil immigrants. The spear-shaped leaves grow on a thin stem. They are slightly serrated, with a pale underside, and are not unlike small bay leaves.

Aroma and flavor

Curry leaves have an intriguing warm fragrance, with just a hint of sweet, green pepper or tangerine. The full flavor is released when the leaves are bruised. When added to curries or braised dishes, they impart a distinctive flavor. Dried curry leaves come a very poor second to fresh, and rapidly lose their fragrance.

Culinary uses

The leaves are used whole or torn in Indian, Malayan and Indonesian curries. Fried in ghee, with mustard seeds, they make a good addition to dhals.

Preparation and cooking techniques

Rinse the leaves and then strip from the stems. Use the leaves whole or chopped as directed in recipes.

Storage

Fresh curry leaves can be bought from shops selling Indian and Gujerati produce. They will keep for several days in the vegetable compartment of the refrigerator, but should be closely wrapped to prevent their distinctive flavor from being transferred to other items. Alternatively—and this is more convenient—open freeze the leaves, then transfer them to a plastic box. Dried leaves do not have much taste, unless you can locate the vacuum-packed variety, which have better color and flavor.

MINT

CHINESE: *PAK HOM HO;* INDONESIAN: *DAUN PUDINA;* THAI: *BAI SARANAI;* VIETNAMESE: *HUNG QUE*

Mint originated in the Mediterranean region, but it spread rapidly throughout the world. There are many types grown in Asia, but the most commonly used is a tropical variety of spearmint, which has grey-green oval leaves.

Aroma and flavor

Mint has a fresh, stimulating aroma. The Asian variety is much more strongly flavored than most European types, and is slightly sweet tasting, imparting a cool aftertaste.

Culinary uses

Mint is an essential ingredient in Vietnamese cooking, and it was they who introduced it to the Thais. Its fresh flavor is enjoyed in many salads, and in the delicious rice paper rolls that go by the name of *goi cuon*. Thai cooks like to add a handful of mint leaves just before serving some of their soups and highly spiced dishes. As it has such a dominant flavor, mint is seldom used with other herbs.

Preparation

Wash the leaves on the stem under cold water, shake off the excess moisture and pat dry using paper towels.

Storage

Wrap loosely in paper towels and keep in the vegetable compartment of the refrigerator, or stand the stems in a pitcher of cold water covered with a plastic bag and keep in the door of the refrigerator.

Below: Mint

BASIL

THAI: *BAI HORAPA* (SWEET BASIL), *BAI KRAPOW* (HOLY BASIL), *BAI MANGLAK* (HAIRY OR LEMON-SCENTED BASIL); INDONESIAN: *INDRING*; JAPANESE: *MEBOKI*

Basil is one of the oldest herbs known to man. It is an annual and is believed to have originated in India. Hindus hold it sacred and often plant it around their holy places.

In India, however, it is not used in cooking as much as it is in the rest of Asia. In Vietnam, Laos and Cambodia it is an important ingredient, but it is in Thailand that basil is most widely used, and it is the varieties of basil favored by the Thais that you will find most frequently in oriental shops in the West. *Horapa* (sweet basil) comes closest to the Mediterranean varieties with which we are most familiar. It has shiny green leaves and the stems are sometimes purple. *Krapow,* commonly known as holy basil, is another sweet basil, but with narrower leaves that tend to be dull rather than shiny. The leaves have serrated red or purple edges. Thais also use a lemon-scented basil—sometimes called hairy basil—but this does not travel well and is seldom seen outside Thailand. If you cannot obtain Asian basil when cooking an oriental dish, any American variety can be used instead, but the flavor will not be the same, and you should use a little more than the amount recommended. Basil is best used fresh, but freeze-dried whole and chopped leaves are also available from larger supermarkets.

Aroma and flavor

Of the Asian basils, *horapa* has a faint aniseed flavor, while holy basil is more pungent. Hairy basil has a lemon scent and is slightly peppery.

Above: Sweet basil

Below: Thai basil

Culinary uses

Sweet basil leaves are added to curries or salads both as an ingredient and also as a garnish. They impart a fresh spicy flavor. Holy basil leaves only release their full flavor when cooked and are therefore frequently used in stir-fries.

Preparation

Strip the leaves from the stem and either tear them into pieces or add them whole to the other ingredients. Avoid chopping basil leaves.

Storage

Wrap bunches of basil loosely in paper towels and keep them in the salad compartment of the refrigerator. Alternatively,

Growing basil

If you have difficulty locating supplies of fresh basil for Thai or Vietnamese recipes, it might be worth growing your own from seed. Many gardeners markets and hardware markets sell the full range of Asian varieties, and they do well wherever the climate is relatively mild. Start them off in pots on a warm window sill, and move them to a sunny patio after the threat of frost has passed.

stand the stems in a jug of water covered with a plastic bag. Keep them in the refrigerator and change the water every day.

SHISO

JAPANESE: *SHISO* (GREEN), *AKA SHISO* (RED); KOREAN: *KKAENNIP*

Also known as *perilla*, this annual nerb is grown in China, Korea, Laos and Vietnam and is very well known in Japan, where is also called *oba*.

The leaves can be green or reddish-purple and often appear wrinkled. When crushed, they release a pungent aroma, similar to that of mint. Japanese cooks use shiso in tempura and when making *umeboshi* (pickled plums). In the presence of an acid, the red-leafed variety dyes ginger root red.

Above: Shiso

CILANTRO

MANDARIN: *XIANGCAI;* CANTONESE: *YUAN SUI;*
BURMESE. *NAN NAN BIN;* THAI: *PAK CHEE*

Also known as Chinese parsley—and
familiar to Europeans as coriander—
cilantro is one of the oldest known
herbs in the world, and also one of
the most popular. Although a native
of southern Europe, fresh cilantro
has become an indispensable
ingredient throughout Asia and
the Middle East, as well as
in Latin America.

Aroma and flavor

Cilantro takes its name from
the Greek *koris,* meaning a bug. The
leaves of the plant are supposed to give
off a smell similar to that of a room
infested with bed bugs, yet the Chinese,
displaying a wicked sense of humour,
call cilantro "fragrant leaves". When
dry-fried, the seeds smell rather like
burnt orange, while the ground seeds
impart a warm, spicy aroma to food.

Culinary uses

Asian cooks use every part of the plant:
the stems are used for flavoring; the
leaves in stir-fries, soups and noodle
dishes; and as a garnish, the seeds for
spice pastes and
in curries. Ground
coriander is widely used, often in
combination with ground cumin.
In Thailand, the roots are
used, too. This can
present problems for
the Western cook,
as the thin, hair-like
roots are usually
removed before the
cilantro reaches the
market. One answer is to
grow your own, but if this
is impractical, use the bottom
portion of the stem as
a substitute.

*Above: Cilantro—
Asian cooks use the
roots as well as the leaves
and stems.*

Below: Ground coriander

Preparation and cooking techniques

Try not to chop fresh
cilantro too finely, or the
beauty of the serrated
leaves will be lost.
Never overcook the
leaves or they will
become limp and
unpalatable; either
use them raw as a
garnish, or add them
to a dish at the very
last moment.
If a recipe calls
for ground

*Left: Coriander
seeds*

coriander, it is preferable to dry-fry
and grind the seeds yourself, as the
aroma and flavor will be much more
pronounced. The seeds and ground
spice are known as coriander in the US.

Storage

Fresh cilantro will not keep for more
than a couple of days unless stood in a
jug of cold water and covered with a
plastic bag, in which case it will stay
fresh for a little longer. Cilantro roots are
seldom available, but if you do locate a
supply, the cleaned roots can be frozen.

Dried coriander seeds keep well, but
the ready-ground powder rapidly loses
its aroma and flavor. Buy small
quantities so that you can replenish
your supplies regularly.

Right: Ground and fresh turmeric

TURMERIC

BURMESE: *HSANWEN;* MANDARIN: *WONG GEUNG;* CANTONESE: *YU CHIN;* JAPANESE: *UKON*

Turmeric comes from the ginger family but does not have the characteristic "heat" associated with fresh ginger. The plant, a rhizome, is indigenous to hot, humid, hilly areas of South-east Asia from Vietnam to Southern India. Frequently referred to as "Indian saffron", it shares with saffron the capacity to tint foods yellow, but is nowhere near as subtle as the much more expensive spice. The bright yellow color, which can clearly be seen when the rhizome is sliced, is also used as a dye of silks and cottons, including the fabric used to make robes for Buddhist monks. When mixed to a paste, turmeric is sometimes smeared on the cheeks to protect the skin from the sun. The world's largest producer of turmeric is India, but Indonesia and China also grow significant quantities of this spice.

The bulk of the turmeric crop is used for domestic consumption or ground and sold as powder.

Aroma and flavor

Fresh turmeric is sometimes available from oriental markets. When cut it has a peppery aroma with a hint of wood in the background. It imparts a warm, slightly musky flavor and a rich color to any food with which it is cooked. The dried spice has similar properties.

Culinary uses

Ground turmeric is an essential ingredient in curry powders, being responsible for the characteristic yellow color. It is also used in the preparation of some blends of mustard powder and is the spice that gives piccalilli its lurid color. A famous Anglo-Indian breakfast dish—kedgeree—contains turmeric, and it is also used in pilau rice, dhals and vegetable dishes. Turmeric has a natural affinity with fish, and is often used in Malayan recipes.

Preparation and cooking methods

Using a sharp knife, slice off the skin, then slice, grate or chop the flesh. It can be ground with other ingredients to make a curry paste. Some people like to wear gloves when preparing fresh turmeric as it can stain the skin. Ground dried turmeric is easy to use as it needs no preparation.

Storage

Fresh turmeric will keep for up to 2 weeks, if stored in a cool, dry place away from strong light. It can be stored in the refrigerator, but must be well wrapped to keep it moist. Like all ground spices, ground turmeric will lose its potency on keeping, so buy only small quantities and keep the powder in an airtight container in a cupboard away from strong light. The only time whole pieces of dried turmeric are likely to be called for is in the preparation of some pickles. Do not attempt to grind the whole dried spice to make powder; the rhizomes are too hard.

Preparing fresh turmeric

1 Using a sharp knife, scrape or slice off the skin.

2 Grate the flesh using a standard box grater, or slice or chop, depending on the recipe.

Above: Star-shaped star anise

STAR ANISE

MANDARIN: *PAK KOK;* CANTONESE: *BOAT GOK;* INDONESIAN: *BUNGA LAWANG;* THAI: *POY KAK BUA*

Star anise is the unusual star-shaped fruit of an evergreen tree native to South-west China and Vietnam. The tree has yellow flowers that resemble narcissus. These give way to the star-like fruits, which are harvested before they ripen. The points of the star contain amber seeds. Both the seeds and the husk are used for the ground spice. In China, one point, the name given to one section of the star, is often chewed after a meal as a digestive.

Aroma and flavor

Star anise both smells and tastes like liquorice. The flavor can also be detected in the alcoholic drinks pastis and anisette.

Culinary uses

The warm aromatic flavor of star anise complements rich meats. It is very popular in Chinese cuisine, especially with pork and duck, and it is used to flavor beef soups in Vietnam. It is also sometimes used in sweet dishes, such as fruit salads. Ground star anise is one of the main ingredients of five spice powder.

Preparation and cooking methods

Star anise can be added whole, and looks so attractive that it is often left in a dish when serving, even though it no longer fulfils any culinary function. When a small quantity is required, the spice can be broken and just one or two points or segments added. It is possible to grind star anise at home, but it should be used sparingly as it has a quite powerful flavor.

Storage

As a whole spice star anise has a long shelf life. Buy the ground spice in small quantities from a shop with a high turnover of stock, and store in a cool, dry place, away from direct light, to retain the maximum aroma and flavor.

Below: The best cloves are plump and unbroken.

CLOVES

MANDARIN: *TING HSIANG;* CANTONESE; *DING HEUNG;* JAPANESE: *CHOJI;* THAI: *KAAN PLOO*

Cloves are the unopened flower buds of a tree that is a member of the myrtle family. They originated in the Spice Islands in Indonesia and were taken to the Seychelles and Mauritius early in the 18th century. The biggest producer now is Zanzibar where the fresh pink buds are picked twice a year. They are then dried on palm leaf mats or over a gentle heat when they turn the familiar reddish brown. The name clove is derived from the Latin *clavus,* meaning a nail.

Aroma and flavor

Cloves have an intense fragrance and an aromatic flavor that can be fiery. They are slightly astringent.

Culinary uses

In Asia, cloves are mainly used in savory dishes. Thai cooks use them to cut the rich flavor of duck, and also use them with tomatoes, salty vegetables and in ham or pork dishes. Ground cloves are an essential ingredient in many spice mixtures, including the famous Chinese five spice powder. They are also one of the ingredients in Worcestershire sauce.

Preparation

Cloves need no preparation. When purchasing them, look for plump, unbroken cloves.

Storage

Whole cloves have a long shelf life if kept in a cool place. Ground cloves should be bought in small quantities and stored in an airtight jar away from strong light, so that the spice retains its color and flavor. To make a small amount of ground cloves, crush the central bud at the top of the clove and use immediately.

CINNAMON

INDONESIAN: *KAYU MANIS PADANG;* THAI: *OB CHUEY*

The best quality cinnamon is grown in Sri Lanka but it also flourishes elsewhere in Asia, particularly on the coastal strip of South India and Burma. The spice is actually the bark of a bushy tree that is a member of the laurel family. After three years, the branches are cut off and a long incision is made in the bark, so that this can be lifted off. The operation is carried out during the rainy season, when the humidity speeds the peeling process. The bark is then dried in the sun and hand rolled to produce the familiar quills or sticks. Ground cinnamon is also produced.

Aroma and flavor

Cinnamon has a delightfully exotic bouquet, sweet and fragrant, thanks to an essential oil, oil of cinnamon, which is used medicinally. The flavor is warm and aromatic.

Culinary uses

Cinnamon has universal appeal as a flavoring both in sweet and savory dishes and in a multitude of cakes and breads. In Asia, the sticks are used in spicy meat dishes, often with star anise, with which cinnamon has an affinity. Indonesian cooks use cinnamon in their famous spiced beef and coconut milk stew known as rendang.

Above: Cinnamon sticks and ground cinnamon

Preparation

Add the whole or broken cinnamon stick as directed in the recipe. The sticks are very hard and it is difficult to grind them at home, so it is preferable to buy ready-ground cinnamon.

Storage

Cinnamon sticks have a long shelf life, and will keep for a year or more in an airtight container. Buy ground cinnamon in small quantities from a store with a high turnover of stock and keep it in an airtight container away from both heat and strong light.

Below: Ground cassia and cassia bark

CASSIA

CHINESE: *KUEI;* JAPANESE: *KEIHI;* THAI: *OB CHOEY*

Cassia is sometimes known as Chinese cinnamon. Like cinnamon, it comes from the bark of a tree which is related to laurel, but whereas cinnamon is native to Sri Lanka, cassia comes from Burma, and is also cultivated in China, Indo-China and Indonesia. It is harvested in much the same way as cinnamon, but the bark is not as fine, so although it curls, it will not form the fine quills we associate with cinnamon.

Aroma and flavor

Cassia smells rather like cinnamon, but is more pungent.

Culinary uses

Chinese cooks make much use of cassia. It is one of the constituents of five spice powder and is also an important ingredient in the elaborate spiced stock known as *lu* which is used throughout China for simmering foods. When this stock is first made, it is very strongly flavored, and is generally used for cooking beef, pot-roast style. The stock is not served with the beef, but is saved to be used again, perhaps with poultry. It may well be boiled up a third time, to simmer

fish or shellfish. In some homes, a pan of *lu* will be kept going for months. Cracked cassia quills and cassia buds (which look like cloves) are used in the East to give a warm aromatic flavor to pickles, curries and spiced meat dishes.

Preparation and cooking methods

Cassia is quite tough. Break the pieces as required with the end of a rolling pin or put them in a mortar and use a stout pestle to shatter them. Where ground cassia is required, it is best to buy it in that form.

Storage

As for cinnamon.

CUMIN

CHINESE: *KUMING;* JAPANESE: *KUMIN;* THAI: *YEERAA*

Cumin has been cultivated since earliest times. It is believed to have originated in the Eastern Mediterranean, but is now widely cultivated, especially in China, India, Indonesia and Japan. The plant is a member of the parsley family, but only the seeds (whole or ground) are used in cooking.

Above: Small green and large black cardamom pods

Aroma and flavor

Cumin has a sweet spicy aroma and the flavor is pungent and slightly bitter.

Culinary uses

Cumin is often partnered with whole or ground coriander seeds. Indian cooks are particularly partial to cumin, and it was they who introduced the spice to Singapore, Malaysia and Indonesia.

Preparation

To bring out their full flavor, the seeds are often dry-fried. They are then used whole or ground in a spice mill or in a mortar using a pestle.

Storage

Buy the whole spice in small quantities. Store in a cool place away from bright light. For best results dry-fry and grind the whole spice as

Above: Cumin seeds and ground cumin

and when required. You can buy ready ground cumin from supermarkets, but it loses its flavor rapidly.

CARDAMOM

BURMESE: *PHALAZEE;* JAPANESE: *KARUDAMON;* THAI: *LUK KRAVAN*

A native of South India, cardamom is a tall herbaceous perennial belonging to the ginger family. It is largely grown for its pods, although Thai cooks sometimes use the leaves for flavoring. The pods are either added whole to spicy dishes, or opened so that the tiny dark seeds can be extracted. The most familiar pods are pale green, and there are also white pods, which are simply bleached green ones. Black cardamoms, which come from Vietnam and India, are large and coarse, and taste quite different. Cardamom pods are harvested by hand, and this makes them more costly than most other spices.

Aroma and flavor

Cardamoms are sweet, pungent and highly aromatic. They have a pleasantly warm flavor, with hints of lemon and eucalyptus. When chewed after a meal, the pods are said to aid digestion as well as sweeten the breath.

Culinary uses

Indian cooks use cardamom to flavor curries, pilaus and desserts, so it is not surprising that the spice is popular wherever there are Indian communities.

Preparation

The pods can be used whole or bruised and dry-fried to enhance the flavor. If just the seeds are required, discard the outer husks. For ground cardamom, grind the seeds in a mortar using a pestle.

Storage

Buy the whole pods and store in an airtight jar in a cool dry place. Grind seeds as required.

FENNEL SEEDS

MANDARIN: *WOOI HEUNG;* CANTONESE: *HUI XIANG;* THAI: *YIRA*

Although native to the Mediterranean, this member of the parsley family is widely grown in India and Japan. The ridged seeds are sage green in color.

Aroma and flavor

Sweet, warm and aromatic, fennel seeds have a distinct anise flavor.

Culinary uses

Fennel seeds are a constituent in many spice mixtures, especially those that are intended to be used with fish or shellfish. Ground fennel is one of the constituents of Chinese five spice powder.

Preparation

Dry-fry before grinding to release the full flavor of the spice.

Storage

Buy small quantities of seeds at a time and store in an airtight jar away from strong light.

Above: Fennel seeds

Chinese five spice powder

Close your eyes as you enter a Chinese supermarket or store and the distinctive aroma of Chinese five spice power seems to dominate. This reddish brown spice mixture is classically composed of equal quantities of Sichuan peppercorns, cassia or cinnamon, cloves, fennel seeds and star anise. Blends vary, however, and ginger, galangal, black cardamom and licorice can be included. Ginger gives the spice blend a sweeter flavor, and this version is used in desserts. Five spice powder is very popular in China, and is particularly complementary when used with duck, pork, red cooked meats (cooked in soy sauce) and barbecued meats such as spareribs. Make your own powder by grinding equal amounts of the five spices with a mortar and pestle, or buy the ready ground powder in small quantities and store in an airtight jar away from strong light. A five spice paste is now available in small jars from many of the larger supermarkets.

Japanese seven spice powder

Seven spice powder, which is also known as *shichimi-togarashi,* seven flavor seasoning or seven taste powder, is a delicious condiment that the Japanese like to shake on to food at the table much as we would use salt and pepper. It is especially popular as a seasoning for soups and noodles and other dishes such as sukiyaki and tempura. *Shichimi* is made from a combination of the following ingredients: ground chile, hemp seed, poppy seed, rape seed, *sansho* (the Japanese name for Sichuan pepper-corns), black and white sesame seeds, and dried ground tangerine peel. In some mixes ground nori (seaweed) is added. It would be usual to buy this mixture ready prepared. Blends of this spice mixture vary, from mild to very sharp.

Right: Chinese five spice powder (top) and Japanese seven spice powder (bottom) can be bought ready-ground from supermarkets and Asian markets.

PEPPER

MANDARIN: *HU-CHIAO*; CANTONESE: *WOO JIU*;
INDONESIAN: *MERICA*; THAI: *PRIK THAI*;
VIETNAMESE: *HAT-TRIEU*

Often referred to as the king of spices, pepper has an ancient and illustrious past. Known and valued in India for over 2,000 years, it was introduced into Europe in the 4th century BC. Demand rapidly grew, but transporting the spice across Asia by the caravan routes was costly, and the monopoly meant that the prices remained astronomically high. Even in Roman times there was outrage that the spices were sold at one hundred times their original cost.

It was the demand for pepper that inspired the search for sailing routes to the East which changed the course of history. When the Portuguese explorer Vasco da Gama opened up the sea route to India in the 15th century, Lisbon became the spice capital of the world, but still the prices stayed high. Even today pepper is the most important spice on world markets, both in terms of value and volume.

Pepper is a perennial climbing vine indigenous to the Malabar coast of India where it is said that the best pepper is still produced. It grows best near the equator and is cultivated intensively in Sarawak and Thailand, as well as in tropical Africa and Brazil. In the Malayan state of Sarawak the vines are trained up long ironwood frames or round tree trunks. The vines have to be controled

Green peppercorns

These are simply unripe berries. They are sold on the stem in some Thai supermarkets, and are a popular ingredient in that country. They can be used fresh, but are also dried, pickled or canned. Those that are bottled or canned need to be rinsed and drained, then added whole or crushed as the recipe dictates. Freeze-dried green peppercorns can be ground in a peppermill. Green peppercorns have a less complex flavor than white or black peppercorns but are still quite fiery.

Above: Fresh green peppercorns are sometimes sold on the stem in Thai supermarkets.

to prevent them from climbing too high, which would make harvesting difficult. The leaves are long, green and pointed, and white flowers blossom on the catkins or "spikes".

The plant starts fruiting three to five years after planting, and the harvest continues every three years thereafter for forty years, which is the life of the plant. When the berries are harvested they are still unripe and green. In Sarawak they are dried on mats in the sun, and are raked frequently until the skin shrivels and the berries darken to become the familiar black peppercorns. Another method is to immerse the berries in boiling water, drain them well, and then dry them in kilns.

White peppercorns are husked ripe berries. The berries are picked when they are red or orange. They are soaked in running water for several days, and then they are trampled underfoot to loosen the husks. Finally the

pepper berries are transferred to rattan baskets, where they are washed and the husks and stems removed by hand to leave the white peppercorns. These are then left to dry on mats in the sun for several weeks, or kiln-dried.

Aroma and flavor

Black peppercorns have an earthy aroma, which is particularly noticeable when they are crushed. The flavor is hot and pungent. White peppercorns are slightly milder.

Culinary uses

Pepper is the one spice that is used before, during and after cooking. Its value as a seasoning is legendary, for it not only has its own flavor, but has the ability to enhance the flavor of other ingredients in a dish.

Preparation

Use a peppermill and grind fresh black pepper as it is required. White peppercorns are less pungent and are used where flecks of black might spoil the appearance of a dish, such as a light-colored sauce.

Storage

Buy whole peppercorns. Store in a cool place in an airtight container. They keep for a long time.

*Right:
Black and
white peppercorns*

SICHUAN/SZECHUAN PEPPER

MANDARIN: *FAA JIU;* CANTONESE: *HU CHIAO;*
JAPANESE: *SANSHO*

To call this "pepper" is misleading. This
spice actually comes from the prickly
ash tree, which is native to the Sichuan
province in China, but also grows
elsewhere in Asia. Unusually, it is the
seed pods themselves, not the seeds
they contain, that are used for the
spice. The tiny reddish brown pods or
husks are harvested when ripe, the
bitter black seeds are removed and
discarded, and the pods—Sichuan
peppercorns—are either added whole to
stewed dishes or dried and ground as a
seasoning spice.

The prickly ash also grows in Japan,
where the ripened pods are called
mizansho or Japanese peppercorns.
When ground, the spice is known as
konazansho or *sansho.* The wood of the
prickly ash is sometimes used to make
mortar and pestle sets, which are much
sought after by Japanese cooks who
claim they impart a subtle flavor when
used to grind ingredients.

*Left: Sichuan
peppercorns*

Aroma and flavor

Not as pungent as true
pepper, Sichuan peppercorns have a
warm aroma with a hint of citrus. The
full flavor is released when they are
dry-fried.

Culinary uses

Sichuan peppercorns are immensely
popular in Chinese cuisine. They are
excellent in duck, pork and chicken
dishes. The ground peppercorns are
used in both Chinese five spice powder
and Japanese seven spice powder.

Preparation

The dried seed pods should be picked
over carefully to remove any debris.
Dry-fry the seed pods to heighten their
flavor, then use as directed in recipes.

Storage

Although it is possible to buy ground
Sichuan pepper, it is better to buy the
peppercorns whole and grind them after
dry-frying. Keep them in an airtight jar.

Wasabi

Sometimes described as horseradish
mustard, this has much in common
with both, although it is related to
neither. Wasabi is a Japanese
seasoning, derived from a slow-growing
plant that is found near mountain
streams. The peeled root
reveals vivid green
flesh. This is very
finely grated, preferably on
sharkskin, and then dried or
powdered. When mixed to a cream
with soy sauce or water, it makes
an extremely hot condiment, which
is traditionally served with both sushi
and sashimi.

*Above: A tube of ready-made
apple-green wasabi paste*

*Right: Wasabi powder is mixed to a
paste with a little water or soy sauce*

MUSTARD

MALAY: *BIJI SAVI*

Mustard is one of the oldest spices known to man and has been cultivated as a crop for thousands of years. Both white *(apounda)* and black *(nigra)* mustard seeds are indigenous to the Mediterranean region, while brown mustard seeds *(juncea)* are native to India. The word mustard

Below: Brown, black and white mustard seeds

Dry frying mustard seeds

Mustard seeds have almost no smell until they are heated, so before adding them to dishes, they should be dry-fried to heighten their aroma.

1 Heat a little sunflower oil in a deep, wide pan. Add the seeds and shake the pan over the heat, stirring occasionally, until they start to change color.

2 Have a pan lid ready to prevent the mustard seeds from popping out of the pan.

comes from the Latin *mustum* or *must*, the newly pressed grape juice that Romans mixed with the ground seeds to make what was aptly described as *mustum ardens* (the burning paste).

In Asia, the mustard plant is valued as much for its dark green leaves, which are called mustard greens and are a popular vegetable, as for its seeds. Mustard powders and pastes are not as widely used as they are in the US or Europe.

Aroma and flavor

Mustard seeds have no aroma in their raw state. When they are roasted, however, they develop a rich, nutty smell. Mustard's famous hot taste comes from an enzyme in the seeds, which is only activated when they are crushed and mixed with warm water. Brown mustard seeds, which have largely replaced the black seeds, are not as intensely pungent. White mustard seeds, which are actually a pale honey color, are slightly larger than the other two varieties and a little milder.

Culinary uses

Throughout Asia, mustard seeds are used for pickling and seasoning. The whole seeds are often used in vegetable and dhal dishes, especially in countries such as Malaysia.

Preparation and cooking techniques

Mustard seeds are frequently roasted or fried before being used to bring out their flavor. A southern Indian technique involves spooning the seeds into hot ghee or oil, with a few curry leaves for extra flavor. A lid is placed over the pan to contain the seeds, which soon begin to splutter and pop. The seeds and oil are then poured, still sizzling, on to hot vegetable dishes, soups, stews or dhal as a flavorsome topping. Mustard oil is occasionally used for frying the seeds.

Mustard powder is used as a condiment. When it is mixed with warm water, milk or beer, a chemical reaction begins that allows the mustard to achieve its maximum potency. It takes about 15 minutes for the full flavor to develop. Boiling water or vinegar would inhibit the action of the enzyme responsible for the process, so should not be used.

Storage

Mustard seeds keep well. Store them in an airtight jar in a cool place.

*Left: Tamarind
block*

may suggest using vinegar or lemon juice instead, but the results will not compare with using the real thing.

Preparation

Compressed tamarind This comes in a solid block and looks rather like a packet of dried dates. To prepare it, tear off a piece that is roughly equivalent to 1 tablespoon and soak it in ⅔ cup warm water for about 10 minutes. Swirl the tamarind around with your fingers so that the pulp is released from the seeds. Using a nylon strainer, strain the juice into a pitcher. Discard the contents of the strainer and use the

TAMARIND

CHINESE: *ASAM KOH;* INDONESIAN: *ASAM JAVA;* THAI: *MAK KHAM;* BURMESE: *MA-GYI-THI*

The handsome tamarind tree, commonly called the "date of India", is believed to be a native of East Africa but is now cultivated in India, Southeast Asia and the West Indies. The brown fruit pods are about 6–8 inches long. Inside, the seeds are surrounded by a sticky brown pulp. This does not look very prepossessing, but is one of the treasures of the East. It has a high tartaric acid content, and is widely used as a souring agent.

dried tamarind have been around for a while, but it is now also possible to buy jars of fresh tamarind and cartons of tamarind concentrate and paste. There is no substitute for tamarind. Some recipes

Aroma and flavor

Tamarind doesn't have much of an aroma, but the flavor is wonderful. It is tart and sour without being bitter, and fruity and refreshing.

Culinary uses

Tamarind is used in many curries, chutneys and dhals, and is an essential ingredient of Thai hot and sour soups. It is also one of the ingredients in Worcestershire sauce. Tamarind is available in a variety of forms. Blocks of compressed tamarind and slices of

*Above,
from top:
Tamarind
paste,
tamarind pods
and dried
tamarind slices*

Stir-fried Shrimp with Tamarind

Tamarind is used in many Thai dishes to give them a characteristic sour, tangy flavor. Fresh tamarind pods from the tamarind tree can sometimes be bought, but preparing them for cooking is a laborious process. The Thais, usually prefer to use compressed blocks of tamarind paste, which is simply soaked in warm water and then strained.

SERVES 4–6

2 ounces compressed tamarind
2/3 cup boiling water
2 tablespoons vegetable oil
2 tablespoons chopped onion
2 tablespoons palm sugar
2 tablespoons chicken stock
1 tablespoon fish sauce
6 dried red chiles, fried
1 pound raw shelled shrimp
1 tablespoon fried chopped garlic
2 tablespoons fried sliced shallots
chopped scallions, to garnish

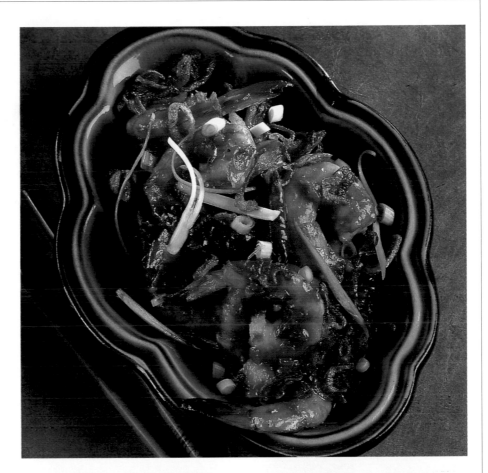

1 Put the tamarind in a bowl, pour over the boiling water and stir well to break up any lumps. Leave for 10 minutes. Meanwhile, heat the oil in a wok. Add the chopped onion and stir-fry until golden brown.

2 Strain the tamarind, pushing as much of the juice through as possible. Measure 6 tablespoons of the juice. Add the sugar, chicken stock, fish sauce, dried chiles along with the tamarind juice, stirring well until the sugar dissolves.

3 Bring to a boil over medium-high heat. Add the shrimp, garlic and shallots, and stir-fry about 3–4 minutes, or until the shrimp are only just cooked. Scatter over the scallions and serve.

liquid as required. Any leftover liquid can be stored in the refrigerator and used for another recipe.
Tamarind slices These look a little like dried apple slices. Place them in a small bowl, then pour over enough warm water to cover and leave to soak

for about 30 minutes to extract the flavor, squeeze the tamarind slices with your fingers, then strain the juice.
Tamarind concentrate or paste Mix 1 tablespoon with 4–6 tablespoons warm water. Stir until dissolved, then use as required.

Storage

Compressed tamarind and tamarind slices will keep perfectly well in a cool dry place. Jars labeled fresh tamarind, or tamarind concentrate or paste must be kept in the refrigerator once opened, and used within one or two months.

CURRY POWDERS AND PASTES

CURRY POWDERS

The word curry evolved from the Tamil word *kari,* meaning any food cooked in a sauce. There is little doubt that curry powder, a ready-made blend of spices, was an early convenience food, prepared for merchants, sailors and military men who had served in the East and wished to bring these exotic flavors home. In India, the spices would have been prepared in the kitchen on a daily basis.

Over the decades and centuries these spice and curry mixtures have changed and developed, as have our tastes, so that today our supermarket shelves carry a wealth of different spice mixtures from all parts of the globe.

For enthusiastic cooks it is fun and a creative challenge to make up your own curry powder. Keep experimenting until you find the balance of spicing which suits you and your family. Of course, it is perfectly possible to mix ground spices, but it is more satisfying (and more satisfactory in terms of flavor) to start with whole spices where possible.

Left: Curry powder

Dry-frying

Many whole spices benefit from being dry-fried before they are ground. This not only makes sure that no surface moisture remains, but also heightens and develops the flavor. Use a heavy-based pan, shaking it constantly so the spices do not scorch. Purists dry-fry spices separately, but they can be heated together as long as you watch them closely. All spices react differently to heat, so here are some guidelines:

Coriander seeds often provide the dominant flavor, especially in powders from Southern India and Singapore.

Shake the pan to keep the seeds on the move, and remove them from the heat when they give off a mild, sweet, orangey perfume.

Dried chiles can be roasted in a cool oven, but it is better to sear them in a heavy-based pan, where you can keep an eye on them. Place the pan over a medium heat for 2–3 minutes, until the chiles soften and puff up. Do not let them burn, or the flavor will be ruined.

Cumin seeds should be dry-fried in a pan, and will be ready for grinding when the seeds have a nutty smell.

Black peppercorns need gentle dry-frying, just to heighten the flavor.

Fenugreek needs to be watched carefully as it will become bitter if it is dry-fried for too long. It is ready when it turns brownish yellow.

Curry leaves can be dry-fried over cool to medium heat when fresh. Grind or pound them, using a mortar and pestle, to release their characteristic flavor, then mix them with the other spices. This works well if you are making a curry powder or paste that is to be used immediately, but if it is to be kept, make up the powder, then add the whole fresh or frozen leaves just before you are ready to use it. Remove the leaves before serving the curry. Avoid using dried curry leaves if possible, as they will have lost most of their flavor.

Right: Curry spices

Simple curry powder

This Malayan Chinese spice mixture is good for poultry, especially chicken, and robust fish curries.

MAKES ABOUT 4 TABLESPOONS

2 dried red chiles
6 whole cloves
1 small cinnamon stick
1 teaspoon coriander seeds
1 teaspoon fennel seeds
2 teaspoons Sichuan peppercorns
1/2 teaspoon grated nutmeg
1 teaspoon ground star anise
1 tsp ground turmeric

COOK'S TIPS

• If you prefer a very hot and punchy spice mixture, then add some or all of the chile seeds and dry-fry with the other spices.
• Ensure that you wash your hands, and the chopping board and other utensils thoroughly after preparing chiles.
• If your skin is particularly sensitive, then you should wear rubber gloves while you are preparing the chiles.

1 Remove the seeds from the dried chiles using the point of a knife, and discard any stems.

2 Put the chiles, cloves, cinnamon, coriander seeds, fennel seeds and Sichuan peppercorns in a heavy-based skillet. Dry-fry the spices, tossing them frequently until they give off a rich, spicy aroma.

3 Grind the spices to a smooth powder in a mortar, using a pestle. Alternatively, use a spice grinder, or an electric coffee grinder that is reserved for blending spices.

4 Add the grated nutmeg, star anise and turmeric. Use at once or store in an airtight jar away from strong light.

CURRY PASTES

On market stalls throughout South-east Asia are mounds of pounded wet spices: lemongrass, chile, ginger, garlic, galangal, shallots and tamarind. After purchasing meat, chicken or fish all the cook has to do is to call on the spice seller. He or she will ask a few questions: "What sort of curry is it to be? Hot or mild? How many servings?" Having ascertained the answers and perhaps exchanged a few more pleasantries (the buying of spices is a serious yet sociable affair) the appropriate quantities of each spice will be scooped on to a banana leaf and folded into a neat cone, ready to be taken home.

We may not be able to buy our ingredients in such colorful surroundings, but supermarkets stock some very good ready-made pastes, or you can make your own. By experimenting, you will find the balance of flavors you like, and can then make up one or more of your favourite mixtures in bulk.

If you grind wet spices a lot, you may wish to invest in a traditional, large oriental mortar with a rough, pitted or ridged bowl, which helps to "hold" the ingredients while they are being pounded with the pestle.

Alternatively, for speed, you can use a food processor or blender instead of a mortar and pestle. Store any surplus curry paste in plastic tubs in the freezer.

Above: Thai curry pastes

Malay spice paste for chicken rendang

This is a fairly pungent spice paste. It can be made milder by leaving out some of the chiles.

MAKES ABOUT 12 OUNCES

 6 fresh red chiles, seeded
  and sliced
 12 shallots, roughly
  chopped
 4 garlic cloves
 1-inch piece fresh turmeric root,
  peeled and sliced or
  1 teaspoon ground turmeric
 10 macadamia nuts
 1-inch cube shrimp paste
  (blachan), prepared
 3 lemongrass stems

1 Place the chiles, shallots, garlic, turmeric, nuts and shrimp paste (blachan) in a food processor.

2 Trim the root end from the lemongrass and slice the lower 2 inches of the stem into thin slices using a sharp knife.

3 Add the lemongrass to the remaining ingredients in the food processor and process them to a fine paste, scraping down the side of the bowl once or twice during processing.

COOK'S TIP

Use the curry paste at once or spoon into a glass jar, seal it tightly and store in the refrigerator for up to 3 or 4 days. Alternatively, transfer the paste to a plastic tub and store in the freezer.

Thai mussaman curry paste

This hot and spicy paste is used to make the Thai version of a Muslim curry, which is traditionally made with beef, but can also be made with other meats such as chicken or lamb.

MAKES ABOUT 6 OUNCES

 12 large dried red chiles
 1 lemongrass stem
 4 tablespoons chopped shallots
 5 garlic cloves, roughly chopped
 2 teaspoons chopped
  fresh galangal
 1 teaspoon cumin seeds
 1 tablespoon coriander seeds
 2 cloves
 6 black peppercorns
 1 teaspoon shrimp paste
  (blachan), prepared
 1 teaspoon salt
 1 teaspoon granulated sugar
 2 tablespoons oil

1 Remove the seeds from the dried chiles and discard. Soak the chiles in hot water for about 15 minutes.

2 Trim the root end from the lemongrass stem and slice the lower 2 inches of the stem into small pieces.

3 Place the chopped lemongrass in a dry wok and then add the chopped shallots, garlic and galangal and dry-fry for a moment or two.

4 Stir in the cumin seeds, coriander seeds, cloves and peppercorns and dry-fry over low heat for 5–6 minutes, stirring constantly. Spoon the mixture into a large mortar.

5 Drain the chiles and add them to the mortar. Grind finely, using the pestle, then add the prepared shrimp paste (blachan), salt, sugar and oil and pound again until the mixture forms a rough paste. Use as required, then spoon any leftover paste into a jar, seal tightly and store in the refrigerator for up to 4 months.

COOK'S TIPS

• Preparing a double or larger quantity of paste in a food processor makes the blending of the ingredients much easier and the paste will be smoother.
• For the best results, before you start to process the ingredients, slice them up in the following order: galangal, lemongrass, fresh ginger and turmeric, chiles, nuts, shrimp paste, garlic and shallots. Add some of the oil (or coconut cream if that is to be your frying medium) to the ingredients in the food processor if the mixture is a bit sluggish. If you do this, however, remember to use less oil or coconut cream when you fry the curry paste to eliminate the raw taste of the individual ingredients before adding the meat, poultry, fish or vegetables.
• Shrimp paste (blachan) is made from fermented shrimp. It can be bought in Asian markets. Unless it is to be fried as part of a recipe, it is always lightly cooked before use. If you have a gas cooker, simply mould the shrimp paste on to the end of a metal skewer and rotate over low to medium gas flame, or heat under the broiler of an electric cooker, until the outside begins to look crusty, but not burnt.

COOKING FATS AND OILS

CHINESE: *SHI YOU*

Animal fats and vegetable oils are regarded as essential ingredients the world over, but in Asia they play a particularly important role, largely because so much of the food is fried. Animal fat or lard was historically the medium for frying (and remains so in China), but vegetable oils are valued because they can be heated to much higher temperatures without smoking, something that is essential for quick stir-frying, in which a high degree of heat is absolutely essential. Similarly, most deep-fried food also requires a high temperature in order to achieve the desired crispness.

Oil can be extracted from sources as diverse as radishes and poppies. Rape seed (canola) oil was a popular cooking medium in China until the Portuguese introduced pea-nuts during the 16th century.

It was not immediately appreciated that the new crop could be a source of oil, but by the 19th century peanut oil was firmly established throughout Asia, a position it continues to hold despite competition from corn oil. In Japan, sesame oil originally held sway, but Japanese cooks soon appreciated that cooking with a mixture of sesame oil and peanut oil gave better results, especially when cooking their beloved tempura (a deep-fried vegetable and seafood dish introduced by Portuguese missionaries), as the mixed oil could be heated to higher temperatures without smoking.

Coconut and palm oil are common in South-east Asia, although both are less popular than they once were, as they are high in saturated fats.

Aroma and flavor

Fats and oils all have their own distinct aroma and flavor; some are quite strong, others fairly mild. Both lamb and beef fat, for instance are more strongly flavored than lard (pork fat) or chicken fat, while peanut oil and rape seed (canola) oil have more taste than soy, cottonseed or sunflower oils.

Culinary uses

In the East, fats and oils are mainly used as a cooking medium, but are sometimes ingredients in their own right. In some Chinese dishes, for instance, pure lard is often stirred in shortly before serving, much as Western cooks would use cream.

Left: Sunflower oil and peanut oil

Above: Palm oil

Preparation and cooking techniques

Although many Asian recipes depend for their success on fats and oils, it is not considered appropriate for the flavor of the fat to dominate. A technique frequently employed to neutralize the flavor of an oil is to season it. The method is quite simple. While the oil is being heated, small pieces of aromatic ingredients such as fresh ginger, scallion and garlic are added. When these have flavored the oil, they are then removed before other ingredients are added to the wok or pan. The technique prevents the finished dish from tasting "oily".

Storage

In normal conditions, fats and oils exposed to the air gradually become rancid due to oxidation. Cooking oil should be stored in a cool, dark place. Oil that has been heated several times in a deep-fryer may acquire an unpleasant flavor. Chinese cooks heat the oil with some fresh ginger after every use to neutralize any off flavors. You may find that you have to discard the oil after using it three or four times.

FLAVORING OILS

CHINESE: *TIAOWEI YOU*

Several types of flavoring oils are used in Asian cooking for dips and dressings, the most common one being sesame oil, but chili oil is also popular.

SESAME OIL

MANDARIN: *ZHIMA YOU*; CANTONESE: *MA YOU*; JAPANESE: *GAMA-ABURA*

The type of sesame oil used for flavoring is quite different from the sesame oil used for cooking in India and the Middle East. In both China and Japan, the preferred oil for flavoring is a rich flavored oil made from processed sesame seeds, which have been roasted or toasted to bring out their flavor.

Right: Toasted sesame oil

Aroma and flavor

Sesame oil from roasted seeds has a wonderfully nutty aroma and taste. It is much stronger than either walnut oil or olive oil. Blended sesame oil has a milder flavor and is much paler in color.

Culinary uses

Because processed sesame oil smokes easily when heated, it is not really suitable for frying. It is used for salads and dipping sauces, and is added to soups or stir-fries.

Cooking techniques

Heating helps to intensify the aroma of sesame oil, but it should never be heated for too long. It is usual to add a few drops to a soup or stir-fry shortly before serving.

Storage

Always store bottled sesame oil in a cool, dark place, because it will lose its strong aroma if exposed to heat and strong light. It becomes rancid much sooner than ordinary cooking oils, so buy in small quantities.

CHILI OIL

CHINESE: *LA YOU*; JAPANESE: *YU*

Chili oil is made by infusing chopped dried red chiles, red chopped onions, garlic and salt in hot vegetable oil for several hours. There is also an "XO chili oil", which is flavored with dried

Blended sesame oil (above) and chili oil

scallops, and is much more expensive. Chili oil is easy to make at home; simply put about 20 seeded and chopped dried chiles in a heatproof container. Heat 1 cup peanut or corn oil until it just reaches smoking point, then leave to cool for 5 minutes. Carefully pour the hot oil into the heatproof container and leave to stand for at least an hour or two. Strain the oil, then use as required.

Aroma and flavor

Chili oil has a pleasant aroma with a fiery taste that is much stronger than the flavor of either chili bean paste or chili sauce.

Culinary uses

Chili oil is always used as a dipping sauce, never for cooking. In some South-east Asian countries, it is used as a dressing, and it is drizzled on top of the Burmese fish soup, mohinga. In Thai cooking, it is added to stir-fried shrimp just before serving.

Storage

Store bottles of chili oil in a cool and dark place; the oil will keep for many months in the refrigerator.

VINEGARS

RICE VINEGAR

MANDARIN: *MICU*; CANTONESE: *HUCK TSO*;
JAPANESE: *SU*

Vinegar fermented from rice, or distilled from rice grains is used extensively in oriental cooking. The former is dark amber in color and is referred to in China as red or black vinegar; the latter is clear, so is called white vinegar. The raw ingredients used for making rice vinegar consist of glutinous rice, long grain rice, wheat, barley, and rice husks. It is fermented twice and is matured for up to 6–7 months. Japan has a brown rice vinegar —*gaen mae su*—which is dark and heady. This vinegar, which has been likened to balsamic vinegar, is robust yet wonderfully smooth.

Aroma and flavor

Red or black vinegar has a pleasant fragrant aroma with a mild, sweetish flavor. The distilled white vinegar is much stronger. It smells vinegary and tastes quite tangy and tart. Japanese brown rice vinegar has a distinctive sweet and sour flavor.

Using sushi vinegar

The rice that is used to make sushi is moistened and flavored with a mixture of hot rice vinegar, sugar and salt. The technique is simple, but it is important to use Japanese rice and good quality vinegar. The cooked rice is spread out in a shallow dish and the hot vinegar mixture is added. The rice is turned with a spatula until the grains are coated, and the mixture is simultaneously fanned so that it cools quickly and develops an attractive sheen. The rice is then covered until it cools completely before being molded.

Above: Rice vinegar

Culinary uses

There's an old Chinese saying that goes something like this: "On rising in the morning, first check that you have the seven daily necessities for the kitchen: fuel, rice, oil, salt, soy sauce, vinegar and tea." Vinegar has always played a vital role in Chinese cookery, and in some parts of the country, particularly in the north, it is added to almost every dish as a matter of course, although the amounts are sometimes so minute as to be barely detectable. Rice vinegar is an important ingredient in the world-renowned sweet and sour sauce, which originated in northern China, and also in the popular hot and sour sauce from Sichuan.

Throughout Asia, rice vinegar also features in Thai cucumber sauce and dipping sauces, such as the Vietnamese vinegar and garlic fish sauce. It is also widely used in preserving and pickling.

Thai cooks add rice vinegar to several dishes, including their famous hot and sour soup. In Japan, rice vinegar is famously used for sushi rice.

Cooking techniques

If rice vinegar is heated for too long, its fragrance will be lost, the food will taste extremely tart and rather unpleasant. In Asian cooking, therefore, vinegar is generally the last item to be stirred into a dish. It is also important not to use too much vinegar; in a good sweet and sour sauce the key ingredients should be in perfect balance, the sour having a slight edge on the sweet.

Storage

Bottled rice vinegar will keep for a very long time, provided it is not exposed to either heat or strong light.

OTHER VINEGARS

Coconut vinegar Made from coconut nectar or "toddy" tapped from the flower sheaths of mature coconut palms, this amber vinegar is highly regarded in the Philippines.
Pon vinegar This Japanese vinegar is made from the juice of citrus fruit that resemble limes.

Coconut vinegar (right) and pon vinegar

SAUCES AND PASTES

SOY SAUCE

MANDARIN: *JIANG YOU*; CANTONESE: *CHI YOU*;
JAPANESE: *SHOYU*; INDONESIAN: *KECAP*;
KETJAP; MALAY: *KICHUP*; *TAUYU*;
THAI: *SIEW*

Soy sauce is
made from
fermented
soybeans,
and is
one of
Asia's
most
important
contributions to
the global pantry. It
is used all over the world,
not merely as a condiment in place of
salt, but as an ingredient in a host of
homemade and manufactured foods.

Making soy sauce involves quite a
lengthy process. The soybeans are
initially cleaned, soaked until soft and
then steamed before being mixed with a
yeast culture and wheat flour. The
mixture is then fermented for up to two
years before being filtered and bottled.
There is no short cut to making soy
sauce of high quality, and while some
modern products may cost less than
others, they have inferior flavor and
should be avoided.

Aroma and flavor

There are basically three types of
Chinese soy sauce on the market. **Light
soy sauce** is the initial extraction, like
the first pressing of virgin olive oil. It
has the most delicate flavor and is light
brown in color with a lovely "beany"
fragrance. **Dark soy sauce** is left to
mature further, and has caramel added
to it, so it is slightly sweeter and has a
much darker color with a powerful
aroma. Then there is the regular soy
sauce, which is a blend of the two.
There are several different types of
Japanese soy sauce too: **Usukuchi soy
sauce** is light in color and tastes less
salty than the Chinese light soy. **Tamari**
is dark and thick with a strong flavor,
and is even less salty than the light
type. **Shoyu** is a full-flavored sauce that
is aged for up to 2 years. In between,

*Above: Dark (top)
and light soy
sauces*

there is the very
popular **Kikkoman**,
which is a brand
name for the
equivalent of the
Chinese regular soy
sauce—not too weak,
nor too strong. It is ideal as
a dipping sauce to be used at
the table, rather than for cooking.
The Indonesian **kecap manis** is thick
and black, with a powerful aroma, but a
surprisingly sweet taste. The light
variety, **kecap asin,** is quite thin and
weak, and is sometimes described as
"white soy". Indonesian cooks also
use the medium-bodied **kecap
sedang,** but this is less popular
than kecap manis.

*Above: There is
a range of Japanese soy
sauces, from dark and thick
to lighter, less rich types.*

Above: Kecap manis (top) and kecap asin are Indonesian soy sauces

Right: Tamari sauce

sauce. When soy sauce is used in a dressing for a salad or similar cold dish, the dressing should be added only just before the dish is served.

Storage

Naturally fermented soy sauce will not keep for ever; it starts to lose its aroma and flavor as soon as it is exposed to the air for any length of time. Sealed bottles can be stored for a year or two, but once the bottle has been opened, soy sauce will deteriorate fairly rapidly. Try to use it up as fast as you can, certainly before the expiry date on the label. Check the label, too, for advice on storage. Some bottles do not contain preservatives and must be kept in the refrigerator once opened.

Culinary uses

As a rule, light soy sauce is used for seafood, white meats, vegetables and soups, while the darker sauce is ideal for red meats, stews, barbecues and gravy. If you are serving soy sauce as a dip, choose the regular variety, or use a blend of three parts light sauce with two parts dark. This proportion also applies to marinades.

Cooking techniques

When soy sauce is used for cooking, it should be stirred in towards the end of the cooking time to avoid dulling the color of the food, and so that the natural flavor of the principal ingredient is not overwhelmed. This point applies to soups, stews, stir-fries and quick-braised dishes, but not to slow-braised dishes, where the ingredients are simmered for a long time in a sauce that includes only a small amount of soy

Chicken Yakitori

There are several classic marinades and sauces that have soy sauce as the main ingredient. This Japanese dish uses soy sauce, which is combined with sake and sugar, and thickened with flour, as a marinade for chicken kebabs. If you like, you can make twice the quantity of sauce and reserve half to serve with the cooked kebabs.

SERVES 4

6 boneless chicken thighs, cut into chunks
1 bunch scallions, cut into short batons
Japanese seven spice powder, to serve

For the yakitori sauce
$2/3$ cup soy sauce
$1/2$ cup sugar
5 teaspoons sake
1 tablespoon all-purpose flour

1 To make the sauce, place the soy sauce, sugar, sake and flour in a small pan and stir well. Bring to a boil, stirring all the time, then reduce the heat and simmer for 10 minutes, until the sauce in reduced by a third. Set aside.

2 Thread the chicken and scallion pieces alternately on to 12 bamboo skewers. Broil for 5–10 minutes until the chicken is cooked through, brushing generously with the sauce once or twice during cooking.

3 Sprinkle the kebabs with Japanese seven spice powder and serve at once, with a little extra yakitori sauce, if you like.

FISH SAUCE

CHINESE: *YU LU*; THAI: *NAM PLA*;
VIETNAMESE: *NUOC MAM*

Fish sauce is an essential seasoning for Thai and Vietnamese cooking, in much the same way that soy sauce is important to the Chinese and the Japanese. In Vietnam it is often made using shrimp, but in Thailand, the sauce is more often made using salted, fermented fish.

Aroma and flavor

All types of fish sauce have a pungent flavor and aroma and are very salty. Thai *nam pla* has a slightly stronger flavor and aroma than the Vietnamese or Chinese versions. The color of fish sauce can vary considerably; lighter-colored sauces are considered to be better than darker versions.

Culinary uses

Fish sauce is used extensively throughout Asia as a seasoning in all kinds of savory dishes. It is also used to make a dipping sauce, when it is blended with extra flavorings such as finely chopped garlic and chiles, and sugar and lime juice.

Right: Fish sauce

Storage

Fish sauce generally comes in either glass or plastic bottles. Once opened it should be kept in a cool, dark place where it will keep for up to a year.

OYSTER SAUCE

MANDARIN: *HAOYOU*; CANTONESE: *HO YOW*

Oyster sauce is a Cantonese specialty. This thick, brown, soy-based sauce is flavored with oyster juice, salt and caramel, and is thickened with cornstarch. It is thicker than soy sauce and fish sauce, but lighter in color.

Above: Oyster sauce

Aroma and flavor

Oyster sauce has a pleasant, fragrant aroma, and has a delicious and delicate flavor that, surprisingly, doesn't taste of fish at all.

Culinary uses

Oyster sauce is a highly versatile flavoring and can be used in a wide variety of dishes. It is especially good with fairly bland foods, such as chicken and beancurd, but also works very well with more strongly flavored ingredients such as beef and seafood. It can be used as a garnish and is often sprinkled over the top of cooked dishes such as rice and noodles.

Cooking techniques

The bottled sauce is only used as a cooking ingredient, and it is never served as a dip or sauce at the table. Oyster sauce is best added to dishes towards the end of the cooking time.

Storage

There are a number of different brands of this sauce, and the more expensive versions are usually far superior, and have a much richer flavor than cheaper versions. Once opened, the bottle should be stored in the refrigerator where the sauce will keep for a very long time, although it is best used before the expiry date.

*Above:
Dark hoisin
sauce*

*Above:
Light
hoisin sauce*

HOISIN SAUCE

MANDARIN: *HAIXIAN JIANG;* CANTONESE: *HOY SIN JIONG;* VIETNAMESE: *TUONG-DEN*

Another Cantonese specialty, hoisin is also known as barbecue sauce. Its Chinese name literally means "sea-flavor", which is a reflection on just how delicious it is, rather than an indication of its ingredients. Hoisin sauce does not contain so much as a trace of seafood, unlike oyster sauce and fish sauce.

Aroma and flavor

The main components of this very popular Chinese sauce are fermented beans, sugar, vinegar, salt, chile, garlic and sesame oil, but there is no standard formula, so the aroma and flavor of brands can vary considerably. A good quality product should have a fragrant aroma with a rich, warm, sweet yet salty flavor.

Culinary uses

Hoisin sauce is quite versatile and makes a valuable contribution to the kitchen. Mainly intended as a marinade, it can be used at the table as a dipping sauce, but should not accompany Peking duck as is the practice in some restaurants.

Cooking techniques

When used as a marinade, hoisin sauce can be spooned straight from the jar over spareribs, chicken or similar foods.

Storage

Hoisin sauce usually comes in glass jars or cans. Once opened, jars should be stored in the refrigerator, where the sauce will keep for several months. Canned hoisin should be decanted into non-metallic containers before being stored in the refrigerator.

CHILI SAUCE

MANDARIN: *LAJIAO JIANG;* CANTONESE: *LA JYEW JYEUNG;* THAI: *SOD PRIK*

The best known Asian chili sauce comes from China, although the Vietnamese have a very hot version and there is also a thick, spicy chili sauce made in Thailand.

Aroma and flavor

This Chinese bottled chili sauce is quite hot and spicy, with a touch of fruitiness, as it is made from fresh red chiles, salt, vinegar and apples or plums. The Thai version includes both hot and sweet chiles, and adds ginger, spices and vinegar. There is also a thick Chinese sauce, which is made exclusively from chiles and salt. This is usually sold in jars and is much hotter than the bottled sauce.

Culinary uses

The bottled sauce is used both for cooking and as a dip, but the thicker sauce is mainly used for cooking as an alternative to chili bean paste.

Cooking techniques

Use chili sauce sparingly. It can be quite fiery.

Storage

Once chili sauce has been opened it should be stored in the refrigerator, where it will keep almost indefinitely. Use before the expiry date.

Below: Sweet chili sauce (top) and chili sauce

PLUM SAUCE

MANDARIN: *MEIZI JIANG;* CANTONESE: *SHWIN MEI JIONG;* VIETNAMESE: *CUONG NGOT*

Made from plum juice with sugar, salt, vinegar and a thickening agent, plum sauce is a sort of sweet and sour sauce. It is generally associated with Chinese food. Thai cooks are partial to plum sauce, but they tend to make their own, using preserved plums and sugar.

Aroma and flavor

There seems to be no standard recipe for the commercially made plum sauce. The various brands all seem to use slightly different seasonings and some even add garlic, ginger or chili to give it extra tang. Taste before use, as some brands can be quite fiery.

Culinary uses

One of the common uses for plum sauce in the West is to serve it with Peking duck. It is also used as a dip for spring rolls and other dim sum.

Storage

Plum sauce is usually sold in glass jars. One opened, the jar should be kept in the refrigerator.

LEMON SAUCE

MANDARIN: *NINGMENG JIANG;* CANTONESE: *NING MUNG JIONG*

Lemon sauce is one of those condiments that was especially created for the Western market. It probably originated in Hong Kong, like black bean sauce. Thick, smooth and velvety, it has an immediate appeal for the Western palate.

Aroma and flavor

The sauce has a rather piquant citrus aroma with a spicy and tangy sweet flavor. It is another sauce from the sweet and sour stable, but with the difference that it is made from fresh lemon juice and rind. Salt and sugar are added, and starch is used for thickening. Most brands have artificial coloring added to give the sauce a bright color.

Above, from top: oyster, plum and hoisin sauces

Culinary uses

The use of lemon sauce in cooking seems to be limited to a single dish, lemon chicken, which is on the menu of most Cantonese restaurants. Other than that, it can be served with deep-fried food, particularly seafood.

Storage

Once opened, the bottle or jar of sauce should be stored in the refrigerator. The fresh flavor of the sauce may be dulled if it is kept for too long, so use it before the expiry date.

Above: Lemon sauce

BLACK BEAN SAUCE

MANDARIN: *CHIZI JIANG;* CANTONESE: *SI JIR JIONG*

A mixture of puréed salted black beans with soy sauce, sugar and spice, this popular sauce is especially manufactured for the convenience of Western cooks, since people in China and South-east Asia generally use only whole fermented beans, and make their own sauce by crushing the beans in the wok while cooking.

Aroma and flavor

Fermented black beans have a powerful "fragrance" and a strong flavor that does not always appeal to the untutored Western palate, but once introduced to its rather earthy taste, many people grow to like it immensely.

Culinary uses

Black bean sauce should not be used cold straight from the jar or bottle, but should always be heated first. It is usually blended with other strongly flavored seasonings such as scallions, garlic, ginger and chiles before being added to stews, stir-fries, and braised or steamed dishes. Ready-made black bean sauces seasoned either with garlic or chiles are available too. These should also be heated before being used, to bring out the aroma and flavor.

Storage

Once opened, the jar should be stored in the refrigerator. Black bean sauce keeps well.

YELLOW BEAN SAUCE

MANDARIN: *HUANG JIANG:* CANTONESE: *MO SHIH JIONG;* THAI: *TAO JIEW KAOW*

Also known as brown bean sauce or ground bean sauce, this Chinese favorite consists of crushed fermented soybeans which have been mixed with salt, wheat flour and sugar to make a paste that is not only useful on its own, but is also the basis of numerous more elaborate sauces. hoisin sauce, chu hou sauce, Guilin chili sauce, Sichuan hot sauce and Peking duck sauce all owe their ancestry to yellow bean sauce.

Aroma and flavor

Regular yellow bean sauce has a wonderfully "beany" aroma with a delectable flavor. It is not as salty as black bean sauce, and cooks in every region of China add

Left: Fermented yellow beans and yellow bean sauce

Above: Fermented black beans, which Chinese cooks use to make their own black bean sauce.

their own spices and seasonings to make individual blends.

Culinary uses

Yellow bean sauce is very versatile in the kitchen. It adds an extra dimension to most meat, poultry, fish and even some vegetable dishes, whether in stir-fries, braised dishes or roasts. It is also the ideal basis for a marinade, usually with additional ingredients such as garlic, scallions and rice wine.

Storage

Once a can or jar of yellow bean sauce has been opened, the contents should be transferred to a lidded plastic tub and stored in the refrigerator. Like black bean sauce, it keeps very well.

CHILI BEAN PASTE

MANDARIN: *DOUBAN JIANG;* CANTONESE: *TOBAN DJAN*

This is a Sichuan specialty. What makes it unique is the fact that the beans used are not soybeans, but a type of broad bean, hence the name *douban* or *toban* in Chinese. Outside China the sauce is sold under various names, including chili bean sauce, hot bean sauce or just plain Sichuan sauce.

Aroma and flavor

There are several chili bean pastes on the market, ranging from mild to hot, but all have a lovely "beany" aroma with a rich flavor. The genuine Pixian paste made in Sichuan is seldom seen in the West, which is a pity, for it is superior in quality to the majority of brands made in Hong Kong, Taiwan or Singapore.

Above: Chili bean paste

Right: Red bean paste

Miso

One of the best known Japanese ingredients, miso is the collective name for several different types of soybean paste, made from steamed soybeans fermented with the aid of various natural yeasts. Some of these starter molds are based upon rice, others on wheat or barley, and yet more on soybeans themselves. The pastes come in different colors, textures and flavors, depending on the yeast used and the length of the fermentation process. Red miso, the most popular paste, is more strongly flavored than the sweeter white miso. Miso is the key ingredient in a soup served at almost every Japanese meal, and the paste is also stirred into sauces. When mixed with mayonnaise it makes the increasingly popular miso-mayo.

Culinary uses

Chili bean paste and chili sauce are not interchangeable; each has its own distinct flavor and consistency. Chili bean paste is slightly thicker than chili sauce and is an indispensable seasoning in Sichuan cooking. It is used to add flavor to stir-fries and braised dishes.

Cooking techniques

Chili bean paste must be thoroughly heated before being used and should never be served cold at the table as a dipping sauce.

Storage

Once opened, the jar should be stored in the refrigerator. Chili bean paste keeps well, but should be used before the expiry date on the jar.

RED BEAN PASTE

MANDARIN: *DOUSHA;* CANTONESE: *DOW SA*

Made from either red kidney beans or aduki beans, this is a thick, smooth paste, which is sweetened with rock sugar. The paste comes in small cans and is only available from Asian and oriental markets.

Aroma and flavor

The paste has a pleasant, mild fragrance with a subtle flavor. Although it is sweetened, the sauce is never cloying, and oriental cooks often add extra sugar to intensify the flavor. Occasionally, other flavorings such as essence of sesame seeds or ground cassia is blended in.

Culinary uses

Red bean paste is mainly used in sweet dishes and is a popular filling for cakes and steamed buns. It is also spread on pancakes, which are then deep-fried.

Storage

Once the can has been opened, the contents should be transferred to a sealed plastic tub and stored in the refrigerator, where the paste will keep for several months. Make a note of the use-by date on the can.

Left: Shrimp paste

SHRIMP PASTE

MALAY: *BLACHAN; BALACHAN;* INDONESIAN: *TERASI; TRASSI;* THAI: *KAPI;* BURMESE: *NGAPI*

Whether you call it *blachan, terasi, kapi* or *ngapi,* shrimp paste is an essential ingredient in scores of savory dishes throughout South-east Asia. It is made from tiny shrimp which have been salted, dried, pounded and then left to ferment in the hot humid conditions until the aroma is very pungent. The color of the paste can be anything from oyster pink to purplish brown, depending upon the type of shrimp and the precise process used. It is compressed and sold in block form or packed in tiny tubs or jars.

Aroma and flavor

There's no disguising the origin of this paste. The moment you unwrap it or lift the lid, the smell of rotten fish is quite overwhelming. Do not let this put you off, however. The odor vanishes when the paste is cooked, and this is one of those ingredients that really does make a difference to the food, contributing depth, pungency and a recognizable South-east Asian signature.

Culinary uses

Shrimp paste is good source of protein and vitamin C. It is used to flavor rice dishes, is stirred into satay sauces and gives depth to salad dressings, dipping sauces, curries and braised dishes. It is the key ingredient in the famous *nam prik,* a dipping sauce whose other ingredients include garlic, chiles and fish sauce, and which appears as a condiment at almost every Thai meal. Burmese cooks use it to intensify the flavor of *balachaung,* a spicy dried shrimp mixture forked into rice.

Preparation

Before using shrimp paste in a sambal, dressing or salad, it is necessary to heat it to temper the raw flavor (see right).

Storage

If you buy the paste in block form, store it in a screwtop jar in a cool place. It will keep for several months. Jars of paste should be kept in the refrigerator.

Sesame paste

The sesame paste used in oriental cooking is not the same as tahini, the ingredient that frequently crops up in recipes from the Middle East. Whereas tahini is made from raw sesame seeds, sesame paste is derived from seeds that have been dry fried or roasted to bring out the rich nutty flavor. If an oriental recipe calls for sesame paste, don't be tempted to try tahini, therefore. Instead, use peanut butter with a little sesame oil stirred in to approximate the correct flavor.

Preparing shrimp paste

Shrimp paste can be used straight from the packet if it is to be fried with other ingredients, but it needs to be heated to temper its raw taste before using in sambals, dressings and salads.

1 Cut off a small piece of shrimp paste and shape it into a ½-inch cube. Mold the paste on to the end of a metal skewer.

2 Holding the end of the skewer in an oven glove, rotate the paste over a low to medium gas flame, or under an electric broiler until the outside begins to look dry, but not burnt. This method works well but gives off a very strong smell.

3 Alternatively, to avoid the strong smell, wrap the cube of paste in a piece of foil and dry-fry in a skillet for about 5 minutes, turning it occasionally.

SAMBALS

In the West, sambals have come to mean the side dishes served with a curry, but this is several steps away from the original South-east Asian term, which was, and still is, applied to a number of hot, spicy relishes, sauces and similar accompaniments that are based on chiles. Sambals are particularly popular in Indonesia, and feature strongly in the famous *Rijstafel*, a veritable feast that includes dozens of different dishes, and which was developed in the days when Indonesia was still the Dutch East Indies. Thanks to the connection, *Rijstafel* is also well known and loved in the Netherlands, and bottled sambals are widely available in that country.

In Indonesia, a sambal can also be a main dish. *Sambal goreng*, for instance is a spicy chile sauce, which may include a variety of foods such as tiny meat balls, cubes of fish, wedges of hard-cooked eggs or vegetables.

Culinary uses

In Malaysia, Singapore and Indonesia *sambal blachan* (chile and shrimp paste sambal) is a favorite. Fresh red chiles are roughly chopped, then pounded with a little salt and prepared shrimp paste *(blachan)*. A little lime or lemon juice is added to the mixture to loosen it slightly. *Sambal blachan* is extremely hot—especially when the seeds have been left in the chiles—so deserves to be served with a health warning! *Sambal oelek* is similar, but a little brown sugar is added to the chopped chiles to bring out the flavors. Sometimes labeled "chopped chile", this product is now sold in jars in many supermarkets. One teaspoonful is equivalent to 1 small chile. After use, the jar should be closed tightly and kept in the refrigerator.

At a typical Thai meal there may be one or two sambals in addition to the much loved *nam prik,* a combination of dried shrimp, shrimp paste (blachan), garlic, chiles, fish sauce, lemon juice and brown sugar. *Nam prik* complements raw, steamed, fried or boiled vegetables and is often simply stirred into a bowl of plain boiled or steamed Thai rice. Another popular sambal is made from fish sauce, lemon juice, shallots and chiles; a blend that enhances all kinds of fish and seafood dishes.

Sambal oelek

This chile sambal will keep for about 6 weeks in a sealed jar in the refrigerator, so it is worth making up a reasonable quantity at a time if you frequently cook Indonesian-style dishes. Use a stainless steel or plastic spoon to measure out the sauce as required. This sauce is fiercely hot, and it will irritate the skin, so should you get any on your fingers, immediately wash them well in soapy water.

MAKES ABOUT 12 OUNCES
 1 pound fresh red chiles
 2 teaspoons salt

1 Cut the chiles in half, scrape out the seeds using the point of a sharp knife and discard with the stems. Plunge the chiles into a pan of boiling water and cook them for 5–8 minutes.

2 Drain the chiles, then place them in the bowl of a food processor or blender and process until finely chopped. The paste should be fairly coarse, so stop processing before it gets too smooth.

3 Spoon the chile paste into a glass jar, stir in the salt and cover with a piece of waxed paper or plastic wrap before screwing on the lid.

4 Store in the refrigerator. Spoon into small dishes to serve as an accompaniment, or use it as suggested in recipes.

Left: Sambal oelek (left), sambal blachan (front) and nam prik sauce are very hot chile sauces.

Below: Nuoc cham

In Vietnam the salt and pepper of the Western table is replaced by *nuoc cham*. This is a piquant sambal made from, chiles, garlic, sugar, lime juice or rice vinegar, and fish sauce and is the classic combination of hot, sweet, sour and salt flavors that is so typical of Vietnamese cooking.

Sambals and sauces are usually served in small bowls or saucers. At a family meal pieces of cooked meat, fish or vegetables may be dipped into a communal bowl or a tiny spoonful of the sambal may be put on each diner's plate, but on special occasions small individual dishes are used. These little dishes are sold in many Asian markets and oriental supermarkets.

Preparation

For the freshest flavors mix the sambal ingredients just before serving. Use a food processor or blender to blend the wet ingredients and a pestle and mortar to grind the dry ingredients.

Storage

Any leftover sambals are best stored in a glass jar in the refrigerator. Before putting on the lid, cover the jar with a piece of waxed paper or plastic wrap to protect the lid from corrosion.

Nuoc cham

This spicy Vietnamese sambal makes a delicious, if fiery, dipping sauce and is good served with crisp, fried spring rolls.

MAKES ABOUT 7 TABLESPOONS

2 fresh red chiles, seeded
2 garlic cloves, crushed
1 tablespoons sugar
3 tablespoons fish sauce
juice of 1 lime or ½ lemon

1 Place the chiles in a large mortar and pound to a paste using a pestle.

2 Transfer the chiles to a bowl and add the garlic, sugar and fish sauce. Stir in lime or lemon juice to taste.

COOK'S TIP

Be careful, when handling either fresh or dried chiles; they contain capsaicin, an oily substance which can cause intense irritation to sensitive skin, so wash your hands thoroughly after handling them, or wear latex gloves. And do not touch or rub your eyes.

Sambal kecap

This Indonesian sauce or sambal can be served as a dip for satays instead of the usual peanut sauce, particularly with beef and chicken, and it is also very good served with pieces of deep-fried chicken.

MAKES ABOUT ⅔ CUP

1 fresh red chile, seeded and
  finely chopped
2 garlic cloves, crushed
4 tablespoons dark soy sauce
4 teaspoons lemon juice or
  1 tablespoon tamarind juice
2 tablespoons hot water
2 tablespoons deep-fried onion slices
  (optional)

1 Place the chopped chile, crushed garlic, soy sauce, and lemon juice or tamarind juice in a small bowl with the hot water and mix together well.

2 Stir in the deep-fried onion slices, if using, and leave the sambal to stand at room temperature for about 30 minutes before serving.

Sambal blachan

Serve this hot and pungent sambal as an accompaniment to rice meals.

MAKES ABOUT 2 TABLESPOONS

2–4 fresh red chiles, seeded
salt
½-inch cube of shrimp paste
  (blachan)
juice of ½ lemon or lime

1 Place the chiles in a mortar, add a little salt and pound them to a paste using a pestle.

2 Cut off a small piece of shrimp paste (blachan) and shape it into a ½-inch cube. Mold the paste on to the end of a metal skewer.

3 Holding the end of the skewer in a cloth or oven glove, rotate the paste over a low gas flame, or under an electric broiler until the outside begins to look dry, but not burnt.

4 Add the shrimp paste to the chiles and pound to mix well. Add lemon or lime juice to taste.

PRESERVED AND PICKLED VEGETABLES

Preserved and pickled food plays an important part in the oriental diet. In the days before refrigeration and rapid transportation, fresh food had to be preserved for the lean months, and so that it could be conveyed to regions that were often a long way from the source of supply.

Preserved and pickled vegetables and, to a lesser extent, fruit are used all over Asia. Some of the more famous examples include *chow chow,* the Chinese sweet mixed pickles that are now an American favorite, and *kimchee,* the tart, garlicky pickle that is served at almost every Korean meal. In Japan, pickled vegetables are hugely popular, as are pickled plums, while Indonesian cooks relish *atjar kuning,* a yellow mixed pickle which is mildly hot.

There are several ways of preserving and pickling food. The most common way is to use salt as a preservative, then dry the food in the sun or by another source of heat. Another age-old method is to partially dry the food, then pickle it in brine or a soy-based solution.

Below: Pickled mustard greens

Below: A selection of Chinese pickles

SICHUAN PRESERVED VEGETABLE

MANDARIN: *ZHACAI;* CANTONESE: *JA CHOI*

This pickle, made from the stems of mustard cabbage, originated in Sichuan province, but is now made in other parts of China. The stems are dried in the sun, then pickled in brine. After being trimmed and cleaned, they are pressed to extract excess liquid (the Mandarin name *zhacai* means "pressed vegetable"), before being blended with chiles and spices, and stored in sealed urns to mature.

Aroma and flavor

Sichuan preserved vegetable has a pungent aroma that may not appeal to the uninitiated. It has a smooth and crunchy texture and tastes quite salty and peppery.

Culinary uses

Unlike most other types of preserved and pickled vegetables, Sichuan preserved vegetable is a very versatile ingredient. It is not merely served raw as a relish, but is also cooked with other foods in stir-fries, soups and steamed dishes.

Preparation and cooking techniques

Because of its strong hot and salty flavor, Sichuan preserved vegetable is often rinsed in water to remove some of the excess salt and chiles before it is finely sliced or shredded for use.

Storage

Sichuan preserved vegetable is normally sold in cans, although you may be able to buy the pickle loose in some oriental markets. Any unused pickle should be transferred to an airtight container and stored in the refrigerator, where it will keep almost indefinitely.

CHINESE PICKLES

There is a wide range of Chinese pickles available in the West. Some appear in packages, some in jars, and some in cans. A pickle may consist of a single ingredient such as ginger, garlic, scallion bulbs, chiles, cabbage, cucumber, gourd, runner beans, bamboo shoots, carrots or daikon (Chinese radish or mooli) or a mixture. Individual items are generally pickled in a dark soy solution, while mixed vegetables tend to be pickled in clear brine to which sugar, Sichuan

Below: Cucumbers are a popular pickled vegetable in many Asian countries. These are from Korea.

peppercorns, distilled spirit and fresh ginger have been added, with chiles and vinegar as optional ingredients. The cleaned vegetables are pickled in the solution in a sealed earthenware urn. This is left in a cool, dark place for at least a week in summer, or up to a month in winter. The longer the pickling process, the better the taste.

JAPANESE PICKLES

JAPANESE: *TSUKEMONO*

There are many varieties of the Japanese pickles known as *tsukemono*. The vegetables that are used are more or less the same as those used in China, but the method of pickling is somewhat different. To start with, instead of earthenware urns, only

Below: Chow chow— Chinese sweet mixed pickles

wooden barrels are used in Japan and, instead of being pickled in a brine solution, the vegetables are layered with salt. When the barrel is full, a lid is put on top, and this is weighted down with a large stone or similar weight. The combined effect of the salt and the compression forces the liquid out of the vegetables and they are pickled in their own juices.

Other methods include pickling in sake, miso or rice bran, and the most popular types of vegetable used are daikon (mooli), bok choy, cucumber, eggplant, horseradish and the bulbs of scallions. Thinly sliced pink pickled ginger (gari) is traditionally served with sushi and sashimi.

Japanese pickles form an essential part of a meal. They are served as a relish to accompany the cooked food, as well as a dessert or a means of cleansing the palate at the end. They are either served singly or in groups of two or three, always beautifully arranged in small individual dishes.

Umeboshi These small pickled plums (below) are a particular Japanese delicacy. The plums are picked before they are ripe and are pickled in salt, with red shiso leaves to give them their distinctive color. They have a sharp and salty taste and are often chopped and used as a filling for rice balls.

Pickled bamboo shoots A delicacy in Vietnam, this consists of sliced bamboo shoots in spiced vinegar. The shoots are quite sour and should be soaked in water to remove some of the bitterness. They are mainly used in soups and stocks, and are often served with duck.

Pickled garlic This is a favorite in Thailand. The small bulbs are pickled whole in a sweet and sour brine (below).

Pickled limes Whole limes preserved in brine or a mixture of soy sauce, sugar, salt and vinegar are another Thai specialty.

COCONUT MILK AND CREAM

Coconut milk is an essential ingredient in South-east Asian cooking. There is an old saying that "he who plants a coconut palm, plants food and drink, vessels and clothing, a habitation for himself and a heritage for his children". Once mature, the palms will go on producing coconuts for 75–100 years, which helps to explain why they are so highly prized.

The coconut was called the nut of India until the Portuguese, struck by its appearance, changed its name to "coco", meaning clown or monkey. Fresh coconuts are available at certain times of the year in oriental markets and supermarkets. The liquid you can hear sloshing about inside the nut when it is shaken is coconut juice, not coconut milk. As any traveller who has tasted it will attest, the juice makes a refreshing drink, especially when tapped from a fresh green coconut. It can also be made into palm wine, which can be pretty potent.

An average size coconut weighs about 1½ pounds. If it is fresh, it will be full of liquid, so test by shaking well before buying. To open a coconut, hold

Below: Coconut milk

Below: A fresh coconut will break neatly into two pieces if you hit it in just the right place.

it in the palm of your left hand, with the "eyes" just above your thumb. The fault line runs between the eyes. Hold the coconut over a bowl to catch the juice, then carefully strike the line with the unsharpened side of a cleaver or a hammer. If you have done this correctly, the coconut will break neatly into two pieces. Taste a little of the white flesh to make sure that the coconut is fresh, as on rare occasions the flesh may have become rancid. Slip a palette knife between the outer husk and the flesh and prize out the pieces of fresh

coconut. The thin brown skin on these pieces can be removed with a potato peeler, if you like.

Coconut milk and cream are both made from the grated flesh of the coconut, and in the East, it is possible to buy bags of freshly grated coconut for just this purpose. Warm water is added and the coconut is squeezed repeatedly until the mixture is cloudy and has a wonderful coconut flavor. When strained, this is coconut milk. If the milk is left to stand, coconut cream will float to the surface in much the same way as regular cream does on whole milk.

Coconut milk is now available in cartons and cans, and even in countries with a plentiful supply of coconuts cooks often use these products for convenience and speed. The quality is excellent, and it is even possible to buy a version that is 88 per cent fat free.

Creamed coconut comes in 7-ounce blocks. This is a very useful product, as small quantities can be cut off and added to dishes to supply a little richness just before serving. When a very small quantity of coconut milk is called for simply dissolve 2 ounces creamed coconut in a scant ½ cup hot water.

Above: Creamed coconut block

Coconut cream can be made in the same way, but the amount of creamed coconut should be increased to 3 ounces. Ready-to-use coconut cream comes in cartons and is a magical ingredient where a rich coconut aroma and flavor are required. In many Thai curries the spices are initially fried in bubbling coconut cream instead of the more usual oil.

Culinary uses

Coconut is widely used in South-east Asian cooking. The milk is used as a cooking medium instead of stock in a variety of dishes, and it is also added at the end of cooking to enrich stews and curries. It can be cooked with rice, to make a savory accompaniment, or as the basis for rice cakes, and also to make a delicious creamy rice pudding. In Thailand, coconut milk is often used to make aromatic soups.

Below: Coconut cream

Making coconut milk

Coconut milk can be made at home, from dried shredded coconut. Although the procedure takes time, it has plenty of advantages. Dried shredded coconut is readily available and is an item which many cooks routinely stock in their pantries. You can make as much or as little as you like—although the method is more practical for large quantities—and coconut milk made this way is less expensive than any of the alternatives.

2 Place a strainer lined with cheesecloth over a large bowl in the sink. Ladle some of the softened coconut into the cheesecloth.

1 Tip 2⅔ cups dried unsweetened shredded coconut into the bowl of a food processor and pour over 2 cups boiling water. Process for about 20–30 seconds and allow the mixture to cool a little. If making several batches transfer immediately to a large bowl and repeat the process.

3 Bring up the ends of the cloth and twist it over the strainer to extract as much of the liquid as possible. Discard the spent coconut. Use the coconut milk as directed in recipes.

COOK'S TIPS

• When making coconut milk, instead of discarding the spent coconut, it can be re-used to make a second batch of coconut milk. This will be of a poorer quality and should only be used to extend a good quality first quantity of coconut milk.
• Any unused coconut milk or cream can be transferred to a plastic tub and stored in the refrigerator for a day or two, or poured into a freezer container and frozen for use on another occasion.
• Before using newly made coconut milk, leave it to stand for 10 minutes or more, and the coconut cream will float to the top. Skim off the cream using a large spoon if needed, or leave it to enrich the milk.

BEER, WINE AND SPIRITS

The art of making alcoholic beverages is an ancient one. Man has been making alcoholic drinks ever since the discovery that a grain and water mash would ferment if left to stand, producing a sour brew that would intoxicate.

Archaeological finds in northern China provide evidence that the Chinese were using separate drinking cups and bowls for different beverages as long ago as the 22nd century BC. Historians

Below: Leading Japanese beers include Sapporo and Asahi, both of which are widely available in the West.

agree that a considerable length of time must have elapsed from the beginning of the making and drinking of a primitive type of "wine" to the sophistication of using vessels in a variety of shapes for specific purposes, so the Chinese may well have been imbibing some form of alcoholic beverage at the dawn of their civilisation more than 5,000 years ago. By the time of the Shang Dynasty (*c.* 1600–1100 BC), a dark wine

Above: Chinese beers include Five Star beer and the light Pilsener, Tsingtao.

was being brewed from millet, and was ceremonially served in elaborate bronze drinking vessels.

A new development in the art of brewing was achieved during the early part of the 12th century BC, where textual evidence records that a form of barm or leaven was used in wine-making. With this discovery, the Chinese were able to control both the flavor and alcoholic content of a variety of wines made from different fruits and grains. Wine continues to be an important drink, although its popularity has now been overtaken by beer.

BEER

MANDARIN: *PI JIU;* CANTONESE: *PI CHIEW*

Beer brewing was not introduced into China and Japan until towards the end of the 19th century, but it rapidly became an extremely popular drink. Today, beer is the favorite alcoholic beverage in Asia, and almost every country in the region has breweries producing beers for export as well as for domestic consumption.

The style of beer most favored by Asian drinkers is a bottom-fermented brew in the style of Pilsener (Pils), a pale, golden-colored lager with a characteristically well-hopped palate and 4.5–5 per cent alcohol by volume.

Chinese beers

Without doubt, the best known Chinese beer is **Tsingtao**, a light, dry Pilsener-type beer, which is brewed from the sweet spring water of Laoshan, using

Chinese barley and hops. It has a refreshing and delicate taste, and enjoys a huge popularity abroad, not just with expatriate Chinese, but among Westerners as well.

In 1898, part of the Shandong Peninsula was ceded to Germany as a colony. Besides the winery in Yantai, the Germans also established a brewery at Tsingtao in 1903, which was called the

Below: Singaporean Tiger beer is popular all over the world.

Anglo-German Brewery Company. Because of the vicissitudes of history, it went through a number of different owners—Britain, Germany and Japan—until after World War II, when it was taken over by the People's Republic of China. Since then a number of breweries have been established all over China, but Tsingtao Brewery remains the largest and most productive brewer in the land.

Other brands that can occasionally be seen in the West are **Beijing Beer**, **Shanghai Beer**, **Snowflake** and **Yu Chuan** ("Jade Spring") **Beer**. These all are Pilsener-type lagers, each with their own individual flavor.

Japanese beers

The huge beer industry of Japan also owes its origins to foreign investment. In 1869, the American firm of Wiegrand and Copeland started an experimental brewery at Yokohama. Soon afterwards, the Japanese Government sent a researcher to Germany to acquire technical know-how, and subsequently the Copeland operation was passed to Japanese management, taking the name Kirin in 1888.

Today, the Kirin Brewery Company has became one of the biggest brewers in the world. It is part of Japan's Mitsubishi conglomerate, and its output even surpasses that of Heineken. Kirin has nine breweries in different parts of Japan, and **Kirin Beer** is exported to almost every country in the world. It used to enjoy 60 per cent of domestic sales, but has recently been pushed down to about 40 per cent, partly oweing to the surge of its chief rival **Asahi Beer**, which has rapidly increased its export market in recent years. Other strong contenders for the crown of the

Left: Canned Thai beer

Japanese beer industry are **Sapporo Beer,** which also challenges Kirin's claim of being the oldest brewer; and the newcomer **Suntory Beer**, which only started brewing in 1963.

South-east Asian beers

The world-renowned **Tiger Beer** of Singapore came into being by accident. The breweries were established after Heineken failed to reach an agreement with the Dutch Colonial Government to set up their breweries in Java in 1929, so established the Malayan Breweries in Singapore and later in Kuala Lumpur instead. Tiger Beer is now brewed by Asia Pacific Breweries of Singapore, and has achieved worldwide sales figures envied by all its competitors.

From Thailand, the biggest selling lager is **Singha**, brewed by Boon Rawd Brewery. The name Singha is a reference to the elegant but fearsome lion-like creature of local mythology.

Perhaps not that many people are aware that the Philippines is the home of one of the world's major brewing groups—**San Miguel**. This group has three breweries in the Philippines, one in Hong Kong, and one in Papua New Guinea. Outside of Asia, San Miguel has three breweries in Spain, but ironically these are only offshoots of its headquarters in the Philippines.

Dutch colonial links are still evident in Indonesia, where **Heineken** eventually did establish an associate company in Java to produce a Pilsener-style beer. Elsewhere in Asia, popular beers include the Vietnamese **"33"**; **Taiwan Beer** from Taiwan; and **OB** and **Crown** from Korea, but these are seldom seen in the West.

WINE

MANDARIN: *JIU*; CANTONESE: *CHIEW*

In contrast to their sophisticated approach to food, the Chinese, as a whole, are remarkably indiscriminating when it comes to alcoholic beverages. Unless they are connoisseurs, the Chinese often fail to distinguish between table wine, in which the alcoholic content is low, and distilled spirits, in which it is high. In everyday usage, the Chinese character *jiu* or *chiew* means any alcoholic beverage.

Chinese wines

As can be expected in a country where rice is the staple food, rice wine leads the field. There are hundreds of different varieties of rice wine in China, but only a few of these are exported.

Chinese rice wine is generally known as **huang jiu** (yellow wine) in Chinese, because of its golden amber color. The best known and best quality rice wine is **Shao Xing**, named after the district where it is made. Shao Xing, or Shao Hsing is situated south of Hangzhou in Zhejiang province, and its wine-making history dates back to 470 BC. The main grains used for making Shao Xing are glutinous rice, millet and ordinary rice, and the water comes from a large lake

Left: Sake

Below: Shao Xing

Above: Glutinous rice wine

which is fed by the fountains and streams that flow down the sandy mountains on one side, and the dense bamboo-forested hills on the other. The water is so clear and the surface so smooth that the lake is known locally as "the mirror".

There are several varieties of Shao Xing wines, ranging in color from golden amber to dark brown, and in the percentage of alcohol by volume from 14–16 per cent. The aroma is always quite distinctive, smelling subtly fragrant and smoky. Shao Xing should be drunk warm, and always with food. It is also used in cooking, and is added to the food towards the end of the cooking time so that the aroma is retained. One of the most famous Shao Xing wines is **Hua Tiao**, meaning "carved flower". This is a reference to the pretty patterns carved on the urns in which the wine is stored in underground cellars to mature.

As in beer brewing and whisky distilling, what distinguishes Shao Xing rice wine from all its imitators is the water used, which just cannot be replicated elsewhere. So beware of Shao

Xing/Hsing wine made in Taiwan, which pales, literally, by comparison. Read the small print on the label; if it says "made in ROC (Republic of China)" it is a fake.

China also produces some quite good grape wines. Several of these are exported to the West. The names to look for are **Dynasty, Great Wall** and **Huadong**. The whites (Riesling and Chardonnay) seem to be more successful than the red Cabernet Sauvignon. China may well become an important wine region in the future.

Mirin

This is a sweet rice wine with a low alcohol content. It is widely used in cooking, and is usually added towards the end, so that the subtle flavor is retained. Mirin is now available in the West. If you cannot locate it, dry sherry can be used instead, but the results will not be the same.

Pears with Chinese White Wine, Star Anise and Ginger

Star anise and ginger complement these sweet, wine-poached pears.

SERVES 4

6 tablespoons sugar
1¼ cups white wine
thinly pared rind and juice of
   1 lemon
3-inch piece fresh ginger
   root, bruised
5 star anise
10 cloves
2½ cups cold water
6 slightly unripe pears
1 ounce stem ginger, sliced
plain yogurt, to serve

1 Place the sugar, wine, lemon rind and juice, fresh ginger root, star anise, cloves and water into a large pan. Bring to a boil.

2 Meanwhile, peel the pears. Add them to the wine mixture and ensure that they are covered in liquid, then lower the heat. Cover and simmer for 15 minutes or until the pears are tender.

3 Lift out the pears with a slotted spoon and keep them warm. Boil the wine syrup until reduced by half, then pour over the pears. Cool, then chill. Slice the pears and arrange on serving plates. Remove the ginger root from the sauce and add the stem ginger, then spoon the sauce over the pears.

Japanese wines

It is widely known that **sake** is the national drink of Japan. There are many varieties of this rice-based brew, but only a few are exported to the West. Unlike Chinese rice wine, sake is almost colorless, and it tastes slightly sweeter. It usually has an alcohol content of about 15 per cent. Like Chinese rice wine, sake should be drunk with food. Most types of sake are served warm, with the exception of **Ginjo**, a fine, dry wine which is invariably served chilled.

The traditional way of serving sake is in a porcelain pitcher, which is immersed in hot water until the wine is judged to be at the right temperature for serving. It is then poured into small cups. The host lifts a cup in both hands and passes it to his guest with a courteous bow. The cup must not be passed in one hand, as this shows disrespect. Having received the cup, also in both hands, the guest bows and downs the wine in one swift movement.

Good quality grape wines are also produced in Japan, but the output is quite small, owing to the scarcity of land available for growing vines and the extreme climate, all of which make wine-making difficult.

The three big names are **Suntory, Mercian** and **Mann's.** All these companies produce both white and red wines, but very little of the wine output is exported overseas.

SPIRITS

Chinese spirits

The Chinese name for distilled spirit—*bai jiu*—means "white wine" and stems from the fact that it is colorless, as opposed to the "yellow" rice wine. Asking for white wine in China can, therefore, lead to some interesting and potentially disastrous social occasions, as most Chinese spirits have an alcohol content of over 50 per cent.

Most Chinese spirits are distilled from a variety of grains, the commonest of these is sorghum, which is a cross between rice and millet. China has far more distilled spirits than wines, and

Below: Mou-Tai, which is served at state banquets, and Chu Yeh Ching

some of the spirits are blended with herbs for use as medicinal tonics.

Mou-Tai is undoubtedly China's top spirit, and it is used for toasts at state banquets and other celebrations. It may be an acquired taste, but it was awarded a medal at the 1915 International Trade Fair in Panama, second only to France's cognac, but ahead of Scotch whisky as the world's top three spirits. Mou-Tai, which means "thatched terrace", is the name of a village in Kweichow in south-west China. The world-renowned spirit is distilled from two grains, wheat and sorghum, with the water taken from the stream running through a nearby gorge. The climate is moist and warm, and the thin layer of mist that hovers permanently over the fast-running stream is supposed to give the spirit its distinctive features.

CHU YEH CHING
CHINESE LIQUEUR

Traditionally, good rice wines came from south China, while the best spirits were historically produced in the north. Although the distillery in Mou-Tai was established in 1529, the spirit was relatively indifferent until 1704, when a salt merchant from Shanxi in north China visited the area and was so enchanted by the beauty of the village that he decided to settle down there. Seeking new employment, he discovered the local spirit and set about improving it, employing the techniques of distilling the famous Fen Chiew from his native northern province. Mou-tai was the result.

Fen Chiew—the inspiration for Mou-Tai—is one of a small group of Chinese spirits that are available in the West. It comes from the "apricot blossoms village" of Shanxi province in north China, and is distilled from millet and sorghum with the water from a tributary of the Yellow River. Fen Chiew has a history of well over fifteen hundred years, and has afforded inspiration for many of China's greatest poets. This spirit also forms the basis for the famous **Chu Yeh Ching** ("bamboo leaf green"), a medicinal liqueur which is blended with no fewer than twelve different herbs, including bamboo leaves, which give it a lovely, pale green hue. The liqueur tastes quite refreshing despite being 47 per cent alcohol by volume.

Other popular Chinese spirits are **Wu Liang Ye** ("five-grain liqueur") from Sichuan; **Mei Kuei Lu** ("rose dew"); **Wu Chia Pi** ("five-layer skin"); and **Dong Chiew** ("mellow wine"). All of these are quite heady, as they are usually more than 50 per cent proof.

China also produces Western-style brandy, whisky, vodka, rum and gin, but all these drinks are mainly sold for home consumption.

Japanese spirits

Japan has its own spirit distilled from sake called **Shochu** ("burnt wine"). It is quite rough, and is usually diluted with warm water for drinking, even though its alcohol content is only about 25 per cent by volume. Japan produces a

Above: Suntory whisky

Above: Suntory malt whisky

Other Asian spirits

Taiwan produces many of the mainland Chinese drinks as well as the Japanese-inspired **Shokushu** rice spirit. In Korea, look out for **Ginseng Ju**, which comes with what appears to be a parsnip, but is actually a large ginseng root, in every bottle. In the East Indies, the island states in the South China Sea, the local **arrack** or **raki** is crudely distilled from either coconut palm juice or sugar cane molasses. A common practice is to add rice to the fermenting base juice to boost the alcohol content of the spirit. The result is a drink that bears a strong resemblance to rum, and is often sold as such to unwary tourists.

Below: Ginseng Ju

really good quality whisky, however. The first distillery was established in 1923, and in recent years Japanese whisky has attracted considerable attention on the international market. The model for Japan's whiskies is single malt Scotch, but there are equally successful spirits made in the idiom of blended Scotch. Some distilleries blend the homegrown product with imported Scotch malt whisky.

Suntory is the biggest and best-known brand name. Several different labels are marketed worldwide, including **The Whisky, Excellence, Royal, Special Reserve, Old, Kakubin, Gold Label, Gold 1000, White Label, Red Label, Torys Extra** and **Rawhide**, which

has a bourbon flavor. Suntory's rivals in terms of whisky production are Nikka distilleries (**G & G**, **Super Nikka**, **Black Nikka** and **Hi Nikka**); Kirin Seagram (**Robert Brown** and **Dunbar**); and Sanraku Ocean (**White Label**). Several other distillers and blenders make Japanese whisky, but they only have a very small output. Perhaps the best known of these is **Godo Shusei**.

Suntory also makes good brandy. The leading brands are **Imperial, XO, VSOP, VSO** and **VO**. Liqueurs include **Midori,** a green, melon-flavored liqueur; **Ocha,** a green tea liqueur with a delicate tea fragrance; and the **Creme de Kobai,** a pretty, pale pink liqueur made from Japanese plums.

ASIAN RECIPES

Exotic, exciting and deliciously different — these are the flavors of Asia. You are invited to take a cook's tour through China, Malaysia and Singapore, Thailand, Burma, Indonesia, Vietnam, the Philippines, Japan and Korea. Each has its own distinct cuisine, and the range of Asian ingredients in our supermarkets is ever-increasing, so all these delicious recipes can now be tried at home.

CHINA AND HONG KONG

Chinese food is home cooking to at least a quarter of the world's population, central to the majority of people's way of life. "Have you eaten?" and "Have you taken rice?" are common greetings throughout China. In such a vast country, there is a wealth of different styles of cooking, and many cooks and restaurants in the West are now distinguishing between Cantonese, Sichuan and Peking-style cooking, introducing us all to some of the world's finest food.

HOT AND SOUR SOUP

One of China's most popular soups, this is famed for its clever balance of flavors. The "hot" comes from pepper; the "sour" from vinegar. Similar soups are found throughout Asia, some relying on chiles and lime juice to provide the essential flavor contrast.

SERVES 6

INGREDIENTS

4–6 Chinese dried mushrooms
2–3 small pieces of wood ear
  and a few golden needles (lily
  buds) (optional)
4 ounces pork tenderloin, cut into
  fine strips
3 tablespoons cornstarch
2/3 cup water
1–2 tablespoons sunflower oil
1 small onion, finely chopped
6¼ cups good quality beef or chicken
  stock, or 2 × 11-ounce cans
  consommé made up to the full
  quantity with water
5 ounces drained fresh firm beancurd
  (tofu), diced
4 tablespoons rice vinegar
1 tablespoon light soy sauce
1 egg, beaten
1 teaspoon sesame oil
salt and ground white or black pepper
2–3 scallions, shredded,
  to garnish

1 Place the dried mushrooms in a bowl, with the pieces of wood ear and the golden needles (lily buds), if using. Add sufficient warm water to cover and leave to soak for about 30 minutes. Drain the mushrooms, reserving the soaking water. Cut off and discard the mushroom stems and slice the caps finely. Trim away any tough stem from the wood ears, then chop them finely. Using kitchen string, tie the golden needles into a bundle.

2 Lightly dust the strips of pork tenderloin with some of the cornstarch; mix the remaining cornstarch to a smooth paste with the measured water.

3 Heat the oil in a wok or saucepan and fry the onion until soft. Increase the heat and fry the pork until it changes color. Add the stock or consommé, mushrooms, soaking water, and wood ears and golden needles, if using. Bring to a boil, then simmer for 15 minutes.

4 Discard the golden needles, lower the heat and stir in the cornstarch paste to thicken. Add the beancurd, vinegar, soy sauce, and salt and pepper.

5 Bring the soup to just below boiling point, then drizzle in the beaten egg by letting it drop from a whisk (or to be authentic, the fingertips) so that it forms threads in the soup. Stir in the sesame oil and serve at once, garnished with scallion shreds.

DRUNKEN CHICKEN

AS THE CHICKEN IS MARINATED FOR SEVERAL DAYS, IT IS IMPORTANT TO USE A VERY FRESH BIRD FROM A REPUTABLE SUPPLIER. "DRUNKEN" FOODS ARE USUALLY SERVED COLD AS PART OF AN APPETIZER, OR CUT INTO NEAT PIECES AND SERVED AS A SNACK WITH COCKTAILS.

SERVES 4–6

INGREDIENTS
  1 chicken, about 3 pounds
  1/2-inch piece fresh ginger root,
    peeled and thinly sliced
  2 scallions, trimmed
  7 1/2 cups water or to cover
  1 tablespoon salt
  1 1/4 cups dry sherry
  1–2 tablespoons brandy
    (optional)
  scallions, shredded, and fresh herbs,
    to garnish

1 Rinse and dry the chicken inside and out. Place the ginger and scallions in the body cavity. Put the chicken in a large saucepan or flameproof casserole and just cover with water. Bring to a boil, skim and cook for 15 minutes.

2 Turn off the heat, cover the pan or casserole tightly and leave the chicken in the cooking liquid for 3–4 hours, by which time it will be cooked. Drain well. Pour 1 1/4 cups of the stock into a jug. Freeze the remaining stock for use in the future.

3 Remove the skin from the chicken, joint it neatly. Divide each leg into a drumstick and thigh. Make two more portions from the wings and some of the breast. Finally cut away the remainder of the breast pieces (still on the bone) and divide each breast into two even-size portions.

4 Arrange the chicken portions in a shallow dish. Rub salt into the chicken and cover with plastic wrap. Leave in a cool place for several hours or overnight in the refrigerator.

VARIATION
To serve as a cocktail snack, take the meat off the bones, cut it into bite-size pieces, then spear each piece on a toothpick.

5 Next day, lift off any fat from the stock. Mix the sherry and brandy, if using, in a jug, add the stock and pour over the chicken. Cover again and leave in the refrigerator to marinate for 2 or 3 days, turning occasionally.

6 When ready to serve, cut the chicken through the bone into chunky pieces and arrange on a serving platter garnished with scallion shreds and herbs.

PEKING DUCK <u>WITH</u> MANDARIN PANCAKES

AS THE CHINESE DISCOVERED CENTURIES AGO, THIS IS QUITE THE BEST WAY TO EAT DUCK. THE PREPARATION IS TIME-CONSUMING, BUT IT CAN BE DONE IN EASY STAGES.

SERVES 8

INGREDIENTS
   1 duck, about 5¼ pounds
   3 tablespoons clear honey
   2 tablespoons water
   1 teaspoon salt
   1 bunch scallions, cut into strips
   ½ cucumber, seeded and cut
      into matchsticks

For the mandarin pancakes
   2½ cups white bread flour
   1 teaspoon salt
   3 tablespoons peanut or
      sesame oil
   1 cup boiling water

For the dipping sauces
   ½ cup hoisin sauce
   ½ cup plum sauce

1 Bring a large pan of water to a boil. Place the duck on a trivet in the sink and pour a boiling water over the duck to scald and firm up the skin. Carefully lift it out on the trivet and drain thoroughly. Tie kitchen string firmly around the legs of the bird and suspend it from a butcher's hook from a shelf in the kitchen or cellar, whichever is the coolest. Place a bowl underneath to catch the drips and leave overnight.

2 Next day, blend the honey, water and salt and brush half the mixture over the duck skin. Hang up again and leave for 2–3 hours. Repeat and leave to dry completely for a further 3–4 hours.

3 Make the pancakes. Sift the flour and salt into a bowl or food processor. Add 1 tablespoon of the oil, then gradually add enough of the boiling water to form a soft but not sticky dough. Knead for 2–3 minutes by hand or for 30 seconds in the food processor. Allow to rest for 30 minutes.

4 Knead the dough, then divide it into 24 pieces and roll each piece to a 6-inch round. Brush the surface of half the rounds with oil, then sandwich the rounds together in pairs.

5 Brush the surface of two heavy frying pans sparingly with oil. Add one pancake pair to each pan and cook gently for 2–3 minutes until cooked but not colored. Turn over and cook for 2–3 minutes more.

6 Slide the double pancakes out of the pan and pull them apart. Stack on a plate, placing a square of non-stick baking parchment between each while cooking the remainder. Cool, wrap tightly in foil and set aside.

7 Preheat the oven to 450°F. When it reaches that temperature, put the duck on a rack in a roasting pan and place it in the oven. Immediately reduce the temperature to 350°F and roast the duck for 1¾ hours without basting. Check that the skin is crisp and, if necessary, increase the oven temperature to the maximum. Roast for 15 minutes more.

8 Meanwhile, place the scallion strips in iced water to crisp up. Drain. Pat the cucumber pieces dry on paper towels. Reheat the prepared pancakes by steaming the foil parcel for 5–10 minutes in a bamboo steamer over a wok or saucepan of boiling water. Pour the dipping sauces into small dishes to share among the guests.

9 Carve the duck into 1½-inch pieces. At the table, each guest smears some of the prepared sauce on a pancake, tops it with a small amount of crisp duck skin and meat and adds cucumber and scallion strips before enjoying the rolled-up pancake.

COOK'S TIP
Mandarin pancakes can be cooked ahead and frozen. Simply separate the cooked pancakes with squares of freezer paper and wrap them in a plastic bag. They can be heated from frozen as described in the recipe. If time is short, use ready-made pancakes, available from large supermarkets and oriental stores.

MONGOLIAN FIREPOT

THIS MODE OF COOKING WAS INTRODUCED TO CHINA BY THE MONGOL HORDES WHO INVADED IN THE 13TH CENTURY. IT CALLS FOR PLENTY OF PARTICIPATION ON THE PART OF THE GUESTS, WHO COOK THE ASSEMBLED INGREDIENTS AT THE TABLE, DIPPING THE MEATS IN A VARIETY OF DIFFERENT SAUCES.

SERVES 6–8

INGREDIENTS
  2 pounds boned leg of lamb,
    preferably bought thinly sliced
  8 ounces lamb's liver and/or kidneys
  3³⁄₄ cups lamb stock (see Cook's Tip)
  3³⁄₄ cups chicken stock
  ¹⁄₂ inch piece fresh ginger root,
    peeled and thinly sliced
  3 tablespoons rice wine or
    medium-dry sherry
  ¹⁄₂ head Chinese leaves, rinsed
    and shredded
  2 tomatoes, cut into wedges
  few young spinach leaves
  9 ounces fresh firm beancurd (tofu),
    diced (optional)
  4 ounces cellophane noodles
  salt and ground black pepper

For the dipping sauce
  ¹⁄₄ cup red wine vinegar
  ¹⁄₂ tablespoon dark soy sauce
  ¹⁄₂-inch piece fresh ginger root,
    peeled and finely shredded
  1 scallion, finely shredded

To serve
  steamed flower rolls
  bowls of tomato sauce, sweet chili
    sauce, mustard oil and sesame oil
  dry-fried coriander seeds, crushed

COOK'S TIP
When buying the lamb, ask the butcher for the bones and make your own lamb stock. Rinse the bones and place them in a large pan with water to cover. Bring to a boil and skim the surface well. Add 1 peeled onion, 2 peeled carrots, ¹⁄₂-inch piece of peeled and bruised ginger, 1 teaspoon salt and ground black pepper to taste. Bring back to a boil, then simmer for about an hour until the stock is full of flavor. Strain, leave to cool, then skim and use.

1 When buying the lamb, ask your butcher to slice it thinly on a slicing machine, if possible. If you have had to buy the lamb in the piece, however, put it in the freezer for about an hour, so that it is easier to slice thinly.

2 Trim the liver and remove the skin and core from the kidneys, if using. Place them in the freezer too. If you managed to buy sliced lamb, keep it in the refrigerator until needed.

3 Mix both types of stock in a large pan. Add the sliced ginger and rice wine or sherry, with salt and pepper to taste. Heat to simmering point; simmer for 15 minutes.

4 Slice all the meats thinly and arrange them attractively on a large platter.

5 Place the shredded Chinese leaves, tomatoes, spinach leaves and the diced beancurd (tofu) on a separate platter. Soak the noodles in warm or hot water, following the instructions on the packet.

6 Make the dipping sauce by mixing all the ingredients in a small bowl. The other sauces and the crushed coriander seeds should be spooned into separate small dishes and placed on a serving tray. Have ready a basket of freshly steamed flower rolls.

7 Fill the moat of the hotpot with the simmering stock. Alternatively, fill a fondue pot and place it over a burner. Each guest selects a portion of meat from the platter and cooks it in the hot stock, using chopsticks or a fondue fork. The meat is then dipped in one of the sauces and coated with the coriander seeds (if liked) before being eaten with a steamed flower roll.

8 When all or most of the meat has been eaten, top up the stock if necessary, then add the vegetables, beancurd and drained noodles. Cook for a minute or two, until the noodles are tender and the vegetables retain a little crispness. Serve the soup in warmed bowls, with any remaining steamed flower rolls.

ICED FRUIT MOUNTAIN

THIS DRAMATIC DISPLAY OF FRUIT ARRANGED ON A "MOUNTAIN" OF ICE CUBES IS BOUND TO DELIGHT YOUR GUESTS. CUT THE PIECES OF FRUIT LARGER THAN FOR A FRUIT SALAD AND SUPPLY TOOTHPICKS FOR SPEARING.

SERVES 6–8

INGREDIENTS
  1 star fruit
  4 kumquats
  6 physalis
  8 ounces seedless black grapes
  8 ounces large strawberries
  1 apple and/or Asian pear
  2 large oranges, peeled
  8 fresh lychees, peeled (optional)
  1 Charentais melon and/or
  1/2 watermelon
  superfine sugar, for dipping
  wedges of kaffir lime, to decorate

COOK'S TIP
The list of fruits is just a suggestion. Use any seasonal fruits, keeping the display as colorful as possible.

1 Slice the star fruit and halve the kumquats. Leave the hulls on the strawberries. Cut the apple and/or Asian pear into wedges and the oranges into segments. Use a melon baller for the melon or, alternatively, cut the melon into neat wedges. Chill the fruit.

2 Prepare the ice cube "mountain". Choose a wide, shallow bowl that, when turned upside down, will fit neatly on a serving platter. Fill the bowl with crushed ice cubes. Put it in the freezer, with the serving platter. Leave in the freezer for at least 1 hour.

3 Remove the serving platter, ice cubes and bowl from the freezer. Invert the serving platter on top of the bowl of ice, then turn platter and bowl over. Lift off the bowl and arrange the pieces of fruit on the "mountain".

4 Decorate the mountain with the sprigs of mint leaves or borage flowers, if you like, and serve the fruit at once, handing round a bowl of sugar separately for guests with a sweet tooth.

CHINESE HONEYED APPLES

THESE SCRUMPTIOUS TREATS ARE BEST PREPARED FOR A SELECT NUMBER AS THEY REQUIRE THE COOK'S COMPLETE ATTENTION. THE HONEY COATING CRISPENS WHEN THE FRITTERS ARE DIPPED IN ICED WATER.

SERVES 4–5

INGREDIENTS
  4 crisp eating apples
  juice of 1/2 lemon
  1/4 cup cornstarch
  sunflower oil, for deep frying
  toasted sesame seeds,
    for sprinkling

For the fritter batter
  1 cup all-purpose flour
  generous pinch of salt
  1/2–2/3 cup water
  2 tablespoons sunflower oil
  2 egg whites

For the sauce
  1 cup clear honey
  1/2 cup sunflower oil
  1 teaspoon white wine vinegar

1 Peel, core and cut the apples into eighths, brush each piece lightly with lemon juice then dust with cornstarch. Make the sauce. Heat the honey and oil in a pan, stirring until blended. Remove from the heat and stir in the vinegar.

2 Sift the flour and salt into a bowl, then stir in the water and oil. Whisk the egg whites until stiff; fold into the batter.

3 Spear each piece of apple in turn on a skewer, dip in the batter and fry in hot oil until golden. Drain on paper towels, place in a dish and pour the sauce over. Transfer the fritters to a lightly oiled serving dish. Sprinkle with sesame seeds. Serve at once, offering bowls of iced water for dipping.

CRISPY SHANGHAI SPRING ROLLS

IT IS SAID THAT THESE FAMOUS SNACKS WERE TRADITIONALLY SERVED WITH TEA WHEN VISITORS CAME TO CALL AFTER THE CHINESE NEW YEAR. AS THIS WAS SPRINGTIME, THEY CAME TO BE KNOWN AS SPRING ROLLS. BUY FRESH OR FROZEN SPRING ROLL WRAPPERS FROM ORIENTAL SHOPS.

MAKES 12

INGREDIENTS
   12 spring roll wrappers, thawed
      if frozen
   2 tablespoons all-purpose flour mixed
      to a paste with water
   sunflower oil, for deep frying

For the filling
   6 Chinese dried mushrooms, soaked
      for 30 minutes in warm water
   5 ounces fresh firm beancurd (tofu)
   2 tablespoons sunflower oil
   8 ounces finely minced pork
   8 ounces peeled cooked shrimp,
      roughly chopped
   1/2 teaspoon cornstarch, mixed to a
      paste with 1 tablespoon light
      soy sauce
   3 ounces each shredded bamboo
      shoot or grated carrot, sliced water
      chestnuts and bean sprouts
   6 scallions or 1 young leek, finely
      chopped
   a little sesame oil

For the dipping sauce
   scant 1/2 cup light soy sauce
   1 tablespoon chili sauce or finely
      chopped fresh red chile
   a little sesame oil
   rice vinegar, to taste

1 Make the filling. Drain the mushrooms. Cut off and discard the stems and slice the caps finely. Cut the beancurd (tofu) into slices of a similar size.

2 Heat the oil in a wok and stir-fry the pork for 2–3 minutes or until the color changes. Add the shrimp, cornstarch paste and bamboo shoot or carrot. Stir in the water chestnuts.

COOK'S TIP
Thaw frozen spring roll wrappers at room temperature, open the package and separate with a palette knife. Cover with a damp cloth until needed.

3 Increase the heat, add the bean sprouts and scallions or leek and toss for 1 minute. Stir in the mushrooms and beancurd. Off the heat, season, then stir in the sesame oil. Cool quickly on a large platter.

4 Separate the spring roll wrappers (see Cook's Tip). Place a wrapper on the work surface with one corner nearest you. Spoon some of the filling near the center of the wrapper and fold the nearest corner over the filling. Smear a little of the flour paste on the free sides, turn the sides to the middle and roll up. Repeat this procedure with the remaining wrappers and filling.

5 Deep fry the spring rolls in batches in oil heated to 375°F until they are crisp and golden. Drain on paper towels and serve at once with the dipping sauce, made by mixing all the ingredients in a bowl.

LION'S HEAD MEAT BALLS

THESE LARGER-THAN-USUAL PORK MEAT BALLS ARE FIRST FRIED, THEN SIMMERED IN STOCK. THEY ARE TRADITIONALLY SERVED WITH A FRINGE OF GREENS SUCH AS PAK-CHOI TO REPRESENT THE LION'S MANE.

SERVES 2–3

INGREDIENTS

1 pound lean pork, ground finely with
  a little fat
4–6 drained canned water chestnuts,
  finely chopped
1 teaspoon finely chopped fresh
  ginger root
1 small onion, finely chopped
2 tablespoons dark soy sauce
beaten egg, to bind
2 tablespoons cornstarch,
  seasoned with salt and ground
  black pepper
2 tablespoons peanut oil
1¼ cups chicken stock
½ teaspoon sugar
4 ounces pak-choi, stalks trimmed
  and the leaves rinsed
salt and ground black pepper

1 Mix the pork, water chestnuts, ginger and onion with 1 tablespoon of the soy sauce in a bowl. Add salt and pepper to taste, stir in enough beaten egg to bind, then form into eight or nine balls. Toss a little of the cornstarch into the bowl and make a paste with the remaining cornstarch and water.

VARIATION
Crab meat or shrimp can be used instead of some of the pork in this recipe. Alternatively, you could try substituting ground lamb or beef for the ground pork used here.

2 Heat the oil in a large frying pan and brown the meat balls all over. Using a slotted spoon, transfer the meat balls to a wok or deep frying pan.

3 Add the stock, sugar and the remaining soy sauce to the oil that is left in the pan. Heat gently, stirring to incorporate the sediment on the bottom of the pan. Pour over the meat balls, cover and simmer for 20–25 minutes.

4 Increase the heat and add the pak-choi. Continue to cook for 2–3 minutes or until the leaves are just wilted.

5 Lift out the greens and arrange on a serving platter. Top with the meat balls and keep hot. Stir the cornstarch paste into the sauce. Bring to a boil, stirring, until it thickens. Pour over the meat balls and serve at once.

TEA EGGS

THESE MARBLED EGGS WITH THEIR MAZE OF FINE LINES, HAVE AN ANTIQUE PORCELAIN APPEARANCE. TEA EGGS CAN BE SERVED AS A SNACK WITH CONGEE, A POPULAR CHINESE SOFT RICE DISH. THEY ALSO MAKE PERFECT PICNIC FARE; SHELL THEM JUST BEFORE EATING SO THAT THEY STAY MOIST.

MAKES 6

INGREDIENTS
6 eggs
2 tablespoons dark soy sauce
1 teaspoon salt
1/2 star anise
2 tea bags

COOK'S TIPS
• The soy sauce and tea not only colors the eggs but adds a subtle flavor as well. Use dark soy sauce, which has a stronger flavor.
• Make sure that the eggs simmer very gently and watch them carefully so that the soy sauce liquid doesn't evaporate too much. Keep topping up the liquid with recently boiled water from the kettle so that the eggs are always covered.

1 Add the eggs to a pan of cold water. Heat it to simmering point and hard cook the eggs for 20 minutes.

2 Drain the eggs and pour enough fresh cold water into the pan to cover. Set the eggs aside. When they are cold, gently roll the eggs to craze the shells without breaking them.

3 Stir the soy sauce, salt and star anise into the pan of water. Add the tea bags and eggs. Bring to a boil, cover and simmer for 1 1/2–2 hours. Top up the water to keep the eggs covered.

4 Allow the eggs to cool in the liquid overnight, then shell carefully. Quarter and serve as part of a meal.

ANITA WONG'S DUCK

THE CHINESE ARE PASSIONATELY FOND OF DUCK AND REGARD IT AS ESSENTIAL AT CELEBRATORY MEALS. TO THE CHINESE, DUCK DENOTES MARITAL HARMONY.

SERVES 4–6

INGREDIENTS
1 duck with giblets, about
   5–5 1/4 pounds
4 tablespoons vegetable oil
2 garlic cloves, chopped
1-inch piece fresh ginger root, peeled
   and thinly sliced
3 tablespoons bean paste
2 tablespoons light soy sauce
1 tablespoon dark soy sauce
1 tablespoon sugar
1/2 teaspoon five-spice powder
3 star anise points
scant 2 cups duck stock
   (see Cook's Tip)
salt
shredded scallions, to garnish

1 Make the stock (see Cook's Tip), strain into a bowl and blot with paper towels to remove excess fat. Measure scant 2 cups into a jug.

2 Heat the oil in a large pan. Fry the garlic without browning, then add the duck. Turn frequently until the outside is slightly brown. Transfer to a plate.

3 Add the ginger to the pan, then stir in the bean paste. Cook for 1 minute, then add both soy sauces, the sugar and the five-spice powder. Return the duck to the pan and fry until the outside is coated. Add the star anise and stock, and season to taste. Cover tightly; simmer gently for 2–2 1/2 hours or until tender. Skim off the excess fat. Leave the duck in the sauce to cool.

4 Cut the duck into serving portions and pour over the sauce. Garnish with scallion curls and serve cold.

COOK'S TIP
To make stock, put the duck giblets in a pan with a small onion and a piece of bruised ginger. Cover with 2 1/2 cups water, bring to a boil and then simmer, covered, for 20 minutes.

SICHUAN CHICKEN WITH KUNG PO SAUCE

THIS RECIPE, WHICH HAILS FROM THE SICHUAN REGION OF WESTERN CHINA, HAS BECOME ONE OF THE CLASSIC RECIPES IN THE CHINESE REPERTOIRE.

SERVES 3

INGREDIENTS
    2 skinless boneless chicken breasts,
      total weight about 12 ounces
    1 egg white
    2 teaspoons cornstarch
    1/2 teaspoon salt
    2 tablespoons yellow salted beans
    1 tablespoon hoisin sauce
    1 teaspoon light brown sugar
    1 tablespoon rice wine or
      medium-dry sherry
    1 tablespoon wine vinegar
    4 garlic cloves, crushed
    2/3 cup chicken stock
    3 tablespoons peanut oil or
      sunflower oil
    2–3 dried chilies, broken into
      small pieces
    4 ounces roasted cashew nuts
    fresh cilantro, to garnish

1 Cut the chicken into neat pieces. Lightly whisk the egg white in a dish, whisk in the cornstarch and salt, then add the chicken and stir until coated.

COOK'S TIP
Peanuts are the classic ingredient in this dish, but cashew nuts have an even better flavor and have become popular both in home cooking and in restaurants.

2 In a separate bowl, mash the beans with a spoon. Stir in the hoisin sauce, brown sugar, rice wine or sherry, vinegar, garlic and stock.

3 Heat a wok, add the oil and then fry the chicken, turning constantly, for about 2 minutes until tender. Drain over a bowl in order to collect excess oil.

4 Heat the reserved oil and fry the chili pieces for 1 minute. Return the chicken to the wok and pour in the bean sauce mixture. Bring to a boil and stir in the cashew nuts. Spoon into a heated serving dish and garnish with cilantro.

SICHUAN NOODLES <u>WITH</u> SESAME SAUCE

THIS TASTY VEGETARIAN DISH RESEMBLES THAMIN LETHOK, *A BURMESE DISH, WHICH ALSO CONSISTS OF FLAVORED NOODLES SERVED WITH SEPARATE VEGETABLES THAT ARE TOSSED AT THE TABLE. THIS ILLUSTRATES NEATLY HOW RECIPES MIGRATE FROM ONE COUNTRY TO ANOTHER.*

SERVES 3–4

INGREDIENTS

1 pound fresh or 8 ounces dried
   egg noodles
1/2 cucumber, sliced lengthwise,
   seeded and diced
4–6 scallions, finely shredded
8 ounces mooli, peeled and
   coarsely grated
a bunch of radishes about 4 ounces,
   halved and finely sliced
2 cups beansprouts, rinsed then left
   in iced water and drained
4 tablespoons peanut oil or
   sunflower oil
2 garlic cloves, crushed
3 tablespoons toasted sesame paste
1 tablespoon sesame oil
1 tablespoon light soy sauce
1–2 teaspoons chili sauce, to taste
1 tablespoon rice vinegar
1/2 cup chicken stock or water
1 teaspoon sugar, or to taste
salt and ground black pepper
roasted cashew nuts, to garnish

1 If using fresh noodles, cook them in boiling water for 1 minute then drain, rinse in fresh water and drain again. Cook dried noodles according to the instructions on the packet, draining and rinsing them as for fresh noodles.

2 Sprinkle the diced cucumber with salt, leave for 15 minutes, then rinse, drain and dry on paper towels. Place in a large salad bowl.

3 Cut the scallions into fine shreds. Cut the radishes in half and slice finely. Coarsely grate the mooli using a mandolin or food procesor. Add all the vegetables to the cucumber

4 Heat half the oil in a wok or frying pan and stir-fry the noodles for about 1 minute. Using a slotted spoon, transfer the noodles to a large serving bowl and keep warm.

5 Add the remaining oil to the wok. When it is hot, fry the garlic to flavor the oil. Remove from the heat and stir in the sesame paste, with the sesame oil, soy and chili sauces, vinegar and stock or water. Add a little sugar and season to taste. Warm through over a gentle heat. Do not overheat or the sauce will thicken too much. Pour the sauce over the noodles and toss well. Garnish with cashew nuts and serve with the vegetables.

SICHUAN SPICED EGGPLANT

THIS STRAIGHTFORWARD YET VERSATILE VEGETARIAN DISH CAN BE SERVED HOT, WARM OR COLD, AS THE OCCASION DEMANDS. TOPPED WITH A SPRINKLING OF TOASTED SESAME SEEDS, IT IS EASY TO PREPARE AND TASTES ABSOLUTELY DELICIOUS.

SERVES 4–6

INGREDIENTS
2 eggplant, total weight about
  1 pound 6 ounces, cut into
  large chunks
1 tablespoon salt
1 teaspoon chili powder or to taste
5–6 tablespoons sunflower oil
1 tablespoon rice wine or
  medium-dry sherry
scant ½ cup water
5 tablespoons chili bean sauce
  (see Cook's Tip)
salt and ground black pepper
a few toasted sesame seeds,
  to garnish

1 Place the eggplant chunks on a plate, sprinkle them with the salt and leave to stand for 15–20 minutes. Rinse well, drain and dry thoroughly on paper towels. Toss the eggplant cubes in the chili powder.

2 Heat a wok and add the oil. When the oil is hot, add the eggplant chunks, with the rice wine or sherry. Stir constantly until the eggplant chunks start to turn a little brown. Stir in the water, cover the wok and steam for 2–3 minutes. Add the chili bean sauce and cook for 2 minutes. Season to taste, then spoon on to a serving dish, scatter with sesame seeds and serve.

COOK'S TIP
If you can't get hold of chili bean sauce, use 1–2 tablespoons chili paste mixed with 2 crushed garlic cloves, 1 tablespoon each of dark soy sauce and rice vinegar, and 2 teaspoons light soy sauce.

KAN SHAO GREEN BEANS

A PARTICULAR STYLE OF COOKING FROM SICHUAN, KAN SHAO MEANS "DRY-COOKED" – IN OTHER WORDS USING NO STOCK OR WATER. THE SLIM GREEN BEANS AVAILABLE ALL THE YEAR ROUND FROM SUPERMARKETS ARE IDEAL FOR USE IN THIS QUICK AND TASTY RECIPE.

SERVES 6

INGREDIENTS
¾ cup sunflower oil
1 pound fresh green beans, trimmed
  and cut in half
2 × ½-inch piece fresh ginger root,
  peeled and cut into matchsticks
1 teaspoon sugar
2 teaspoons light soy sauce
salt and ground black pepper

VARIATION
This simple recipe works just as well with other fresh green vegetables such as baby asparagus spears and okra.

1 Heat the oil in a wok. When the oil is just beginning to smoke, carefully add the beans and stir-fry them for 1–2 minutes until just tender.

2 Lift out the green beans on to a plate lined with paper towels. Using a ladle carefully remove all but 2 tablespoons oil from the wok.

3 Reheat the remaining oil, add the ginger and stir-fry for a minute or two to flavor the oil.

4 Return the green beans to the wok, stir in the sugar, soy sauce and salt and pepper, and toss together quickly to ensure the beans are well coated. Serve the beans at once.

BANG BANG CHICKEN

What a descriptive name this special dish from Sichuan has! Use toasted sesame paste to give the sauce an authentic flavor, although crunchy peanut butter can be used instead. Bang Bang Chicken is perfect for parties and ideal for a buffet.

SERVES 4

INGREDIENTS

   3 skinless boneless chicken breasts,
     total weight about 1 pound
   1 garlic clove, crushed
   1/2 teaspoon black peppercorns
   1 small onion, halved
   1 large cucumber, peeled, seeded
     and cut into thin strips
   salt and ground black pepper

For the sauce

   3 tablespoons toasted sesame paste
   1 tablespoon light soy sauce
   1 tablespoon wine vinegar
   2 scallions, finely chopped
   2 garlic cloves, crushed
   2 × 1/2-inch piece fresh ginger
     root, peeled and cut into
     matchsticks
   1 tablespoon Sichuan peppercorns,
     dry fried and crushed
   1 teaspoon light brown sugar

For the chili oil

   4 tablespoons peanut oil
   1 teaspoon chili powder

2 Make the sauce by mixing the toasted sesame paste with 3 tablespoons of the chicken stock, saving the rest for soup. Add the soy sauce, vinegar, scallions, garlic, ginger and crushed peppercorns to the sesame mixture. Stir in sugar to taste.

3 Make the chili oil by gently heating the oil and chili powder together until foaming. Simmer for 2 minutes, cool, then strain off the red-colored oil and discard the sediment.

4 Spread out the cucumber batons on a platter. Cut the chicken breasts into pieces of about the same size as the cucumber strips and arrange them on top. Pour over the sauce, drizzle on the chili oil and serve.

VARIATION

Crunchy peanut butter can be used instead of sesame paste, if preferred. Mix it with 2 tablespoons sesame oil and proceed as in Step 2.

1 Place the chicken in a saucepan. Just cover with water, add the garlic, peppercorns and onion and bring to a boil. Skim the surface, stir in salt and pepper to taste, then cover the pan. Cook for 25 minutes or until the chicken is just tender. Drain, reserving the stock.

CRISPY WONTON SOUP

THE FRESHLY COOKED CRISP WONTONS ARE SUPPOSED TO SIZZLE AND "SING" IN THE HOT SOUP AS THEY ARE TAKEN TO THE TABLE.

SERVES 6

INGREDIENTS
  2 wood ears, soaked for 30 minutes
    in warm water to cover
  5 cups homemade chicken stock
  1-inch piece fresh ginger root,
    peeled and grated
  4 scallions, chopped
  2 rich-green inner spring greens
    leaves, finely shredded
  2 ounces drained canned bamboo
    shoots, sliced
  1 1/2 tablespoons dark soy sauce
  1/2 teaspoon sesame oil
  salt and ground black pepper

For the filled wontons
  1 teaspoon sesame oil
  1/2 small onion, finely chopped
  10 drained canned water chestnuts,
    finely chopped
  4 ounces finely minced pork
  24 wonton wrappers
  peanut oil, for deep frying

1 Make the filled wontons. Heat the sesame oil in a small pan, add the onion, water chestnuts and pork and fry, stirring occasionally, until the meat is no longer pink. Tip into a bowl, season to taste and leave to cool.

COOK'S TIP
The wontons can be filled up to two hours ahead. Place them in a single layer on a baking sheet dusted with cornstarch to prevent them from sticking and leave in a cool place.

2 Place the wonton wrappers under a slightly dampened dish towel so that they do not dry out. Next, dampen the edges of a wonton wrapper. Place about 1 teaspoon of the filling in the center of the wrapper. Gather it up like a purse and twist the top or roll up as you would a baby spring roll. Fill the remaining wontons in the same way.

3 Make the soup. Drain the wood ears, trim away any rough stems, then slice thinly. Bring the stock to a boil, add the ginger and the scallions and simmer for 3 minutes. Add the sliced wood ears, shredded spring greens, bamboo shoots and soy sauce. Simmer for 10 minutes, then stir in the sesame oil. Season to taste with salt and pepper, cover and keep hot.

4 Heat the oil in a wok to 375°F and fry the wontons, in batches if necessary, for 3–4 minutes or until they are crisp and golden brown all over. Ladle the soup into six warmed soup bowls and share the wontons among them. Serve immediately.

EGG FOO YUNG – CANTONESE STYLE

HEARTY AND FULL OF FLAVOR, THIS CAN BE COOKED EITHER AS ONE LARGE OMELET OR AS INDIVIDUAL OMELETS. EITHER WAY, IT IS A CLEVER WAY OF USING UP LEFTOVERS SUCH AS COOKED HAM, SEAFOOD, CHICKEN, PORK OR VEGETABLES. SERVE IT CUT INTO PIECES.

2 Beat the eggs in a bowl. Add the meat and vegetables and mix well.

3 Wipe the frying pan and heat the remaining oil. Pour in the egg mixture and tilt the pan so that it covers the base. When the omelet has set on the underside, sprinkle the top with salt, pepper and sugar.

SERVES 3–4

INGREDIENTS

   6 Chinese dried mushrooms soaked
     for 30 minutes in warm water
   1 cup beansprouts
   6 drained canned water chestnuts,
     finely chopped
   2 ounces baby spinach leaves,
     washed
   4 tablespoons sunflower oil
   2 ounces roast pork, cut into
     thin strips
   4 eggs
   1/2 teaspoon sugar
   1 teaspoon rice wine or
     medium-dry sherry
  salt and ground black pepper
  fresh cilantro sprigs, to garnish

1 Drain the mushrooms, cut off and discard the stems; slice the caps finely and mix them with the remaining vegetables. Heat half the oil in a large heavy frying pan. Add the pork and the vegetables and toss the mixture over the heat for 1 minute.

4 Invert a plate over the pan, turn both over, and slide it back into the pan to cook on the other side. Drizzle with rice wine or sherry and serve immediately, garnished with sprigs of cilantro.

CANTONESE FRIED NOODLES

CHOW MEIN IS HUGELY POPULAR WITH THE THRIFTY CHINESE WHO BELIEVE IN TURNING LEFTOVERS INTO TASTY DISHES. FOR THIS DELICIOUS DISH, BOILED NOODLES ARE FRIED TO FORM A CRISPY CRUST, WHICH IS TOPPED WITH A SAVORY SAUCE CONTAINING WHATEVER TASTES GOOD AND NEEDS EATING UP.

SERVES 2–3

INGREDIENTS

8 ounces lean beef steak or
   pork tenderloin
8-ounce can bamboo shoots, drained
1 leek, trimmed
1 ounce Chinese dried mushrooms,
   soaked for 30 minutes in ½ cup
   warm water
5 ounces Chinese leaves
1 pound cooked egg noodles
   (8 ounces dried), drained well
6 tablespoons vegetable oil
2 tablespoons dark soy sauce
1 tablespoon cornstarch
1 tablespoon rice wine or
   medium-dry sherry
1 teaspoon sesame oil
1 teaspoon caster sugar
salt and ground black pepper

1 Slice the beef or pork, bamboo shoots and leek into matchsticks. Drain the mushrooms, reserving 6 tablespoons of the soaking water. Cut off and discard the stems, then slice the caps finely. Cut the Chinese leaves into 1-inch diamond-shaped pieces and sprinkle with salt. Pat the noodles dry with paper towels.

2 Heat a third of the oil in a large wok or frying pan and sauté the noodles. After turning them over once, press the noodles evenly against the bottom of the pan with a wooden spatula until they form a flat, even cake. Cook over medium heat for about 4 minutes or until the noodles at the bottom have become crisp.

3 Turn the noodle cake over with spatula or fish slice or invert on to a large plate and slide back into the wok. Cook for 3 minutes more, then slide on to a heated plate. Keep warm.

4 Heat 2 tablespoons of the remaining oil in the wok. Add the strips of leek, then the meat strips and stir-fry for 10–15 seconds. Sprinkle over half the soy sauce and then add the bamboo shoots and mushrooms, with salt and pepper to taste. Toss over the heat for 1 minute, then transfer this mixture to a plate and set aside.

5 Heat the remaining oil in the wok and sauté the Chinese leaves for 1 minute. Return the meat and vegetable mixture to the wok and sauté with the leaves for 30 seconds, stirring constantly.

6 Mix the cornstarch with the reserved mushroom water. Stir into the wok along with the rice wine or sherry, sesame oil, sugar and remaining soy sauce. Cook for 15 seconds to thicken. Divide the noodles among 2–3 serving dishes and pile the meat and vegetables on top.

STEAMED FISH <u>WITH</u> FIVE WILLOW SAUCE

A FISH KETTLE WILL COME IN USEFUL FOR THIS RECIPE. CARP IS TRADITIONALLY USED, BUT ANY CHUNKY FISH THAT CAN BE COOKED WHOLE SUCH AS SALMON OR SEA BREAM CAN BE GIVEN THIS TREATMENT. MAKE SURE YOU HAVE A SUITABLE LARGE PLATTER FOR SERVING THIS SPECTACULAR DISH.

SERVES 4

INGREDIENTS
    1–2 carp or similar whole fish, total
        weight about 2¼ pounds, cleaned
        and scaled
    1-inch piece fresh ginger root, peeled
        and thinly sliced
    4 scallions, cut into thin strips
    ½ teaspoon salt

For the five willow sauce
    13-ounce jar chow chow (Chinese
        sweet mixed pickles)
    1¼ cups water
    2 tablespoons rice vinegar
    1½ tablespoons sugar
    1½ tablespoons cornstarch
    1 tablespoon light soy sauce
    1 tablespoon rice wine or
        medium-dry sherry
    1 small green bell pepper, seeded
        and diced
    1 carrot, peeled and cut into
        matchsticks
    1 tomato, peeled, seeded and diced

2 Fold up one or two pieces of foil to make a long wide strip. You will need one for each fish. Place the fish on the foil and then lift the fish on to the trivet. Lower the trivet into the fish kettle and tuck the ends of the foil over the fish.

3 Pour boiling water into the fish kettle to a depth of 1 inch. Bring to a full rolling boil, then lower the heat and cook the fish until the flesh flakes, topping up the kettle with boiling water as necessary. See Cook's Tip for cooking times.

5 In a small bowl, mix the cornstarch to a paste with the remaining water. Stir in the soy sauce and rice wine or sherry.

6 Add the mixture to the sauce and bring to a boil, stirring until it thickens and becomes glossy. Add all the vegetables, the chopped pickles and the pickle liquid and cook over a gentle heat for 2 minutes.

7 Using the foil strips as a support, carefully transfer the cooked fish to a platter, then ease the foil away. Spoon the warm sauce over the fish and serve.

1 Rinse the fish inside and out. Dry with paper towels. Create a support for each fish by placing a broad strip of oiled foil on the work surface. Place the fish on the foil. Mix the ginger, scallions and salt, then tuck the mixture into the body cavity.

4 Meanwhile, prepare the sauce. Tip the chow chow (Chinese sweet mixed pickles) into a strainer placed over a bowl and reserve the liquid. Cut each of the pickles in half. Pour 1 cup of the water into a pan and bring to a boil. Add the vinegar and sugar and stir until dissolved.

COOK'S TIP
If using one large fish that is too long to fit in a fish kettle, cut it in half and cook it on a rack placed over a large roasting tin. Pour in a similar quantity of boiling water as for the fish kettle, cover with foil and cook on top of the stove. Allow about 20–25 minutes for a 2¼ pound fish; 15–20 minutes for a 1½ pound fish. Reassemble the halved fish before coating it with the sauce.

DUCK BREASTS WITH PINEAPPLE AND GINGER

USE THE BONELESS DUCK BREASTS THAT ARE WIDELY AVAILABLE OR ALTERNATIVELY DO AS THE CHINESE AND USE A WHOLE BIRD, SAVING THE LEGS FOR ANOTHER MEAL AND USING THE CARCASS TO MAKE STOCK FOR SOUP. MUCH MORE IN LINE WITH CHINESE FRUGALITY!

SERVES 2–3

INGREDIENTS
  2 boneless duck breasts
  4 scallions, chopped
  1 tablespoon light soy sauce
  8-ounce can pineapple rings
  5 tablespoons water
  4 pieces drained Chinese stem ginger
    in syrup, plus 3 tablespoons syrup
    from the jar
  2 tablespoons cornstarch mixed to a
    paste with a little water
  1/4 each red and green bell pepper,
    seeded and cut into thin strips
  salt and ground black pepper
  cooked thin egg noodles, baby
    spinach and green beans, blanched,
    to serve

1 Strip the skin from the duck breasts. Select a shallow bowl that will fit into your steamer and that will accommodate the duck breasts side by side. Spread out the chopped scallions in the bowl, arrange the duck breasts on top and cover with baking parchment. Set the steamer over boiling water and cook the duck breasts for about 1 hour or until tender. Remove the breasts from the steamer and leave to cool slightly.

2 Cut the breasts into thin slices. Place on a plate and moisten them with a little of the cooking juices from the steaming bowl. Strain the remaining juices into a small saucepan and set aside. Cover the duck slices with the baking parchment or foil and keep warm.

3 Drain the canned pineapple rings, reserving 5 tablespoons of the juice. Add this to the reserved cooking juices in the pan, together with the measured water. Stir in the ginger syrup, then stir in the cornstarch paste and cook, stirring until thickened. Season to taste.

4 Cut the pineapple and ginger into attractive shapes. Put the cooked noodles, baby spinach and green beans on a plate, add slices of duck and top with the pineapple, ginger and pepper strips. Pour over the sauce and serve.

SPICY SHREDDED BEEF

THE ESSENCE OF THIS RECIPE IS THAT THE BEEF IS CUT INTO VERY FINE STRIPS. THIS IS EASIER TO ACHIEVE IF THE PIECE OF BEEF IS PLACED IN THE FREEZER FOR 30 MINUTES UNTIL IT IS VERY FIRM BEFORE BEING SLICED WITH A SHARP KNIFE.

SERVES 2

INGREDIENTS
    8 ounces rump or tenderloin of beef
    1 tablespoon each light and dark
        soy sauce
    1 tablespoon rice wine or
        medium-dry sherry
    1 teaspoon dark brown soft sugar
    6 tablespoons vegetable oil
    1 large onion, thinly sliced
    1-inch piece fresh ginger root, peeled
        and grated
    1–2 carrots, cut into matchsticks
    2–3 fresh or dried chilies, halved,
        seeded (optional) and chopped
    salt and ground black pepper
    fresh chives, to garnish

1 With a sharp knife, slice the beef very thinly, then cut each slice into fine strips or shreds.

2 Mix together the light and dark soy sauces with the rice wine or sherry and sugar in a bowl. Add the strips of beef and stir well to ensure they are evenly coated with the marinade.

3 Heat a wok and add half the oil. When it is hot, stir-fry the onion and ginger for 3–4 minutes, then transfer to a plate. Add the carrot, stir-fry for 3–4 minutes until slightly softened, then transfer to a plate and keep warm.

4 Heat the remaining oil in the wok, then quickly add the beef, with the marinade, followed by the chilies. Cook over high heat for 2 minutes, stirring all the time.

5 Return the fried onion and ginger to the wok and stir-fry for 1 minute more. Season with salt and pepper to taste, cover and cook for 30 seconds. Spoon the meat into two warmed bowls and add the strips of carrots. Garnish with fresh chives and serve.

COOK'S TIP
Remove and discard the seeds from the chilies before you chop them—unless, of course, you like really fiery food. In which case, you could add some or all of the seeds with the chopped chilies.

STEAMED FLOWER ROLLS

THESE ATTRACTIVE LITTLE ROLLS ARE TRADITIONALLY SERVED WITH MONGOLIAN FIREPOT.

<u>MAKES 16</u>

INGREDIENTS
    1 quantity basic dough (below) made
      using 1 teaspoon sugar
    1 tablespoon sesame seed oil
    chives, to garnish

1 Divide the risen and knocked back
dough into two equal portions. Roll each
into a rectangle measuring 12 x 8-inches.
Brush the surface of one with sesame oil
and lay the other on top. Roll up like a

COOK'S TIP
When lining the steamer, fold the paper
several times, then cut small holes like a
doily. This lets the steam circulate, yet
prevents the steamed flower rolls from
sticking to the steamer.

2 Take each dough roll in turn and
press down firmly on the rolled side
with a chopstick. Place the rolls on the
work surface, coiled side uppermost.

3 Pinch the opposite ends of each roll
with the fingers of both hands, then pull
the ends underneath and seal. The
dough should separate into petals.

4 Place the buns on non-stick baking
paper in a steamer and leave to double
in size. Steam over rapidly boiling water
for 30–35 minutes. Serve the buns hot,
garnished with chives.

PORK-STUFFED STEAMED BUNS

*THESE TREATS ARE JUST ONE EXAMPLE OF DIM SUM, FEATHERLIGHT STEAMED BUNS WITH A RANGE OF
TASTY FILLINGS. THEY ARE NOW A POPULAR SNACK THE WORLD OVER.*

<u>MAKES 16</u>

INGREDIENTS
For the basic dough
    1 tablespoon sugar
    about 1¼ cups warm water
    1½ tablespoons dried yeast
    4 cups white bread flour
    1 teaspoon salt
    1 tablespoon lard
    chives, to garnish

For the filling
    2 tablespoons oil
    1 garlic clove, crushed
    8 ounces roast pork, very finely chopped
    2 scallions, chopped
    2 teaspoons yellow bean
      sauce, crushed
    2 teaspoons sugar
    1 teaspoon cornstarch mixed to a
      paste with water

1 Make the dough. In a small bowl,
dissolve the sugar in half the water.
Sprinkle in the yeast. Stir well, then
leave for 10–15 minutes until frothy. Sift
the flour and salt into a bowl and rub
in the lard. Stir in the yeast mixture with
enough of the remaining water to make
a soft dough. Knead on a floured
surface for 10 minutes. Transfer to an
oiled bowl and cover. Leave in a warm
place for 1 hour until doubled in bulk.

2 Meanwhile, make the filling. Heat the
oil and fry the garlic until golden, then
add the pork, scallions, bean sauce and
sugar. Stir in the cornstarch paste and
cook, stirring, until slightly thickened.
Leave to cool.

3 Punch down the dough. Knead it for
2 minutes, then divide into 16 pieces.
Roll out each piece on a floured work
surface to a 3–4-inch round.

4 Place a spoonful of filling in the
center of each, gather up the sides and
twist the top to seal. Secure with string.

5 Set on baking parchment in a
steamer and leave in a warm place to
double in size. Steam over rapidly
boiling water for 30–35 minutes. Serve
hot, garnished with chives.

CONGEE WITH CHINESE SAUSAGE

CONGEE—SOFT RICE—IS COMFORT FOOD. GENTLE ON THE STOMACH, IT IS FREQUENTLY EATEN FOR BREAKFAST OR SERVED TO INVALIDS. THROUGHOUT THE EAST, PEOPLE WILL FREQUENTLY HAVE JUST A CUP OF TEA ON RISING; LATER THEY WILL SETTLE DOWN TO A BOWL OF CONGEE OR ITS REGIONAL EQUIVALENT.

SERVES 2–3

INGREDIENTS
generous 1/2 cup long grain rice
3 tablespoons glutinous rice
5 cups water
1/2 teaspoon salt
1 teaspoon sesame oil
thin slice of fresh ginger root, peeled
  and bruised
2 Chinese sausages
1 egg, lightly beaten (optional)
1/2 teaspoon light soy sauce
roasted peanuts, chopped, and thin
  shreds of scallion, to garnish

1 Wash both rices thoroughly. Drain and place in a large pan. Add the water, bring to a boil and immediately reduce to very low heat, using a heat diffuser if you have one.

2 Cook gently for 1 1/4–1 1/2 hours, stirring from time to time. If the congee thickens too much, stir in a little boiling water. It should have the consistency of creamy pouring porridge.

3 About 15 minutes before serving, add salt to taste and the sesame oil, together with the piece of ginger.

4 Steam the Chinese sausages for about 10 minutes, then slice and stir into the congee. Cook for 5 minutes.

5 Just before serving, remove the ginger and stir in the lightly beaten egg, if using. Serve hot, garnished with the peanuts and scallions and topped with a drizzle of soy sauce.

VARIATION
If you prefer, use roast duck instead of Chinese sausages. Cut the cooked duck into bite-sized pieces and add once the rice is cooked. Congee is also popular with tea eggs.

SALT AND PEPPER SHRIMP

THESE SUCCULENT SHELLFISH BEG TO BE EATEN WITH THE FINGERS, SO PROVIDE FINGER BOWLS OR HOT CLOTHS FOR YOUR GUESTS.

SERVES 3–4

INGREDIENTS
- 15–18 large raw shrimp, in the shell, about 1 pound
- vegetable oil, for deep frying
- 3 shallots or 1 small onion, very finely chopped
- 2 garlic cloves, crushed
- ½-inch piece fresh ginger root, peeled and very finely grated
- 1–2 fresh red chiles, seeded and finely sliced
- ½ teaspoon sugar or to taste
- 3–4 scallions, shredded, to garnish

For the fried salt
- 2 teaspoons salt
- 1 teaspoon Sichuan peppercorns

2 Carefully remove the heads and legs from the raw shrimp and discard. Leave the body shells and the tails in place. Pat the prepared shrimp dry with sheets of paper towel.

3 Heat the oil for deep frying to 375°F. Fry the shrimp for 1 minute, then lift them out and drain thoroughly on paper towels. Spoon 2 tablespoons of the hot oil into a large frying pan, leaving the rest of the oil to one side to cool.

4 Heat the oil in the frying pan. Add the fried salt, with the shallots or onion, garlic, ginger, chiles and sugar. Toss together for 1 minute, then add the shrimp and toss them over the heat for 1 minute more until they are coated and the shells are impregnated with the seasonings. Serve at once, garnished with the scallions.

1 Make the fried salt by dry frying the salt and peppercorns in a heavy frying pan over medium heat until the peppercorns begin to release their aroma. Cool the mixture, then tip into a mortar and crush with a pestle.

COOK'S TIP
"Fried salt" is also known as "Cantonese salt" or simply "salt and pepper mix". It is widely used as a table condiment or as a dip for deep fried or roasted food, but can also be an ingredient, as here. Black or white peppercorns can be substituted for the Sichuan peppercorns. It really is best made when required.

FRAGRANT HARBOR FRIED RICE

FRAGRANT HARBOR IS THE CHINESE NAME FOR HONG KONG, THE CROSSROADS FOR SO MANY STYLES OF COOKING. FRIED RICE IS EVER POPULAR AS YET ANOTHER WAY OF USING UP LITTLE BITS OF THIS AND THAT TO MAKE A VERITABLE FEAST. COOK THE RICE THE DAY BEFORE IF POSSIBLE.

SERVES 4

INGREDIENTS

generous 1 cup long grain rice
about 6 tablespoons vegetable oil
2 eggs, beaten
4 Chinese dried mushrooms,
    soaked for 30 minutes in warm
    water to cover
8 shallots or 2 small onions, sliced
4 ounces peeled cooked shrimp,
    thawed if frozen
3 garlic cloves, crushed
4 ounces cooked pork, cut into
    thin strips
4 ounces Chinese sausage
2 tablespoons light soy sauce
1 cup frozen peas, thawed
2 scallions, shredded
1–2 fresh or dried red chilies,
    seeded (optional)
salt and ground black pepper
cilantro leaves, to garnish

1 Bring a large saucepan of lightly salted water to a boil. Add the rice and cook for 12–15 minutes until just tender. Drain and leave to go cold. Ideally use the next day.

2 Heat about 1 tablespoon of the oil in a large frying pan over medium heat, pour in the beaten eggs and allow to set without stirring. Slide the omelet on to a plate, roll it up and cut into fine strips. Set aside.

3 Drain the mushrooms, cut off and discard the stems and slice the caps finely. Heat a wok, add 1 tablespoon of the remaining oil and, when hot, stir-fry the shallots or onions until crisp and golden brown. Remove with a slotted spoon and set aside.

4 Add the shrimp and garlic to the wok, with a little more oil if needed, and fry for 1 minute. Remove the shrimp and garlic and set aside. Add 1 tablespoon more oil to the wok.

5 Stir-fry the shredded pork and mushrooms for 2 minutes; lift out and reserve. Steam the Chinese sausage in a strainer for 5 minutes or until it plumps up. Trim and slice at an angle.

6 Wipe the wok, reheat with the remaining oil and stir-fry the rice, adding more oil if needed so the grains are coated. Stir in the soy sauce, salt and pepper, plus half the cooked ingredients.

7 Add the peas and half the scallions and toss over the heat until the peas are cooked. Pile the fried rice on a heated platter and arrange the remaining cooked ingredients on top, with the remaining scallions. Add the chili, if using, and the cilantro leaves, to garnish.

COOK'S TIP
There are many theories on the best way to cook rice. This gives excellent results every time: Put generous 1 cup long grain rice in a strainer and rinse thoroughly in cold water. Place in a large bowl, add salt to taste and pour in just under 2½ cups boiling water. Cover with microwave plastic wrap, leaving a gap and cook in a 675 watt microwave on full power for 10 minutes. Leave to stand for 5 minutes more. Cool, then stir with a chopstick.

LETTUCE PARCELS

KNOWN AS SANG CHOY IN HONG KONG, THIS IS A POPULAR "ASSEMBLE-IT-YOURSELF" TREAT. THE FILLING—AN IMAGINATIVE BLEND OF TEXTURES AND FLAVORS—IS SERVED WITH CRISP LETTUCE LEAVES, WHICH ARE USED AS WRAPPERS.

SERVES 6

INGREDIENTS

2 boneless chicken breasts, total weight about 12 ounces
4 Chinese dried mushrooms, soaked for 30 minutes in warm water to cover
2 tablespoons vegetable oil
2 garlic cloves, crushed
6 drained canned water chestnuts, thinly sliced
2 tablespoons light soy sauce
1 teaspoon Sichuan peppercorns, dry fried and crushed
4 scallions, finely chopped
1 teaspoon sesame oil
vegetable oil, for deep frying
2 ounces cellophane noodles
salt and ground black pepper (optional)
1 crisp lettuce and 4 tablespoons hoisin sauce, to serve

1 Remove the skin from the chicken breasts, pat dry and set aside. Chop the chicken into thin strips. Drain the soaked mushrooms. Cut off and discard the mushroom stems; slice the caps finely and set aside.

2 Heat the oil in a wok or large frying pan. Add the garlic, then add the chicken and stir-fry until the pieces are cooked through and no longer pink.

3 Add the sliced mushrooms, water chestnuts, soy sauce and peppercorns. Toss for 2–3 minutes, then season, if needed. Stir in half of the scallions, then the sesame oil. Remove from the heat and set aside.

4 Heat the oil for deep frying to 375°F. Cut the chicken skin into strips, deep fry until very crisp and drain on paper towels. Add the noodles to the hot oil, deep fry until crisp. Transfer to a plate lined with paper towels.

5 Crush the noodles and put in a serving dish. Top with the chicken skin, chicken mixture and the remaining scallions. Wash the lettuce leaves, pat dry and arrange on a large platter.

6 Toss the chicken and noodles to mix. Invite guests to take one or two lettuce leaves, spread the inside with hoisin sauce and add a spoonful of filling, turning in the sides of the leaves and rolling them into a package. They are traditionally eaten in the hand.

MALAYSIA AND SINGAPORE

The food of Malaysia is a rich blend of three of the world's most exciting cuisines: Malay, Chinese and Indian. The result is the Malayan melange—a mixture of flavors, some cool, some fiery, but always in perfect harmony. Singapore promises sophistication as well as sumptuous flavors, and introduces Nonya cooking, which is famously hot and spicy.

LAKSA LEMAK

THIS SPICY SOUP IS NOT A DISH YOU CAN THROW TOGETHER IN 20 MINUTES, BUT IT IS MARVELOUS PARTY FOOD. GUESTS SPOON NOODLES INTO WIDE SOUP BOWLS, ADD ACCOMPANIMENTS OF THEIR CHOICE, TOP UP WITH SOUP AND THEN TAKE A FEW SHRIMP CRACKERS TO NIBBLE.

SERVES 6

INGREDIENTS
1 1/2 pounds small clams
1 3/4 cups canned coconut milk
2 ounces ikan bilis (dried anchovies)
3 3/4 cups water
4 ounces shallots, finely chopped
4 garlic cloves, chopped
6 macadamia nuts or blanched
   almonds, chopped
3 lemongrass stalks, root trimmed
6 tablespoons sunflower oil
1/2-inch cube shrimp paste (blachan)
1/4 cup mild curry powder
a few curry leaves
2–3 eggplant, total weight about
   1 1/4 pounds, trimmed
1 1/2 pounds raw peeled shrimp
2 teaspoons sugar
1 head Chinese leaves, thinly sliced
2 cups beansprouts, rinsed
2 scallions, finely chopped
2 ounces crispy fried onions
4 ounces fried beancurd (tofu)
1 1/2 pounds mixed noodles
   (laksa, mee and behoon) or one
   type only
shrimp crackers, to serve

1 Scrub the clams and then put in a large pan with 1/2 inch water. Bring to a boil, cover and steam for 3–4 minutes until all the clams have opened. Drain. Make up the coconut milk to 5 cups with water. Put the ikan bilis (dried anchovies) in a pan and add the water. Bring to a boil and simmer for 20 minutes.

2 Meanwhile, put the shallots, garlic and nuts into a mortar. Cut off the lower 2 inches of two of the lemongrass stalks, chop finely and add to the mortar. Pound the mixture to a paste.

3 Heat the oil in a large heavy pan, add the shallot paste and fry until the mixture gives off a rich aroma. Bruise the remaining lemongrass stalk and add to the pan. Toss over the heat to release its flavor. Mix the shrimp paste (blachan) and curry powder to a paste with a little of the coconut milk, add to the pan and toss the mixture over the heat for 1 minute, stirring all the time, and keeping a very low heat. Stir in the remaining coconut milk. Add the curry leaves and leave the mixture to simmer while you prepare the accompaniments.

4 Strain the stock into a pan. Discard the ikan bilis, bring to a boil, then add the eggplant; cook for about 10 minutes or until tender and the skins can be peeled off easily. Lift out of the stock, peel and cut into thick strips.

5 Arrange the eggplant on a serving platter. Sprinkle the shrimp with sugar, add to the stock and cook for 2–4 minutes until they turn pink. Remove and place next to the eggplant. Add the Chinese leaves, beansprouts, scallions and crispy fried onions to the platter, along with the clams.

6 Gradually stir the remaining ikan bilis stock into the pan of soup and bring to a boil. Rinse the fried beancurd in boiling water, cool slightly and squeeze to remove excess oil. Cut each piece in half and add to the soup. Lower the heat to a very gentle simmer.

7 Cook the noodles according to the instructions, drain and pile in a dish. Remove the curry leaves and lemongrass from the soup. Place the noodles, soup and the platter of seafood and vegetables on the table, along with a bowl of shrimp crackers. Guests can then help themselves.

VARIATION
You could substitute mussels for clams if preferred. Scrub them thoroughly, removing any beards, and cook them in lightly salted water until they open. Like clams, discard any that remain closed.

COOK'S TIP
Dried shrimp paste, also called blachan, is sold in small blocks and is available from Asian markets.

CHICKEN SATAY

ONE OF THE CLASSIC FOODS OF THE EAST. THE PIECES OF MEAT SHOULD NOT BE MORE THAN A DELICATE MOUTHFUL OTHERWISE THEY WILL NOT ABSORB THE MARINADE SATISFACTORILY.

SERVES 4

INGREDIENTS
    4 boneless, skinless chicken breasts
    2 teaspoons light brown sugar

For the marinade
    1 teaspoon cumin seeds
    1 teaspoon fennel seeds
    1½ teaspoons coriander seeds
    6 shallots or small onions, chopped
    1 garlic clove, crushed
    1 lemongrass stalk, root trimmed
    3 macadamia nuts or 6 cashew nuts
    ½ teaspoon ground turmeric

For the peanut sauce
    4 shallots or small onions, sliced
    2 garlic cloves, crushed
    ½-inch cube shrimp paste (blachan)
    6 cashew nuts or almonds
    2 lemongrass stalks, trimmed, lower
      2 inches sliced
    3 tablespoons sunflower oil
    1–2 teaspoons chili powder
    1¾ cups canned coconut milk
    4–5 tablespoons tamarind water
      or 2 tablespoons tamarind
      concentrate mixed with
      3 tablespoons water
    1 tablespoon soft brown sugar
    ½ cup crunchy peanut butter

1 Cut the chicken into thin strips, sprinkle with the sugar and set aside.

2 Make the marinade. Dry fry the spices, then grind them to a powder. Put the shallots or onions in a mortar or a food processor and add the garlic. Roughly chop the lower 2 inches of the lemongrass and add it to the mortar or processor with the nuts, ground spices and turmeric. Grind to a paste and place in a bowl.

COOK'S TIP
Soaking the bamboo skewers for about 30 minutes in a large bowl of warm water before use ensures that they won't scorch when placed under the broiler.

3 Add the chicken pieces and stir well until coated. Cover loosely with plastic wrap and leave to marinate for at least 4 hours.

4 Prepare the sauce. Pound or process the shallots or onions with the garlic and shrimp paste (blachan). Add the nuts and the lower parts of the lemongrass stalks. Process to a fine purée. Heat the oil in a wok and fry the purée for 2–3 minutes. Add the chili powder and cook for 2 minutes more.

5 Stir in the coconut milk and bring to a boil slowly. Reduce the heat, stir in the tamarind water, brown sugar and peanut butter and cook over low heat until fairly thick. Keep warm. Prepare the barbecue or preheat the broiler.

6 Thread the chicken on to 16 bamboo skewers. Barbecue or broil for about 5 minutes or until golden and tender, brushing with oil occasionally. Serve with the hot peanut sauce.

CHICKEN RENDANG

THIS MAKES A MARVELOUS DISH FOR A BUFFET. SERVE IT WITH SHRIMP CRACKERS OR WITH BOILED RICE AND DEEP-FRIED ANCHOVIES, ACAR PICKLE OR SAMBAL NANAS.

3 Add the onions, garlic and ginger to the processor. Cut off the lower 2 inches of the lemongrass, chop and add to the processor with the galangal. Process to a fine paste.

4 Heat the oil in a wok or large saucepan and fry the onion mixture for a few minutes. Reduce the heat, stir in the chili powder and cook for 2–3 minutes, stirring constantly. Spoon in ½ cup of the coconut milk and add salt to taste.

5 As soon as the mixture bubbles, add the chicken pieces, turning them until they are well coated with the spices. Pour in the remaining coconut milk, stirring constantly to prevent curdling. Bruise the top of the lemongrass stalks and add to the wok or pan. Cover and cook gently for 40–45 minutes until the chicken is tender.

6 Just before serving stir in the coconut paste. Bring to just below boiling point, then simmer for 5 minutes. Transfer to a serving bowl and garnish with fresh chives and deep fried anchovies.

SERVES 4

INGREDIENTS
    4 boneless chicken breasts, skinned
    1 teaspoon sugar
    1 cup shredded coconut
    4 small red or white onions,
      roughly chopped
    2 garlic cloves, chopped
    1-inch piece fresh ginger root, peeled
      and sliced
    1–2 lemongrass stalks, root trimmed
    1-inch piece fresh galangal, peeled
      and sliced
    5 tablespoons peanut oil or vegetable
      oil
    2–3 teaspoons chili powder or
      to taste
    1¾ cups canned coconut milk
    2 teaspoons salt
    fresh chives and deep-fried
      anchovies, to garnish

1 Halve the chicken breasts, sprinkle with the sugar and leave to stand for about 1 hour.

2 Dry fry the coconut in a wok or large frying pan over medium to low heat, turning all the time until it is crisp and golden. Transfer the fried coconut to a food processor and process to an oily paste. Transfer to a bowl and reserve.

FISH MOOLIE

THIS IS A VERY POPULAR SOUTH-EAST ASIAN FISH CURRY IN A COCONUT SAUCE, WHICH IS TRULY DELICIOUS. CHOOSE A FIRM-TEXTURED FISH SO THAT THE PIECES STAY INTACT DURING THE BRIEF COOKING PROCESS. HALIBUT AND COD WORK EQUALLY WELL.

5 Heat the oil in a wok. Add the onion mixture and cook for a few minutes without browning. Stir in the coconut milk and bring to a boil, stirring constantly to prevent curdling.

SERVES 4

INGREDIENTS

   1¼ pounds monkfish or other firm-textured fish fillets, skinned and cut into 1-inch cubes

   ½ teaspoon salt

   ⅔ cup shredded coconut

   6 shallots or small onions, roughly chopped

   6 blanched almonds

   2–3 garlic cloves, roughly chopped

   1-inch piece fresh ginger root, peeled and sliced

   2 lemongrass stalks, trimmed

   2 teaspoons ground turmeric

   3 tablespoons vegetable oil

   1¾ cups canned coconut milk

   1–3 fresh chiles, seeded and sliced

   salt and ground black pepper

   fresh chives, to garnish

   boiled rice, to serve

1 Spread out the pieces of fish in a shallow dish and sprinkle them with the salt. Dry fry the coconut in a wok or large frying pan over medium to low heat, turning all the time until it is crisp and golden (see Cook's Tip).

2 Transfer the coconut to a food processor and process to an oily paste. Scrape into a bowl and reserve.

3 Add the shallots or onions, almonds, garlic and ginger to the food processor. Cut off the lower 2 inches of the lemongrass stalks, chop them roughly and add to the processor. Process the mixture to a paste.

4 Add the turmeric to the mixture in the processor and process briefly to mix. Bruise the remaining lemongrass and set the stalks aside.

6 Add the cubes of fish, most of the sliced chile and the bruised lemongrass stalks. Cook for 3–4 minutes. Stir in the coconut paste (moistened with some of the sauce if necessary) and cook for a further 2–3 minutes only. Do not overcook the fish. Taste and adjust the seasoning.

7 Remove the lemongrass. Transfer to a hot serving dish and sprinkle with the remaining slices of chile. Garnish with chopped and whole chives and serve with boiled rice.

COOK'S TIP

Dry frying is a feature of Malay cooking. When dry frying do not be distracted. The coconut must be constantly on the move so that it becomes crisp and of a uniform golden color.

STEAMBOAT

THIS DISH IS NAMED AFTER THE UTENSIL IN WHICH IT IS COOKED—A TYPE OF FONDUE WITH A FUNNEL AND A MOAT. THE MOAT IS FILLED WITH STOCK, TRADITIONALLY KEPT HOT WITH CHARCOAL. ELECTRIC STEAMBOATS OR ANY TRADITIONAL FONDUE POTS CAN BE USED INSTEAD.

SERVES 8

INGREDIENTS

  8 Chinese dried mushrooms, soaked
     for 30 minutes in warm water
     to cover
  6¼ cups well-flavored chicken stock,
     homemade if possible
  2 teaspoons rice wine or
     medium-dry sherry
  2 teaspoons sesame oil
  8 ounces each lean pork and rump
     steak, thinly sliced
  1 skinless boneless chicken breast,
     thickly sliced
  2 chicken livers, trimmed and sliced
  8 ounces raw shrimp, peeled
  1 pound white fish fillets, skinned
     and cubed
  7 ounces fish balls (from Asian
     markets)
  4 ounces fried beancurd (tofu), each
     piece halved
  leafy green vegetables, such as
     lettuce, Chinese leaves, spinach
     leaves and watercress, cut into
     6-inch lengths
  8 ounces Chinese rice vermicelli
  8 eggs
  selection of sauces, including soy
     sauce with sesame seeds; soy sauce
     with crushed ginger; chili sauce;
     plum sauce and hot mustard
  ½ bunch scallions, chopped
  salt and ground white pepper

1 Drain the mushrooms, reserving the soaking liquid. Cut off and discard the stems; slice the caps finely.

2 Pour the stock into a large pan, with the rice wine or sherry, sesame oil and reserved mushroom liquid. Bring the mixture to a boil, then season with salt and white pepper. Reduce the heat and simmer gently while you prepare the remaining ingredients.

3 Put the meat, fish, beancurd, green vegetables and mushrooms in bowls on the table. Soak the vermicelli in hot water for about 5 minutes, drain and place in eight soup bowls on a small table. Crack an egg for each diner in a small bowl; place on a side table. Put the sauces in bowls beside each diner.

4 Add the chopped scallions to the pan of stock, bring it to a full boil and fuel the steamboat. Pour the stock into the moat and seat your guests at once. Each guest lowers a few chosen morsels into a boiling stock, using chopsticks or fondue forks, leaves them for a minute or two, then removes them with a small wire mesh ladle, a fondue fork or pair of chopsticks.

5 When all the meat, fish, beancurd and vegetables have been cooked, the stock will be concentrated and wonderfully enriched. Add a little boiling water if necessary. Bring the soup bowls containing the soaked noodles to the table, pour in the hot soup and slide a whole egg into each, stirring until it cooks and forms threads.

SIZZLING STEAK

THIS WAS ORIGINALLY A SPECIALITY OF THE COLISEUM RESTAURANT IN THE BATU ROAD IN KUALA LUMPUR. THE STEAKS WERE BROUGHT TO THE TABLE ON INDIVIDUAL HOT METAL PLATTERS, EACH SET ON A THICK WOODEN BOARD. THIS RECIPE COMES CLOSE TO RECREATING THIS WONDERFUL DISH.

SERVES 2

INGREDIENTS
   2 rump or sirloin steaks, total weight
     about 1 pound
   1–2 tablespoons vegetable oil
   shredded scallion, to garnish

For the marinade and sauce
   1 tablespoon brandy
   1 tablespoon rich brown sauce
   2 tablespoons peanut oil or
     sunflower oil
   a few drops of sesame oil
   2 garlic cloves, halved or crushed
   2/3 cup beef stock
   2 tablespoons tomato ketchup
   1 tablespoon oyster sauce
   1 tablespoon Worcestershire sauce
   salt and sugar

1 Put the steaks side by side in a dish. Mix the brandy, brown sauce, peanut or sunflower oil, sesame oil and garlic in a jug and pour this marinade over the steaks. Cover loosely with plastic wrap and leave for 1 hour, turning once. Drain the meat well, reserving the marinade.

2 Heat the oil in a heavy, ridged frying pan and fry the steaks for 3–5 minutes on each side, depending on how well done you like them. Transfer to a plate and keep warm while preparing the sauce: this allows the meat to relax, making it more tender.

3 Pour the marinade into the frying pan, if liked, discarding any large pieces of garlic.

4 Stir in the beef stock, ketchup, oyster sauce and Worcestershire sauce, with salt and sugar to taste. Bring to a boil, boil rapidly to reduce by half, then taste again for seasoning.

5 Serve each cooked steak on a very hot plate, pouring the sauce over each portion just before serving. Garnish with the shredded scallion.

COOK'S TIP
If you don't have a ridged frying pan, simply use a large, heavy based frying pan instead.

SOTONG SAMBAL

SQUID IS READILY AVAILABLE THESE DAYS, AND IT NOW COMES CLEANED, WHICH IS A DEFINITE BONUS. WASH THOROUGHLY INSIDE THE POCKET TO MAKE SURE THAT ALL THE QUILL HAS BEEN REMOVED.

SERVES 2

INGREDIENTS
8 small squid, each about 4-inches long, total weight about 12 ounces
lime juice (optional)
salt
boiled rice, to serve

For the stuffing
6 ounces white fish fillets, such as sole or plaice, skinned
1-inch piece fresh ginger root, peeled and finely sliced
2 scallions, finely chopped
2 ounces peeled cooked shrimp, roughly chopped

For the sambal sauce
4 macadamia nuts or blanched almonds
1/2-inch piece fresh galangal, peeled, or 1 teaspoon drained bottled galangal
2 lemongrass stalks, root trimmed
1/2-inch cube shrimp paste (blachan)
4 fresh red chiles, or to taste, seeded and roughly chopped
6 ounces small onions, roughly chopped
4–6 tablespoons vegetable oil
1 3/4 cups canned coconut milk

1 Clean the squid, leaving them whole. Set aside with the tentacles. Put the white fish, ginger and scallions in a mortar. Add a little salt and pound to a paste with a pestle. Use a food processor, if preferred.

2 Transfer the fish mixture to a bowl and stir in the shrimp.

3 Divide the filling among the squid, using a spoon or a forcing bag fitted with a plain tube. Tuck the tentacles into the stuffing and secure the top of each squid with a toothpick.

4 Make the sauce. Put the macadamia nuts or almonds and galangal in a food processor. Cut off the lower 2 inches from the lemongrass stalks, chop them roughly and add them to the processor with the shrimp paste, chiles and onions. Process to a paste.

5 Heat the oil in a wok and fry the mixture to bring out the full flavors. Bruise the remaining lemongrass and add it to the wok with the coconut milk. Stir constantly until the sauce comes to a boil, then lower the heat and simmer the sauce for 5 minutes.

6 Arrange the squid in the sauce, and cook for 15–20 minutes. Taste and season with salt and lime juice, if liked. Serve with boiled rice.

MALAYSIAN COCONUT ICE CREAM

THIS ICE CREAM IS DELECTABLE AND VERY EASY TO MAKE IN AN ICE-CREAM MAKER, ESPECIALLY IF YOU USE THE TYPE WITH A BOWL THAT IS PLACED IN THE FREEZER TO CHILL BEFORE THE ICE-CREAM MIXTURE IS ADDED. THE ICE CREAM IS THEN CHURNED BY A MOTORIZED LID WITH A PADDLE.

2 Pour the mixture into the frozen freezer bowl of an ice-cream maker (or follow the appliance instructions) and churn till the mixture has thickened. (This will take 30–40 minutes.)

3 Transfer the mixture to a lidded plastic tub, cover and freeze until the consistency is right for scooping. If you do not have an ice-cream maker, pour the mixture into a shallow container and freeze on the coldest setting.

4 When ice crystals form around the sides of the ice cream, beat the mixture, then return it to the freezer. Do this at least twice. The more you do it, the creamier the mixture will be.

5 Make the sauce. Mix the sugar, measured water and ginger in a saucepan. Stir over medium heat until the sugar has dissolved, then bring the liquid to a boil. Add the pandan leaf, if using, tying it into a knot so that it can easily be removed with the ginger before serving. Lower the heat and simmer for 3–4 minutes. Set aside till required.

6 Serve the ice cream in coconut shells or in a bowl. Sprinkle with the strips of coconut and serve with the gula melaka sauce which can be hot, warm or cold.

SERVES 6

INGREDIENTS
   1³/₄ cups canned coconut milk
   1³/₄ cups canned sweetened
     condensed milk
   ¹/₂ teaspoon salt

For the gula melaka sauce
   ³/₄ cup palm sugar or dark
     brown sugar
   ²/₃ cup water
   ¹/₂-inch slice fresh ginger root,
     bruised
   1 pandan leaf (if available)
   coconut shells (optional) and thinly
     pared strips of coconut, to serve

1 Chill the canned coconut and condensed milk very thoroughly. In a bowl, mix the coconut milk with the condensed milk. Gently whisk together with the salt.

COOK'S TIP
Coconut milk takes longer to freeze than thick cream, so allow plenty of time for the process.

COCONUT CHIPS

COCONUT CHIPS ARE A WONDERFULLY TASTY NIBBLE TO SERVE WITH DRINKS. THE CHIPS CAN BE SLICED AHEAD OF TIME AND FROZEN (WITHOUT SALT), ON OPEN TRAYS. WHEN FROZEN, SIMPLY SHAKE INTO PLASTIC BOXES OR BAGS. YOU CAN THEN TAKE OUT AS FEW OR AS MANY AS YOU WISH FOR THE PARTY.

3 Having opened the coconut, use a broad-bladed knife to ease the flesh away from the hard outer shell. Taste a piece of the flesh just to make sure it is fresh and not rancid. Peel off the brown skin with a potato peeler, if liked.

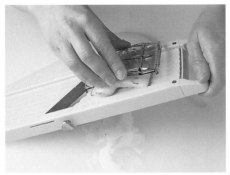

4 Slice the flesh into wafer-thin shavings, using a food processor, mandoline or sharp knife. Scatter these evenly all over one or two baking sheets and sprinkle with salt. Bake for about 25–30 minutes or until crisp, turning them from time to time. Cool and serve. Any leftovers can be stored in airtight containers.

COOK'S TIP
This is the kind of recipe where the slicing blade on a food processor comes into its own. It is worth preparing two or three coconuts at a time, and freezing, surplus chips. The chips can be cooked from frozen, but will need to be spread out well on the baking sheets, before being salted. Allow a little longer for frozen chips to cook.

SERVES 8 AS A SNACK

INGREDIENTS
1 fresh coconut
salt

1 Preheat the oven to 325ºF. First drain the coconut juice, either by piercing one of the coconut eyes with a sharp instrument or by breaking it carefully.

2 Lay the coconut on a board and hit the center sharply with a hammer. The shell should break cleanly in two.

POPIAH

POPIAH ARE THE STRAITS CHINESE OR NONYA VERSION OF THE SPRING ROLL. DO NOT BE PUT OFF BY THE NUMBER OF INGREDIENTS; IT TAKES A LITTLE TIME TO GET EVERYTHING TOGETHER BUT ONCE IT IS ALL ON THE TABLE THE COOK CAN RETIRE AS GUESTS ASSEMBLE THEIR OWN.

MAKES 20–24 PANCAKES

INGREDIENTS
1/3 cup cornstarch
generous 1 3/4 cups all-purpose flour
salt
scant 2 cups water
6 eggs, beaten
lard, for frying

For the cooked filling
2 tablespoons vegetable oil
1 onion, finely chopped
2 garlic cloves, crushed
4 ounces cooked pork, chopped
4 ounces crab meat or peeled cooked
   shrimp, thawed if frozen
4 ounces drained canned bamboo
   shoot, thinly sliced
1 small yam bean, peeled and grated
   or 12 drained canned water
   chestnuts, finely chopped
1–2 tablespoons yellow
   salted beans
1 tablespoon light soy sauce
ground black pepper

For the fresh fillings
2 hard-cooked eggs, chopped
2 Chinese sausages, steamed
   and sliced
4-ounce packet fried beancurd (tofu),
   each piece halved
4 cups beansprouts
4 ounces crab meat or peeled
   cooked shrimp
1/2 cucumber, cut into matchsticks
small bunch of scallions, finely
   chopped
20 lettuce leaves, rinsed and dried
fresh cilantro sprigs, to garnish
selection of sauces, including
   bottled chopped chilies, bottled
   chopped garlic and hoisin sauce,
   to serve

COOK'S TIP
Yam beans are large tubers with a mild sweet texture similar to water chestnuts.

1 Sift the flours and salt into a bowl. Add the measured water and eggs and mix to a smooth batter.

2 Grease a heavy-based frying pan with lard. Heat the pan, pouring off any excess lard, then pour in just enough batter to cover the base.

3 As soon as it sets, flip and cook the other side. The pancakes should be quite thin. Repeat with the remaining batter to make 20–24 pancakes in all. Pile the cooked pancakes on top of each other, with a layer of waxed paper between each to prevent them sticking. Wrap in foil and keep warm in a low oven.

4 Make the cooked filling. Heat the oil in a wok and stir-fry the onion and garlic for 5 minutes until softened but not browned. Add the pork, crab meat or shrimp, bamboo shoot and grated yam bean or water chestnuts. Stir-fry the mixture over a medium heat for 2–3 minutes.

5 Add the salted yellow beans and soy sauce to the wok, with pepper to taste. Cover and cook gently for 15–20 minutes, adding a little water if the mixture starts to dry out. Spoon into a serving bowl and allow to cool.

6 Meanwhile, arrange the chopped hard-cooked eggs, sliced Chinese sausages, sliced beancurd (tofu), beansprouts, crab meat or shrimp, cucumber, scallions and lettuce leaves in piles on a large platter or in separate bowls. Spoon the bottled chopped chilies, bottled chopped garlic and hoisin into small bowls.

7 Each person makes up his or her own popiah by spreading a very small amount of chopped chili, garlic or hoisin sauce on a pancake, adding a lettuce leaf, a little of the cooked filling and a small selection of the fresh ingredients. The pancake wrapper should not be over-filled.

8 The ends can be tucked in and the pancake rolled up in typical spring roll fashion, then eaten in the hand. They also look attractive simply rolled with the filling showing. The popiah can be filled and rolled before guests arrive, in which case, garnish with sprigs of cilantro. It is more fun though for everyone to fill and roll their own.

SAMOSAS

THESE TASTY SNACKS ARE ENJOYED THE WORLD OVER. THROUGHOUT THE EAST, THEY ARE SOLD BY STREET VENDORS, AND EATEN AT ANY TIME OF DAY. FILO PASTRY CAN BE USED IF PREFERRED.

MAKES ABOUT 20

INGREDIENTS

    1 packet 10-inch square spring roll wrappers, thawed if frozen
    2 tablespoons all-purpose flour, mixed to a paste with water
    vegetable oil, for deep frying
    cilantro, to garnish
    cucumber, carrot and celery, cut into matchsticks, to serve (optional)

For the filling

    2 tablespoons ghee or unsalted butter
    1 small onion, finely chopped
    1/2-inch piece fresh ginger root, peeled and chopped
    1 garlic clove, crushed
    1/2 teaspoon chili powder
    1 large potato, about 8 ounces, cooked until just tender and finely diced
    1/2 cup cauliflower florets, lightly cooked, chopped into small pieces
    1/2 cup frozen peas, thawed
    1–2 teaspoons garam masala
    1 tablespoon chopped fresh cilantro (leaves and stems)
    squeeze of lemon juice
    salt

2 Cut the spring roll wrappers into three strips (or two for larger samosas). Brush the edges with a little of the flour paste. Place a small spoonful of filling about 3/4 inch in from the edge of one strip. Fold one corner over the filling to make a triangle and continue this folding until the entire strip has been used and a triangular pastry has been formed. Seal any open edges with more flour and water paste, if necessary adding more water if the paste is very thick.

3 Heat the oil for deep frying to 375°F and fry the samosas, a few at a time, until golden and crisp. Drain well on paper towels and serve hot garnished with cilantro leaves and accompanied by cucumber, carrot and celery matchsticks, if liked.

COOK'S TIP
Prepare samosas in advance by frying until just cooked through and draining. Cook in hot oil for a few minutes to brown and drain again before serving.

1 Heat the ghee or butter in a large wok and fry the onion, ginger and garlic for 5 minutes until the onion has softened. Add the chili powder and cook for 1 minute, then stir in the potato, cauliflower and peas. Sprinkle with garam masala and set aside to cool. Stir in the cilantro, lemon juice and salt.

CHA SHAO

THIS DISH IS OFTEN KNOWN AS BARBECUED PORK AND IS VERY POPULAR IN SOUTHERN CHINA AND MALAYSIA AS WELL AS SINGAPORE. IF YOU LIKE, THE MARINADE CAN BE THOROUGHLY HEATED, THEN SERVED WITH THE MEAT.

SERVES 6

INGREDIENTS
   2 pounds pork tenderloin,
      trimmed
   1 tablespoon clear honey
   3 tablespoons rice wine or
      medium-dry sherry
   scallion curls, to garnish

For the marinade
   2/3 cup dark soy sauce
   6 tablespoons rice wine or
      medium-dry sherry
   2/3 cup well-flavored chicken stock
   1 tablespoon soft brown sugar
   1/2-inch piece fresh ginger root,
      peeled and finely sliced
   2 1/2 tablespoons chopped onion

1 Mix all the marinade ingredients in a pan and stir over medium heat until the mixture boils. Lower the heat and simmer gently for 15 minutes, stirring from time to time. Leave to cool.

2 Put the pork tenderloins in a shallow dish that is large enough to hold them side by side. Pour over 1 cup of the marinade, cover and chill for at least 8 hours, turning the meat over several times.

COOK'S TIP
You will have extra marinade when making this dish. Freeze this and use to baste other broiled dishes or meats such as spare ribs.

3 Preheat the oven to 400°F. Drain the pork, reserving the marinade in the dish. Place the meat on a rack over a roasting pan and pour water into the pan to a depth of 1/2 inch. Place the pan in the oven and roast for 20 minutes.

4 Stir the honey and rice wine or sherry into the marinade. Remove the meat from the oven and place in the marinade, turning to coat. Put back on the rack and roast for 20–30 minutes or until cooked. Serve hot or cold, in slices, garnished with scallion curls.

CHILE CRABS

EAT THESE CRABS SINGAPOREAN STYLE, WITH THE FINGERS. GIVE GUESTS CRAB CRACKERS FOR THE CLAWS AND HAVE SOME FINGER BOWLS OR HOT TOWELS TO HAND AS IT WILL BE MESSY!

SERVES 4

INGREDIENTS
2 cooked crabs, each about
  1¹/₂ pounds
6 tablespoons sunflower oil
1-inch piece fresh ginger root, peeled
  and chopped
2–3 garlic cloves, crushed
1–2 red chiles, seeded and pounded
  to a paste
³/₄ cup tomato ketchup
2 tablespoons soft brown sugar
1 tablespoon light soy sauce
salt
¹/₂ cup boiling water
hot toast and cucumber chunks,
  to serve

COOK'S TIP
Ready-cooked whole crabs are available
from supermarkets and fish shops.

1 To prepare the crabs twist off the large claws, then turn the crab on its back with its mouth and eyes facing away from you. Using both of your thumbs, push the body, with the small legs attached, upwards from beneath the flap, separating the body from the main shell in the process. Discard the stomach sac and grey spongy lungs known as "dead men's fingers".

2 Using a teaspoon scrape the brown creamy meat from the large shell into a small bowl. Twist the legs from the body. Cut the body section in half. Pick out the white meat. If liked, pick out the meat from the legs, or leave for guests to remove at the table.

3 Heat the oil in a wok and gently fry the ginger, garlic and fresh chile paste for 1–2 minutes without browning. Stir in the ketchup, sugar and soy sauce, with salt to taste and heat gently.

4 Stir in the crab meat together with the claws and crab legs, if these were reserved. Pour in a boiling water, stir well and cook over high heat until heated through. Pile with the crab and crab claws mixture on serving plates with the chunks of cucumber and serve with pieces of toast.

NONYA PORK SATAY

WHEN CHINESE MERCHANTS CAME TO SINGAPORE AND PENANG AND TOOK MALAY WIVES, CULINARY TURMOIL ENSUED. THEIR BELOVED PORK WAS FORBIDDEN TO THEIR MUSLIM WIVES. NONYA, THE STYLE OF COOKING THAT EMERGED, IS A TESTAMENT TO COMPROMISE—MOSTLY BY THE WIVES.

SERVES 8–12

INGREDIENTS
1 pound pork tenderloin
1 tablespoon light brown sugar
¹/₂ inch cube shrimp paste (blachan)
1–2 lemongrass stalks
2 teaspoons coriander seeds,
  dry-fried
6 macadamia nuts or blanched
  almonds, if preferred
2 onions, roughly chopped
3–6 fresh red chiles, seeded and
  roughly chopped
¹/₂ teaspoon ground turmeric
1¹/₄ cups canned coconut milk
2 tablespoons peanut oil or
  sunflower oil
salt

1 Soak 8–12 bamboo skewers in water for at least an hour to prevent them from scorching when they are placed under the broiler.

2 Cut the pork into small chunks, then spread it out in a single layer in a shallow dish. Sprinkle with sugar to help release the juices. Fry the shrimp paste (blachan) briefly in a foil parcel in a dry frying pan or warm it on a skewer held over the heat.

COOK'S TIP
Nonya Pork Satay can be served as part of a meal or as a snack, in which case serve with cubes of cucumber, which contrast well with the spicy meat.

3 Cut off the lower 2-inches of the lemongrass stalks and chop finely. Process the dry-fried coriander seeds to a powder in a food processor. Add the nuts and chopped lemongrass, process briefly, then add the onions, chiles, shrimp paste, turmeric and a little salt; process to a fine paste. Pour in the coconut milk and oil. Switch the machine on very briefly to mix. Pour the mixture over the pork and leave to marinate for 1–2 hours.

4 Preheat the broiler or prepare the barbecue. Thread three or four pieces of marinated pork on each bamboo skewer and broil or barbecue for 8–10 minutes until tender, basting frequently with the remaining marinade. Serve at once.

SAMBAL NANAS

SAMBALS ARE THE LITTLE SIDE DISHES SERVED AT ALMOST EVERY MALAY MEAL. IN POORER SOCIETIES, A MAIN MEAL MAY SIMPLY BE A BOWL OF RICE AND A SAMBAL MADE FROM POUNDED SHRIMP PASTE, CHILES AND LIME JUICE. THIS SAMBAL INCLUDES CUCUMBER AND PINEAPPLE.

SERVES 8–10 AS AN ACCOMPANIMENT

INGREDIENTS

1 small or ½ large fresh
   ripe pineapple
½ cucumber, halved lengthwise
2 ounces dried shrimps
1 large fresh red chile, seeded
½-inch cube shrimp paste (blachan),
   prepared (see Cook's Tip)
juice of 1 large lemon or lime
light brown sugar, to taste (optional)

1 Cut off both ends of the pineapple. Stand it upright on a board, then slice off the skin from top to bottom, cutting out the spines. Slice the pineapple, removing the central core. Cut into thin slices and set aside.

2 Trim the ends from the cucumber and slice thinly. Sprinkle with salt and set aside. Place the dried shrimps in a food processor and chop fairly finely. Add the chile, prepared shrimp paste (blachan) and lemon or lime juice and process again to a paste.

3 Rinse the cucumber, drain and dry on paper towels. Mix with the pineapple and chill. Just before serving, spoon in the spice mixture with sugar to taste. Mix well and serve.

COOK'S TIP
The pungent shrimp paste, also called blachan, is popular in many South-east Asian countries, and is available in Asian markets. Since it can taste a bit raw in a sambal, dry fry it by wrapping in foil and heating in a frying pan over a low heat for 5 minutes, turning from time to time. If the shrimp paste is to be fried with other spices, this preliminary cooking can be eliminated.

INDIAN MEE GORENG

*THIS IS A TRULY INTERNATIONAL DISH COMBINING INDIAN, CHINESE AND WESTERN INGREDIENTS.
IT IS A DELICIOUS TREAT FOR LUNCH OR SUPPER AND IN SINGAPORE AND MALAYSIA CAN BE BOUGHT
IN MANY STREETS FROM ONE OF THE MANY HAWKERS' STALLS.*

2 If using fried beancurd, cut each cube in half, refresh it in a pan of boiling water, then drain well. Heat 2 tablespoons of the oil in a large frying pan. If using plain beancurd, cut into cubes and fry until brown, then lift it out with a slotted spoon and set aside.

3 Beat the eggs with the water and seasoning. Add to the oil in the frying pan and cook without stirring until set. Flip over, cook the other side, then slide it out of the pan, roll up and slice thinly.

SERVES 4–6

INGREDIENTS
    1 pound fresh yellow egg noodles
    4–6 tablespoons vegetable oil
    4 ounces fried beancurd (tofu) or
      5 ounces firm beancurd (tofu)
    2 eggs
    2 tablespoons water
    1 onion, sliced
    1 garlic clove, crushed
    1 tablespoon light soy sauce
    2–3 tablespoons tomato ketchup
    1 tablespoon chili sauce (or to taste)
    1 large cooked potato, diced
    4 scallions, shredded
    1–2 fresh green chiles, seeded
      and finely sliced (optional)

1 Bring a large saucepan of water to a boil, add the fresh egg noodles and cook for just 2 minutes. Drain the noodles and immediately rinse them under cold water to halt cooking. Drain again and set aside.

4 Heat the remaining oil in a wok and fry the onion and garlic for 2–3 minutes. Add the drained noodles, soy sauce, ketchup and chili sauce. Toss well over medium heat for 2 minutes, then add the diced potato. Reserve a few scallions for garnish and stir the rest into the noodles with the chiles, if using, and the beancurd.

5 When hot, stir in the omelet. Serve on a hot platter garnished with the remaining scallions.

THAILAND
AND BURMA

*To eat a Thai meal is an exquisite experience. Curries are spicy but subtle; soups are
legendary and even the humble fish cake can be sensational if the product of an
accomplished cook. Burma has a more robust but equally interesting cuisine,
and is famous for one of the world's most delicious fish soups, Mohingha.*

THAI SPRING ROLLS

CRUNCHY SPRING ROLLS ARE AS POPULAR IN THAILAND AS THEY ARE IN CHINA. THAIS FILL THEIR VERSION WITH A DELICIOUS GARLIC, PORK AND NOODLE MIXTURE.

MAKES ABOUT 24

INGREDIENTS
   24 × 6-inch square spring
     roll wrappers
   2 tablespoons all-purpose flour
   vegetable oil, for deep frying
   Thai sweet chili dipping sauce, to
     serve (optional)

For the filling
   4–6 Chinese dried mushrooms,
     soaked for 30 minutes in warm
     water to cover
   2 ounces cellophane noodles
   2 tablespoons vegetable oil
   2 garlic cloves, chopped
   2 fresh red chiles, seeded
     and chopped
   8 ounces ground pork
   2 ounces peeled cooked shrimp,
     thawed if frozen
   2 tablespoons nam pla (fish sauce)
   1 teaspoon sugar
   1 carrot, grated
   2 ounces drained canned bamboo
     shoots, chopped
   1 cup beansprouts
   2 scallions, finely chopped
   1 tablespoon chopped fresh cilantro
   ground black pepper

1 Make the filling. Drain the soaked mushrooms. Cut off the mushroom stems and discard; chop the caps finely.

2 Place the noodles in a large bowl, cover with boiling water and soak for 10 minutes. Drain the noodles and snip them into 2-inch lengths.

3 Heat the oil in a wok, add the garlic and chiles and stir-fry for 30 seconds. Transfer to a plate, add the pork and cook, stirring, until it has browned.

4 Add the noodles, mushrooms and shrimp. Stir in the nam pla (fish sauce) and sugar, then add pepper to taste.

5 Tip the noodle mixture into a bowl and stir in the carrot, bamboo shoots, beansprouts, scallions and chopped cilantro together with the reserved chile mixture.

6 Unwrap the spring roll wrappers. Cover them with a dampened dish towel while you are making the rolls, so that they do not dry out. Put the flour in a small bowl and stir in a little water to make a paste. Place a spoonful of filling in the centre of a spring roll wrapper.

7 Turn the bottom edge over to cover the filling, then fold in the left and right sides. Roll the wrapper up almost to the top then brush the top edge with the flour paste and seal. Fill the remaining wrappers in the same way.

8 Heat the oil in a wok or deep-fryer. Fry the spring rolls, a few at a time, until crisp and golden brown. Drain on paper towels and keep hot while cooking successive batches. Serve hot with Thai sweet chili sauce, if you like.

COOK'S TIP
Fish sauce (nam pla) is made from anchovies, which are salted, then fermented in wooden barrels. The sauce accentuates the flavor of food, and does not necessarily impart a fishy flavor.

CRISP-FRIED CRAB CLAWS

CRAB CLAWS ARE READILY AVAILABLE IN THE FREEZER CABINET IN MANY ORIENTAL STORES AND SUPERMARKETS. THAW OUT THOROUGHLY AND DRY ON PAPER TOWELS BEFORE DIPPING IN THE BATTER.

SERVES 4

INGREDIENTS
 1/3 cup rice flour
 1 tablespoon cornstarch
 1/2 teaspoon sugar
 1 egg
 4 tablespoons cold water
 1 lemongrass stalk, root trimmed
 2 garlic cloves, finely chopped
 1 tablespoon chopped fresh cilantro
 1–2 fresh red chiles, seeded and
   finely chopped
 1 teaspoon nam pla (fish sauce)
 vegetable oil, for frying
 12 half-shelled crab claws
 ground black pepper

For the chile vinegar dip
 3 tablespoons sugar
 1/2 cup water
 1/2 cup red wine vinegar
 1 tablespoon nam pla (fish sauce)
 2–4 fresh red chiles, seeded
   and chopped

1 Make the chile dip. Mix the sugar and water in a saucepan, stirring until the sugar has dissolved then bring to a boil. Lower the heat and simmer for 5–7 minutes. Stir in the rest of the ingredients and set aside.

2 Combine the rice flour, cornstarch and sugar in a bowl. Beat the egg with the cold water, then stir the egg and water mixture into the flour mixture and mix well until it forms a light batter.

3 Cut off the lower 2 inches of the lemongrass stalk and chop it finely. Add the lemongrass to the batter, with the garlic, cilantro, red chiles and nam pla (fish sauce). Stir in pepper to taste.

4 Heat the oil in a wok or deep-fryer. Pat the crab claws dry and dip into the batter. Drop the battered claws into the hot oil, a few at a time. Fry until golden brown. Drain on paper towels and keep hot. Pour the dip into a serving bowl and serve with the crab claws.

FISH CAKES <u>WITH</u> CUCUMBER RELISII

THESE WONDERFUL SMALL FISH CAKES ARE A VERY FAMILIAR AND POPULAR APPETIZER IN THAILAND AND INCREASINGLY THROUGHOUT SOUTH-EAST ASIA. THEY ARE USUALLY SERVED WITH THAI BEER.

MAKES ABOUT 12

INGREDIENTS
  5 kaffir lime leaves
  11 ounces cod, cut into chunks
  2 tablespoons red curry paste
  1 egg
  2 tablespoons nam pla (fish sauce)
  1 teaspoon sugar
  2 tablespoons cornstarch
  1 tablespoon chopped fresh cilantro
  2 ounces green beans, finely sliced
  vegetable oil, for frying
  fresh Chinese mustard cress or
    cilantro leaves, to garnish

For the cucumber relish
  4 tablespoons coconut or rice vinegar
  ¼ cup sugar
  1 head pickled garlic
  1 tablespoon fresh ginger root
  1 cucumber, cut into matchsticks
  4 shallots, finely sliced

1 Make the cucumber relish. Bring the vinegar and sugar to a boil in a small pan with 4 tablespoons water, stirring until the sugar has dissolved. Remove from the heat and cool.

2 Separate the pickled garlic into cloves. Chop these finely along with the ginger and place in a bowl. Add the cucumber and shallots, pour over the vinegar mixture and mix lightly.

3 Reserve two kaffir lime leaves for garnish and thinly slice the remainder. Put the chunks of fish, curry paste and egg in a food processor and process to a smooth paste. Transfer the mixture to a bowl and stir in the nam pla (fish sauce), sugar, cornstarch, sliced kaffir lime leaves, cilantro and green beans. Mix well, then shape the mixture into about twelve ¼-inch thick cakes, measuring about 2 inches in diameter.

4 Heat the oil in a wok or deep-frying pan. Fry the fish cakes, a few at a time, for about 4–5 minutes until cooked and evenly brown.

5 Lift out the fish cakes and drain them on paper towels. Keep each batch hot while frying successive batches. Garnish with the reserved kaffir lime leaves and serve with the cucumber relish.

GINGER, CHICKEN AND COCONUT SOUP

THIS AROMATIC SOUP IS RICH WITH COCONUT MILK AND INTENSELY FLAVORED WITH GALANGAL,
LEMONGRASS AND KAFFIR LIME LEAVES.

SERVES 4–6

INGREDIENTS
    4 lemongrass stalks, roots trimmed
    1¾ cups canned coconut milk
    2 cups chicken stock
    1-inch piece galangal, peeled and
        thinly sliced
    10 black peppercorns, crushed
    10 kaffir lime leaves, torn
    11 ounces skinless boneless chicken
        breasts, cut into thin strips
    1 cup button mushrooms
    ½ cup baby corn cobs, quartered
        lengthwise
    4 tablespoons lime juice
    3 tablespoons nam pla (fish sauce)
    chopped fresh red chiles, scallions
        and fresh cilanro leaves, to garnish

1 Cut off the lower 2 inches from each lemongrass stalk and chop it finely. Bruise the remaining pieces of stalk. Bring the coconut milk and chicken stock to a boil in a large pan. Add all the lemongrass, the galangal, peppercorns and half the lime leaves, lower the heat and simmer gently for 10 minutes. Strain into a clean pan.

2 Return the soup to the heat, then add the chicken, mushrooms and corn. Simmer for 5–7 minutes or until the chicken is cooked.

3 Stir in the lime juice and nam pla (fish sauce), then add the remaining lime leaves. Serve hot, garnished with chiles, scallions and cilantro.

HOT AND SOUR SHRIMP SOUP

THIS IS A CLASSIC THAI SEAFOOD SOUP—TOM YAM KUNG—AND IT IS PROBABLY THE MOST
POPULAR AND WELL-KNOWN SOUP FROM THAT COUNTRY.

SERVES 4–6

INGREDIENTS
    1 pound raw jumbo shrimp, thawed
        if frozen
    4 cups chicken stock or water
    3 lemongrass stalks, root trimmed
    10 kaffir lime leaves, torn in half
    8-ounce can straw mushrooms
    3 tablespoons nam pla (fish sauce)
    4 tablespoons lime juice
    2 tablespoons chopped scallion
    1 tablespoon fresh cilantro
        leaves
    4 fresh red chiles, seeded
        and thinly sliced
    salt and ground black pepper

1 Shell the shrimp, putting the shells in a strainer. De-vein the shrimp and set them aside.

2 Rinse the shells under cold water, then put in a large saucepan with the stock or water. Bring to a boil.

3 Bruise the lemongrass stalks and add them to the stock with half the lime leaves. Simmer gently for 5–6 minutes, until the stock is fragrant.

4 Strain the stock, return it to the clean pan and reheat. Add the drained mushrooms and the shrimp, then cook until the shrimp turn pink.

5 Stir in the nam pla (fish sauce), lime juice, scallions, cilantro, chiles and the remaining lime leaves. Taste and adjust the seasoning. The soup should be sour, salty, spicy and hot.

STIR-FRIED CHICKEN WITH BASIL AND CHILE

THIS QUICK AND EASY CHICKEN DISH IS AN EXCELLENT INTRODUCTION TO THAI CUISINE. THAI BASIL, WHICH IS SOMETIMES KNOWN AS HOLY BASIL, HAS A UNIQUE, PUNGENT FLAVOR THAT IS BOTH SPICY AND SHARP. DEEP FRYING THE LEAVES ADDS ANOTHER DIMENSION TO THIS DISH.

SERVES 4–6

INGREDIENTS

   3 tablespoons vegetable oil
   4 garlic cloves, thinly sliced
   2–4 fresh red chiles, seeded
     and finely chopped
   1 pound skinless boneless chicken
     breasts, cut into bite-size pieces
   3 tablespoons nam pla (fish sauce)
   2 teaspoons dark soy sauce
   1 teaspoon sugar
   10–12 Thai basil leaves
   2 fresh red chiles, seeded and finely
     chopped and about 20 deep-fried
     Thai basil leaves, to garnish

1 Heat the oil in a wok or large frying pan. Add the garlic and chiles and stir-fry over medium heat for 1–2 minutes until the garlic is golden.

2 Add the pieces of chicken to the wok or pan and stir-fry until the chicken changes color.

3 Stir in the nam pla (fish sauce), soy sauce and sugar. Continue to stir-fry the mixture for 3–4 minutes or until the chicken is fully cooked with the sauce.

4 Stir in the fresh Thai basil leaves. Spoon the entire mixture on to a warm serving platter, or individual serving dishes and garnish with the sliced chiles and deep-fried Thai basil.

COOK'S TIP
To deep fry Thai basil leaves, first make sure that the leaves are completely dry or they will splutter when added to the oil. Deep fry the leaves briefly in hot oil until they are crisp and transluscent—this will only take about 30–40 seconds. Lift out the leaves using a slotted spoon or wire basket and leave them to drain on paper towels.

GREEN PAPAYA SALAD

THIS SALAD APPEARS IN MANY GUISES IN SOUTH-EAST ASIA. AS GREEN PAPAYA IS NOT EASY TO GET HOLD OF, FINELY GRATED CARROTS, CUCUMBER OR GREEN APPLE CAN BE USED INSTEAD. ALTERNATIVELY, USE VERY THINLY SLICED WHITE CABBAGE.

2 Put the garlic, shallots, chiles and salt in a large mortar and grind to a paste with a pestle. Add the shredded papaya, a little at a time, pounding until it becomes slightly limp and soft.

3 Add the sliced beans and wedges of tomato to the mortar and crush them lightly with the pestle.

SERVES 4

INGREDIENTS
  1 green papaya
  4 garlic cloves, roughly chopped
  1 tablespoon chopped shallots
  3–4 fresh red chiles, seeded
    and sliced
  1/2 teaspoon salt
  2–3 snake beans or 6 green beans,
    cut into 3/4-inch lengths
  2 tomatoes, cut into thin wedges
  3 tablespoons nam pla (fish sauce)
  1 tablespoon sugar
  juice of 1 lime
  2 tablespoons crushed roasted peanuts
  sliced fresh red chiles, to garnish

1 Cut the papaya in half lengthwise. Scrape out the seeds with a spoon, then peel using a swivel vegetable peeler or a small sharp knife. Shred the flesh finely using a food processor or grater.

4 Season the mixture with the nam pla (fish sauce), sugar and lime juice. Transfer the salad to a serving dish and sprinkle with crushed peanuts and garnish with sliced red chiles.

LARP OF CHIANG MAI

CHIANG MAI IS A CITY IN THE NORTH-EAST OF THAILAND. THE CITY IS CULTURALLY VERY CLOSE TO LAOS AND FAMOUS FOR ITS CHICKEN SALAD, WHICH WAS ORIGINALLY CALLED "LAAP" OR "LARP". DUCK, BEEF OR PORK CAN BE USED INSTEAD OF CHICKEN.

SERVES 4–6

INGREDIENTS
  1 pound ground chicken
  1 lemongrass stalk, root trimmed
  3 kaffir lime leaves, finely chopped
  4 fresh red chiles, seeded
    and chopped
  4 tablespoons lime juice
  2 tablespoons nam pla (fish sauce)
  1 tablespoon roasted ground rice
    (see Cook's Tip)
  2 scallions, chopped
  2 tablespoons fresh cilantro leaves
  thinly sliced kaffir lime leaves, mixed
    salad greens and fresh mint sprigs,
    to garnish

1 Heat a large nonstick frying pan. Add the ground chicken and moisten with a little water. Stir constantly over medium heat for 7–10 minutes until it is cooked. Meanwhile, cut off the lower 2 inches of the lemongrass stalk and chop finely.

2 Transfer the cooked chicken to a bowl and add the chopped lemongrass, lime leaves, chiles, lime juice, nam pla (fish sauce), ground rice, scallions and cilantro. Mix thoroughly.

3 Spoon the chicken mixture into a salad bowl. Scatter sliced kaffir lime leaves over the top and garnish with salad leaves and sprigs of mint.

COOK'S TIP
Use glutinous rice for the roasted ground rice. Put the rice in a frying pan and dry-roast it until golden brown. Remove and grind to a powder, using a pestle and mortar or a food processor. When the rice is cold, store it in a glass jar in a cool and dry place.

THAI BEEF SALAD

A HEARTY MAIN MEAL SALAD, THIS COMBINES TENDER STRIPS OF STEAK WITH A WONDERFUL CHILI AND LIME DRESSING.

SERVES 4

INGREDIENTS
  2 sirloin steaks, each about 8 ounces
  1 lemongrass stalk, root trimmed
  1 red onion, finely sliced
  1/2 cucumber, cut into strips
  2 tablespoons chopped scallion
  2–4 fresh red chiles, seeded and
    chopped
  juice of 2 limes
  1–2 tablespoons nam pla
    (fish sauce)
  Chinese mustard cress or salad cress,
    to garnish

COOK'S TIP
Look out for gui chai leaves in Thai groceries. These look like very thin scallions and are often used as a substitute for the more familiar vegetable.

1 Pan-fry or broil the steaks for 6–8 minutes for medium-rare. Allow to rest for 10–15 minutes. Meanwhile, cut off the lower 2 inches from the lemongrass stalk and chop it finely.

2 When the meat is cool, slice it thinly and put the slices in a large bowl.

3 Add the sliced onion, cucumber, lemongrass, chopped scallion and chiles to the meat slices.

4 Toss the salad and season with the lime juice and nam pla (fish sauce). Transfer to a serving bowl or plate and serve at room temperature or chilled, garnished with Chinese mustard cress or salad cress.

STUFFED THAI OMELETS

*INDIVIDUAL OMELETS CAN BE MADE OR MAKE TWO LARGE OMELET PARCELS TO SERVE FOUR.
THEY ARE REMARKABLY EASY TO MAKE AND MAKE A TASTY LUNCH OR LIGHT SUPPER.*

2 Stir in the nam pla (fish sauce), sugar and tomatoes, with pepper to taste. Simmer for 5–8 minutes, until the sauce thickens. Remove from the heat and stir in the chopped cilantro.

3 Make the omelets. Whisk the eggs and nam pla in a bowl. Heat a little of the oil in a 8-inch omelet pan. Add a quarter or half of the egg mixture, depending on whether you wish to make individual parcels or cut them in half. Tilt the pan to spread the egg into a thin, even sheet. As soon as it sets, spoon some of the filling over the center of the omelet. Fold the top and bottom over, then the right and left sides to make a neat, square package.

4 Slide the omelet out on to a warm serving dish, folded side down, and keep hot while you make the remaining omelet(s). Serve garnished with sprigs of cilantro.

SERVES 3–4

INGREDIENTS
   2 tablespoons vegetable oil
   2 garlic cloves, finely chopped
   1 small onion, finely chopped
   8 ounces ground pork
   2 tablespoons nam pla (fish sauce)
   1 teaspoon sugar
   2 tomatoes, peeled and chopped
   1 tablespoon chopped fresh cilantro
ground black pepper
fresh cilantro sprigs, to garnish

For the omelets
   6 eggs
   1 tablespoon nam pla (fish sauce)
   about 2 tablespoons vegetable oil

1 Heat the oil in a wok or frying pan. Add the chopped garlic and onion and fry for 3–4 minutes until the onion is softened. Add the pork and stir-fry for 7–10 minutes, until broken up and lightly browned.

VARIATION
Replace half the pork with peeled jumbo shrimp or white crab meat.

BARBECUED CHICKEN

BARBECUED CHICKEN IS SERVED ALMOST EVERYWHERE IN THAILAND, FROM PORTABLE ROADSIDE STALLS TO SPORTS STADIUMS AND EVEN ON THE BEACH.

SERVES 4–6

INGREDIENTS
1 chicken, about 3–3½ pounds,
  cut into 8–10 pieces
lime wedges and fresh red chiles,
  to garnish

For the marinade
2 lemongrass stalks, root trimmed
1-inch piece fresh ginger root, peeled
  and thinly sliced
6 garlic cloves, roughly chopped
4 shallots, roughly chopped
½ bunch cilantro roots, chopped
1 tablespoon palm sugar
½ cup coconut milk
2 tablespoons nam pla (fish sauce)
2 tablespoons light soy sauce

1 First make the marinade. Cut off the lower 2 inches of both of the lemongrass stalks and chop them roughly. Put into a food processor along with all the other marinade ingredients and process until the mixture has reached a smooth consistency.

2 Place the chicken pieces in a dish, pour over the marinade and stir to mix well. Cover the dish and leave in a cool place to marinate for at least 4 hours or overnight.

3 Prepare the barbecue or preheat the oven to 400°F. If cooking in the oven, arrange the chicken pieces on a rack over a roasting pan.

4 Barbecue or bake in the oven for 20–30 minutes or until the pieces are cooked and golden brown. Turn the pieces and brush with the marinade once or twice during cooking. Transfer the chicken pieces to a serving platter and garnish with lime wedges and red chiles.

COOK'S TIP
Coconut milk is available fresh or in cans or cartons from most supermarkets.

CRISPY FRIED RICE VERMICELLI

MEE KROB IS USUALLY SERVED AT CELEBRATION MEALS. IT IS A CRISP TANGLE OF FRIED RICE VERMICELLI, WHICH IS TOSSED IN A PIQUANT GARLIC, SWEET AND SOUR SAUCE.

SERVES 4–6

INGREDIENTS
    vegetable oil, for deep frying
    6 ounces rice vermicelli
    1 tablespoon chopped garlic
    4–6 small dried red chilies
    2 tablespoons chopped shallots
    1 tablespoon dried shrimp, rinsed
    4 ounces ground pork
    4 ounces raw peeled shrimp, thawed
      if frozen, chopped
    2 tablespoons brown bean sauce
    2 tablespoons rice wine vinegar
    3 tablespoons nam pla (fish sauce)
    3 ounces palm sugar
    2 tablespoons tamarind juice or
      lime juice
    2 cups beansprouts

For the garnish
    2 scallions, shredded
    2 tablespoons fresh cilantro
    2-egg omelet, rolled and sliced
    2 fresh red chiles, seeded and cut
      into thin strips

1 Heat the oil in a wok. Cut or break the rice vermicelli into small handfuls about 3-inches long. Deep fry these for a few seconds in the hot oil until they puff up. Lift out with a slotted spoon and drain on paper towels.

VARIATION
Pickled garlic can also be used as one of the garnish ingredients. Thai garlic is smaller than European garlic; the heads are pickled whole, in sweet and sour brine.

2 Ladle off all but 2 tablespoons of the oil, pouring it into a pan and setting aside to cool. Reheat the oil in the wok and fry the garlic, chilies, shallots and dried shrimp for about 1 minute.

3 Add the pork and stir-fry for 3–4 minutes, until no longer pink. Add the fresh shrimp and fry for 2 minutes. Spoon into a bowl and set aside.

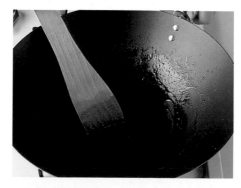

4 Add the brown bean sauce, vinegar, nam pla (fish sauce) and sugar. Heat gently, stirring in any sediment. Bring to a gentle boil, stir to dissolve the sugar and cook until thick and syrupy.

5 Add the tamarind or lime juice to the sauce and adjust the seasoning as necessary. The sauce should be sweet, sour and salty. Lower the heat, then return the pork and shrimp mixture to the wok, add the beansprouts and stir them into the sauce.

6 Add the fried rice noodles to the wok and toss gently to coat them with the sauce without breaking them up too much. Transfer the mixture to a large, warm serving platter or individual serving dishes. Garnish with the shredded scallions, cilantro, omelet strips and fresh red chiles and serve immediately.

COOK'S TIP
Always deep fry rice vermicelli in small quantities, as it puffs up to two or three times its original volume. It cooks in seconds, so be ready to remove from the wok using a slotted spoon or wire basket as soon as it is puffy and before it takes on any color.

RED CHICKEN CURRY WITH BAMBOO SHOOTS

BAMBOO SHOOTS HAVE A LOVELY CRUNCHY TEXTURE. IT IS QUITE ACCEPTABLE TO USE CANNED ONES, AS FRESH BAMBOO IS NOT READILY AVAILABLE IN THE WEST. BUY CANNED WHOLE BAMBOO SHOOTS, WHICH ARE CRISPER AND OF BETTER QUALITY THAN SLICED SHOOTS. RINSE BEFORE USING.

SERVES 4–6

INGREDIENTS
4 cups coconut milk
1 pound skinless, boneless chicken
    breasts, cut into bite-size pieces
2 tablespoons nam pla (fish sauce)
1 tablespoon sugar
8 ounces drained canned bamboo
    shoots, rinsed and sliced
5 kaffir lime leaves, torn
salt and ground black pepper
chopped fresh red chiles and kaffir
    lime leaves, to garnish

For the red curry paste
1 teaspoon coriander seeds
1/2 teaspoon cumin seeds
12–15 fresh red chiles, seeded and
    roughly chopped
4 shallots, thinly sliced
2 garlic cloves, chopped
1 tablespoon chopped galangal
2 lemongrass stalks, chopped
3 kaffir lime leaves, chopped
4 fresh cilantro roots
10 black peppercorns
good pinch of ground cinnamon
1 teaspoon ground turmeric
1/2 teaspoon shrimp paste (blachan)
1 teaspoon salt
2 tablespoons vegetable oil

2 Add the oil, a little at a time, mixing or processing well after each addition. Transfer to a jar and keep in the refrigerator until ready to use.

3 Pour half of the coconut milk into a large heavy-based pan. Bring the milk to a boil, stirring constantly until it has separated.

1 Make the curry paste. Dry fry the coriander and cumin seeds for 1–2 minutes, then put in a mortar or food processor with the remaining ingredients except the oil and pound or process to a paste.

4 Stir in 2 tablespoons of the red curry paste and cook the mixture for 2–3 minutes, stirring constantly. Remaining red curry paste can be kept in the refrigerator for up to 3 months.

5 Add the chicken pieces, nam pla (fish sauce) and sugar to the pan. Stir well, then cook for 5–6 minutes until the chicken changes color and is cooked through, stirring constantly to prevent the mixture from sticking to the bottom of the pan.

6 Pour the remaining coconut milk into the pan, then add the sliced bamboo shoots and torn kaffir lime leaves. Bring back to a boil over medium heat, stirring constantly to prevent the mixture sticking, then taste and add salt and pepper if necessary.

7 To serve, spoon the curry into a warmed serving dish and garnish with chopped chiles and kaffir lime leaves.

VARIATION
Instead of, or as well as, bamboo shoots, use straw mushrooms. These are available in cans from Asian markets. Drain well and then stir into the curry at the end of the recipe.

COOK'S TIP
It is essential to use chicken breasts, rather than any other cut, for this curry, as it is cooked very quickly. Look out for diced chicken or strips of chicken (which are often labelled "stir-fry chicken") in the supermarket.

MUSSAMAN CURRY

THIS DISH IS TRADITIONALLY MADE WITH BEEF, BUT CHICKEN, LAMB OR BEANCURD CAN BE USED. IT HAS A RICH, SWEET AND SPICY FLAVOR AND IS BEST SERVED WITH BOILED RICE. MUSSAMAN CURRY PASTE IS AVAILABLE FROM SPECIALIST STORES OR MAKE YOUR OWN.

SERVES 4–6

INGREDIENTS

2$\frac{1}{2}$ cups canned coconut milk
1$\frac{1}{2}$ pounds stewing steak, cut into
  1-inch chunks
1 cup coconut cream
3 tablespoons Mussaman curry paste
  (see Cook's Tip)
2 tablespoons nam pla (fish sauce)
1 tablespoon palm sugar
4 tablespoons tamarind juice
6 green cardamom pods
1 cinnamon stick
1 large potato, about 8 ounces, cut
  into even-size chunks
1 onion, cut into wedges
$\frac{1}{2}$ cup roasted peanuts

1 Bring the coconut milk to a gentle boil in a large saucepan. Add the beef, lower the heat and simmer for about 40 minutes until tender.

2 Put the coconut cream into a pan and cook for 5–8 minutes, stirring, until it separates. Stir in the Mussaman curry paste and cook rapidly until fragrant. Add to the cooked beef, and mix well.

3 Stir in the nam pla (fish sauce), sugar, tamarind juice, cardamom pods, cinnamon, potato and onion. Simmer for 15–20 minutes or until the potato is cooked. Add the peanuts and mix well. Cook for 5 minutes and serve.

COOK'S TIP
To make Mussaman curry paste, soak 12 large, seeded dried chilies, in hot water for 15 minutes. Chop finely and pound or process with 4 tablespoons shallots, 5 garlic cloves, 1 lemongrass stalk base and 2 tablespoons chopped galangal. Put 1 teaspoon cumin seeds, 1 tablespoon coriander seeds, 2 cloves and 6 black peppercorns in a pan; dry fry over low heat for 1–2 minutes. Grind to a powder; add 1 teaspoon shrimp paste (blachan), 1 teaspoon salt, 1 teaspoon sugar and 2 tablespoons vegetable oil. Stir in the shallot mixture to make a paste.

CURRIED SHRIMP IN COCONUT MILK

ANOTHER WONDERFULLY QUICK AND EASY DISH, THIS FEATURES SHRIMP IN A SPICY COCONUT GRAVY.

SERVES 4–6

INGREDIENTS

2½ cups coconut milk
2 tablespoons yellow curry paste
  (see Cook's Tip)
1 tablespoon nam pla (fish sauce)
½ teaspoon salt
1 teaspoon sugar
1 pound raw jumbo shrimp peeled,
  thawed if frozen
8 ounces cherry tomatoes
fresh yellow and orange peppers,
  seeded and cut into thin strips,
  chives and juice of ½ lime,
  to garnish

VARIATION
Use cooked shrimp for a quick version
of this dish. Add them after the tomatoes
and heat through for a minute or two.

1 Put half the coconut milk in a wok or
saucepan and bring to a boil. Add the
yellow curry paste, stir until it disperses,
then lower the heat and simmer for
about 10 minutes.

2 Add the nam pla (fish sauce), salt,
sugar and remaining coconut milk to
the sauce. Simmer for 5 minutes more.

3 Add the shrimp and cherry tomatoes.
Simmer very gently for about 5 minutes
until the shrimp are pink and tender.

4 Spoon into a serving dish, sprinkle
with lime juice and garnish with strips
of yellow peppers and chives.

COOK'S TIP
To make yellow curry paste, put into a
food processor or blender 6–8 fresh yellow
chiles, the chopped base of 1 lemongrass
stalk, 4 chopped shallots, 4 chopped
garlic cloves, 1 tablespoon chopped
peeled fresh ginger root, 1 teaspoon
coriander seeds, 1 teaspoon mustard
powder, 1 teaspoon salt, ½ teaspoon
ground cinnamon, 1 tablespoon light
brown sugar and 2 tablespoons sunflower
oil. Process to a paste, scrape into a glass
jar, cover and keep in the refrigerator.

STEWED PUMPKIN IN COCONUT CREAM

STEWED FRUIT IS A POPULAR DESSERT IN THAILAND. PUMPKINS, BANANAS AND MELONS CAN ALL BE PREPARED IN THIS WAY, AND YOU CAN EVEN STEW CORN KERNELS, MUNG BEANS OR BLACK BEANS IN COCONUT MILK.

SERVES 4–6

INGREDIENTS
  2¼ pounds kabocha pumpkin
  3 cups coconut milk
  ¾ cup sugar
  pinch of salt
  toasted pumpkin seed kernels and
    fresh mint sprigs, to decorate

COOK'S TIP
To make the garnish, wash the pumpkin seeds to remove any fibers and pat them dry on paper towels. Roast them in a dry frying pan or, alternatively, spread the seeds out on a baking sheet and broil until golden brown; toss them frequently.

1 Cut the pumpkin in half using a large, sharp knife, then cut away and discard the skin. Scoop out the seed cluster and reserve a few seeds. Using a sharp knife, cut the pumpkin flesh into pieces that are about 2 inches long and ¾-inch thick.

2 In a saucepan, bring the coconut milk, sugar and salt to a boil. Add the pumpkin and simmer for about 10–15 minutes until it is tender. Serve warm, in individual dishes. Decorate each serving with a mint sprig and a few toasted pumpkin seed kernels.

MANGOES WITH STICKY RICE

EVERYONE'S FAVORITE DESSERT: MANGOES, WITH THEIR DELICATE FRAGRANCE, SWEET-AND-SOUR FLAVOR AND VELVETY FLESH, BLEND ESPECIALLY WELL WITH COCONUT STICKY RICE. YOU NEED TO START PREPARING THIS DISH THE DAY BEFORE YOU INTEND TO SERVE IT.

SERVES 4

INGREDIENTS
  ⅔ cup white glutinous rice
  ¾ cup thick coconut milk
  3 tablespoons sugar
  pinch of salt
  2 ripe mangoes, peeled and sliced
  strips of lime rind, to decorate

1 Rinse the glutinous rice thoroughly in several changes of cold water, then leave to soak overnight in a bowl of fresh cold water.

COOK'S TIP
Like cream, the thickest and richest part of coconut milk rises to the top. Spoon it off and pour over before serving.

2 Drain the rice and spread evenly in a steamer lined with cheesecloth. Cover and steam over simmering water for 20 minutes or until tender.

3 Reserve 3 tablespoons of the top of the coconut milk. Bring the rest to a boil in a pan with the sugar and salt, stirring until the sugar dissolves. Pour into a bowl to cool.

4 Tip the cooked rice into a bowl and pour over the cooled coconut milk mixture. Stir well, then leave to stand for about 10–15 minutes.

5 Spoon the rice on to individual serving plates. Arrange mango slices on one side and then drizzle with the reserved coconut milk. Decorate with strips of lime rind and serve.

MOHINGHA

BURMESE HOUSEWIVES BUY THIS WELL-KNOWN AND DELICIOUS ONE-COURSE MEAL FROM HAWKERS,
RECOGNIZED BY A BAMBOO POLE CARRIED ACROSS THEIR SHOULDERS. AT ONE END IS A CONTAINER
WITH A CHARCOAL FIRE AND AT THE OTHER END IS EVERYTHING ELSE THEY NEED TO MAKE THE MEAL.

SERVES 8

INGREDIENTS
   1½ pounds cod or mackerel, cleaned
      but left on the bone
   3 lemongrass stalks
   1-inch piece fresh ginger root, peeled
   2 tablespoons fish sauce
   3 onions, roughly chopped
   4 garlic cloves, roughly chopped
   2–3 fresh red chiles, seeded
      and chopped
   1 teaspoon ground turmeric
   5 tablespoons peanut oil, for frying
   1¾ cups canned coconut milk
   3 tablespoons rice flour
   3 tablespoons chick-pea
      flour (besan)
   pieces of banana trunk, or heart,
      if available, or 1 pound 5 ounces
      drained canned bamboo shoot,
      sliced
   salt and ground black pepper
   wedges of hard-cooked egg, thinly
      sliced red onions, finely chopped
      scallions, a few deep fried shrimp
      and fried chilies (see Cook's Tip),
      to garnish
   1 pound dried or fresh rice noodles,
      cooked according to the instructions
      on the packet, to serve

1 Place the fish in a large pan and pour in cold water to cover. Bruise two lemongrass stalks and half the ginger and add to the pan. Bring to a boil, add the fish sauce and cook for 10 minutes. Lift out the fish and allow to cool while straining the stock into a large bowl. Discard any skin and bones from the fish and break the flesh into small pieces.

COOK'S TIP
To make fried chilies, dry roast 8–10 dried red chilies in a heavy frying pan, then pound them, fry in 2 tablespoons peanut oil and stir in 1 ounce dried shrimps (pounded).

2 Cut off the lower 2 inches of the remaining lemongrass stalk and discard; roughly chop the remaining lemongrass. Put it in a food processor with the remaining ginger, the onions, garlic, chiles and turmeric. Process to a smooth paste. Heat the oil in a frying pan and fry the paste until it gives off a rich aroma. Remove from the heat and add the fish.

3 Stir the coconut milk into the reserved fish stock, then add enough water to make up to 10 cups and pour into a large pan. In a jug, mix the rice flour and chick-pea (besan) flour to a thin cream with some of the stock. Stir this into the coconut and stock mixture and bring to a boil, stirring all the time.

4 Add the banana trunk or heart or bamboo shoots and cook for 10 minutes until just tender. Stir in the fish mixture and season. Cook until hot. Guests pour soup over the noodles and add hard-cooked egg, onions, scallions, shrimp and fried chilies as a garnish.

THAMIN LETHOK

THIS IS THE BURMESE WAY OF DEALING WITH LEFTOVERS, AND VERY SUCCESSFUL IT IS TOO. THE NOODLES AND RICE ARE ARRANGED ON PLATTERS WITH SOME OR ALL OF THE ACCOMPANIMENTS. EVERYTHING IS SERVED COLD, SO IT IS PERFECT FOR A SUMMER PARTY.

SERVES 6

INGREDIENTS
  scant 1 cup long grain rice
  1–2 red chiles, seeded and
    roughly chopped
  1 small onion, roughly chopped
  1 tablespoon vegetable oil
  12 ounces potatoes, diced
  4 ounces egg noodles, soaked for
    30 minutes in cold water to cover
  4 ounces rice noodles, soaked for
    at least 10 minutes in cold water
    to cover
  2 ounces cellophane noodles (or
    increase either of the above)
  8 ounces spinach leaves
  3 cups beansprouts
  1½ tablespoons tamarind
    pulp or concentrate, soaked in
    scant 1 cup warm water, or
    6 lemon wedges
  salt

For the accompaniments
  1 very small onion, thinly sliced
  3 scallions, finely shredded
  crisp fried onion
  2 ounces cellophane noodles, fried
    until crisp
  3 tablespoons chick-peas, dry roasted
    and pounded
  3 dried chilies, dry-fried
    and pounded
  fresh cilantro leaves

1 Bring a large pan of water to a boil and cook the rice for 12–15 minutes until tender. Drain, tip into a bowl and set aside. In a mortar, pound the chiles with the onion. Heat the oil in a small frying pan, add the mixture and fry for 2–3 minutes. Stir into the cooked rice.

2 Cook the potatoes in boiling salted water for about 8–10 minutes until just tender; drain and set aside. Drain the noodles and cook them in separate pans of salted, boiling water (see Cook's Tip). Drain, refresh under cold water and drain again.

3 Put the spinach into a large pan with just the water that clings to the leaves after washing. Cover the pan and cook for 2 minutes until starting to wilt. Drain well. Cook the beansprouts in the same way. Leave both to get cold.

COOK'S TIP
Cook noodles following the instructions on the packet: egg noodles need about 4 minutes and rice noodles are ready when the water boils again.

4 Arrange the cold flavored rice, potato cubes, noodles, spinach and beansprouts attractively on a large serving platter. Set out the range of accompaniments. Strain the tamarind juice, if using, into a jug or put the lemon wedges on a plate. Each guest takes a little of whichever main ingredients they fancy, adds some accompaniments and drizzles over a little tamarind juice or a squeeze of lemon juice to taste.

INDONESIA

Over 13,000 islands make up this lush tropical archipelago. Numerous cultures have flourished here, from the early Hindu and Buddhist empires to the rise of Islam. In the following centuries, Portuguese and British merchants set up trading posts, but the Dutch had the strongest impact, occupying the islands for 250 years. This culinary heritage and the abundance of ingredients, such as rice, chiles, limes, tamarind and spices, has led to the development of exciting dishes such as Nasi Goreng, Gado-gado and Beef Rendang.

LAMB SATÉ

THESE TASTY LAMB SKEWERS ARE TRADITIONALLY SERVED WITH DAINTY DIAMOND-SHAPED PIECES OF COMPRESSED RICE, WHICH ARE SURPRISINGLY SIMPLE TO MAKE. OFFER THE REMAINING SAUCE FOR DIPPING.

MAKES 25–30 SKEWERS

INGREDIENTS
  2¼ pounds leg of lamb, boned
  3 garlic cloves, crushed
  1–2 tablespoons chile sambal or
    1–2 teaspoons chili powder
  6 tablespoons dark soy sauce
  juice of 1 lemon
  salt and ground black pepper
  peanut or sunflower oil,
    for brushing

For the sauce
  6 garlic cloves, crushed
  1 tablespoon chile sambal or
    2–3 fresh chiles, seeded and ground
    to a paste
  6 tablespoons dark soy sauce
  1½ tablespoons lemon juice
  2 tablespoons boiling water

To serve
  thinly sliced onion
  cucumber wedges (optional)
  compressed-rice shapes (see
    Cook's Tip)

1 Cut the lamb into neat ½-inch cubes. Remove any pieces of gristle, but do not trim off any of the fat because this keeps the meat moist during cooking and enhances the flavor. Spread out the lamb cubes in a single layer in a shallow bowl.

COOK'S TIP
Make two cheesecloth bags about 6 inches square and put 4 ounces rice in each. Sew up the fourth side. Place in a pan of boiling, salted water and simmer for 1¼ hours until the cooked rice fills each bag like a plump cushion. The bags must be covered with water throughout; use a saucer or plate to weigh them down. Let the bags cool completely before slitting them and removing the slabs of cooked rice. With a sharp, wetted knife, cut each rice slab horizontally in half, then into diamond shapes.

2 Put the garlic, chile sambal or chili powder, soy sauce and lemon juice in a mortar. Add salt and pepper and grind to a paste. Alternatively, process the mixture using a food processor. Pour over the lamb and mix to coat. Cover and leave in a cool place for at least 1 hour. Soak wooden or bamboo skewers in water to prevent them from scorching during cooking.

3 Prepare the sauce. Put the garlic into a bowl. Add the chile sambal or fresh chiles, soy sauce, lemon juice and boiling water. Stir well. Preheat the broiler. Thread the meat on to the skewers. Brush with oil and broil, turning often. Brush with a little sauce and serve hot, with onion, cucumber wedges, if using, rice shapes and the sauce.

BALINESE VEGETABLE SOUP

THE BALINESE BASE THIS POPULAR SOUP ON BEANS, BUT ANY SEASONAL VEGETABLES CAN BE ADDED OR SUBSTITUTED. THE RECIPE ALSO INCLUDES SHRIMP PASTE, WHICH IS KNOWN LOCALLY AS TERASI.

2 Finely grind the chopped garlic, macadamia nuts or almonds, shrimp paste (blachan) and the coriander seeds to a paste using a pestle and mortar or in a food processor.

SERVES 8

INGREDIENTS
8 ounces green beans
5 cups lightly salted water
1 garlic clove, roughly chopped
2 macadamia nuts or 4 almonds,
  finely chopped
½-inch cube shrimp paste (blachan)
2–3 teaspoons coriander seeds,
  dry fried
2 tablespoons vegetable oil
1 onion, finely sliced
1¾ cups coconut milk
2 bay leaves
4 cups beansprouts
8 thin lemon wedges
2 tablespoons lemon juice
salt and ground black pepper

1 Top and tail the beans, then cut them into small pieces. Bring the lightly salted water to a boil, add the beans to the pan and cook for 3–4 minutes. Drain, reserving the cooking water. Set the beans aside.

COOK'S TIP
Dry fry the coriander seeds for about 2 minutes until the aroma is released.

3 Heat the oil in a wok, and fry the onion until transparent. Remove with a slotted spoon. Add the nut paste to the wok and fry it for 2 minutes without allowing it to brown.

4 Pour in the reserved vegetable water. Spoon off 3–4 tablespoons of the cream from the top of the coconut milk and set it aside. Add the remaining coconut milk to the wok, bring to a boil and add the bay leaves. Cook, uncovered, for 15–20 minutes.

5 Just before serving, reserve a few beans, fried onions and beansprouts for garnish and stir the rest into the soup. Add the lemon wedges, reserved coconut cream, lemon juice and seasoning; stir well. Pour into individual soup bowls and serve, garnished with reserved beans, onion and beansprouts.

SPICY SQUID

This aromatically spiced squid dish, Cumi Cumi Smoor, is simple yet delicious. Gone are the days when cleaning squid was such a chore: today they can be bought ready-cleaned from fish shops, market stalls and the fish counters of large supermarkets.

2 Heat a wok and add 1 tablespoon of the oil. When hot, toss in the squid strips and stir-fry for 2–3 minutes, by which time the squid will have curled into attractive shapes or into firm rings. Lift out and set aside.

3 Wipe out the wok, add the remaining oil and heat it. Stir-fry the onion and garlic until soft and beginning to brown. Stir in the tomato, soy sauce, nutmeg, cloves, water and lemon or lime juice. Bring to a boil, lower the heat and add the squid with seasoning to taste.

4 Cook the mixture gently for a further 3–5 minutes stirring from time to time to prevent sticking. Take care not to overcook the squid.

5 Divide boiled rice among 3–4 serving plates and spoon the spicy squid on top. Garnish with cilantro leaves and shredded scallions and serve.

SERVES 3–4

INGREDIENTS

1 1/2 pounds squid
3 tablespoons peanut oil
1 onion, finely chopped
2 garlic cloves, crushed
1 beefsteak tomato, peeled
  and chopped
1 tablespoon dark soy sauce
1/2 teaspoon grated nutmeg
6 cloves
2/3 cup water
juice of 1/2 lemon or lime
salt and ground black pepper
fresh cilantro leaves and shredded
  scallions, to garnish
boiled rice, to serve

1 Rinse and drain the squid, then slice lengthwise along one side and open it out flat. Score the inside of the squid in a lattice pattern, using the blunt side of a sharp knife, then cut it crosswise into long thin strips.

NASI GORENG

ONE OF THE MOST FAMOUS INDONESIAN DISHES, THIS IS A MARVELOUS WAY TO USE UP LEFTOVER RICE, CHICKEN AND MEATS. IT IS IMPORTANT THAT THE RICE BE QUITE COLD AND THE GRAINS SEPARATE BEFORE THE OTHER INGREDIENTS ARE ADDED, SO COOK THE RICE THE DAY BEFORE IF POSSIBLE.

SERVES 4–6

INGREDIENTS

2 eggs
2 tablespoons water
7 tablespoons oil
8 ounces pork or beef tenderloin, cut into neat strips
4 ounces peeled cooked shrimp, thawed if frozen
6–8 ounces cooked chicken, finely chopped
2 fresh red chiles, halved and seeded
½ inch cube shrimp paste (blachan)
2 garlic cloves, crushed
1 onion, roughly chopped
6 cups cold cooked long grain rice, preferably basmati (about 1¾ cups raw rice)
2 tablespoons dark soy sauce or 3–4 tablespoons tomato ketchup
salt and ground black pepper
deep-fried onions, celery leaves and fresh cilantro sprigs, to garnish

2 Put the shrimp paste (blachan) in a food processor. Add the remaining chile, the garlic and the onion. Process to a fine paste. Alternatively, pound the mixture in a mortar, using a pestle.

3 Heat the remaining oil in a wok and fry the paste, without browning, until it gives off a rich, spicy aroma. Add the pork or beef and toss over the heat to seal in the juices, then cook for 2 minutes more, stirring constantly.

4 Add the shrimp and stir-fry for 2 minutes. Finally, stir in the chicken, cold rice, dark soy sauce or ketchup and seasoning to taste. Reheat the rice fully, stirring all the time to keep the rice light and fluffy and prevent it from sticking to the base of the pan.

5 Spoon into individual dishes and arrange the omelet strips and reserved chile on top. Garnish with the deep-fried onions and cilantro sprigs.

1 Put the eggs in a bowl and beat in the water, with salt and pepper to taste. Using a nonstick frying pan make two or three omelets using as little oil as possible for greasing. Roll up each omelet and cut in strips when cold. Set aside. Place the strips of pork or beef in a bowl. Put the shrimp and chopped chicken in separate bowls. Shred one of the chiles and reserve it.

SPICY MEAT BALLS

SERVE THESE SPICY LITTLE PATTIES—PERGEDEL DJAWA—WITH EGG NOODLES AND CHILE SAMBAL.

SERVES 4–6

INGREDIENTS
  ¹/₂-inch cube shrimp paste
    (blachan)
  1 large onion, roughly chopped
  1–2 fresh red chiles, seeded
    and chopped
  2 garlic cloves, crushed
  1 tablespoon coriander seeds
  1 teaspoon cumin seeds
  1 pound lean ground beef
  2 teaspoons dark soy sauce
  1 teaspoon dark brown sugar
  juice of 1¹/₂ lemons
  a little beaten egg
  vegetable oil, for shallow frying
  salt and ground black pepper
  chile sambal, to serve
  1 green and 2 fresh red chiles,
    to garnish

1 Wrap the shrimp paste (blachan) in a piece of foil and warm in a frying pan for 5 minutes, turning a few times. Unwrap and put in a food processor.

COOK'S TIP
When processing the shrimp paste (blachan), onion, chiles and garlic, do not process for too long, otherwise the onion will become too wet and spoil the consistency of the meat balls.

2 Add the onion, chiles and garlic to the food processor and process until finely chopped. Set aside. Dry fry the coriander and cumin seeds in a hot frying pan for 1 minute, to release the aroma. Tip the seeds into a mortar and grind with a pestle.

3 Put the meat in a large bowl. Stir in the onion mixture. Add the ground spices, soy sauce, brown sugar, lemon juice and beaten egg. Season to taste.

4 Shape the meat mixture into small, even-size balls, and chill these for 5–10 minutes to firm them up.

5 Heat the oil in a wok or large frying pan and fry the meatballs for 4–5 minutes, turning often, until cooked through and browned. You may have to do this in batches.

6 Drain the meatballs on paper towels, and then pile them on to a warm serving platter or into a large serving bowl. Finely slice the green chile and one of the red chiles and scatter over the meatballs. Garnish with the remaining red chile, if you like. Serve with the Chile Sambal (see below) handed round separately.

VARIATION
Ground beef is traditionally used for this dish, but ground pork, lamb—or even turkey—would also be good.

CHILE SAMBAL

THIS FIERCE CONDIMENT IS BOTTLED AS SAMBAL OELEK, BUT IT IS EASY TO PREPARE AND WILL KEEP FOR SEVERAL WEEKS IN A WELL-SEALED JAR IN THE REFRIGERATOR. USE A STAINLESS-STEEL OR PLASTIC SPOON TO MEASURE; IF SAUCE DRIPS ON YOUR FINGERS, WASH WELL IN SOAPY WATER IMMEDIATELY.

MAKES POUND

INGREDIENTS
  1 pound fresh red chiles, seeded
  2 teaspoons salt

1 Bring a saucepan of water to a boil, add the seeded chiles and cook them for 5–8 minutes.

2 Drain the chiles and then grind them in a food processor, without making the paste too smooth.

3 Scrape into a screw-top glass jar, stir in the salt and cover with a piece of waxed paper or plastic wrap. Screw on the lid and store in the refrigerator. Spoon into small dishes, to serve as an accompaniment, or to use in recipes as suggested.

SWEET AND SOUR SALAD

ACAR BENING MAKES A PERFECT ACCOMPANIMENT TO MANY SPICY DISHES AND CURRIES, WITH ITS CLEAN TASTE AND BRIGHT, JEWEL-LIKE COLORS, AND POMEGRANATE SEEDS, THOUGH NOT TRADITIONAL, MAKE A BEAUTIFUL GARNISH. THIS IS AN ESSENTIAL DISH FOR A BUFFET PARTY.

SERVES 8

INGREDIENTS

  1 small cucumber
  1 onion, thinly sliced
  1 small, ripe pineapple or 15-ounce
    can pineapple rings
  1 green bell pepper, seeded and
    thinly sliced
  3 firm tomatoes, chopped
  2 tablespoons golden sugar
  3–4 tablespoons white wine vinegar
  $^1\!/_2$ cup water
  salt
  seeds of 1–2 pomegranates,
    to garnish

1 Halve the cucumber lengthwise, remove the seeds, slice and spread on a plate with the onion. Sprinkle with salt. After 10 minutes, rinse and dry.

2 If using a fresh pineapple, peel and core it, removing all the eyes, then cut it into bite-size pieces. If using canned pineapple, drain the rings and cut them into small wedges. Place the pineapple in a bowl with the cucumber, onion, green bell pepper and tomatoes.

3 Heat the sugar, vinegar and measured water in a pan, stirring until the sugar has dissolved. Remove the pan from the heat and leave to cool. When cold, add a little salt to taste and pour over the fruit and vegetables. Cover and chill until required. Serve in small bowls, garnished with pomegranate seeds.

VARIATION
To make an Indonesian-style cucumber salad, salt a cucumber as described in the recipe. Make half the dressing and pour it over the cucumber. Add a few chopped scallions. Cover and chill. Serve scattered with toasted sesame seeds.

FRUIT AND RAW VEGETABLE GADO-GADO

A BANANA LEAF, WHICH CAN BE BOUGHT FROM ASIAN MARKETS, CAN BE USED INSTEAD OF THE MIXED SALAD LEAVES TO LINE THE PLATTER FOR A SPECIAL OCCASION.

SERVES 6

INGREDIENTS
½ cucumber
2 pears (not too ripe) or 6-ounce
  wedge of yam bean
1–2 eating apples
juice of ½ lemon
mixed salad leaves
6 small tomatoes, cut in wedges
3 fresh pineapple slices, cored and
  cut in wedges
3 eggs, hard-cooked and shelled
6 ounces egg noodles, cooked, cooled
  and chopped
deep-fried onions, to garnish

For the peanut sauce
2–4 fresh red chiles, seeded
  and ground, or 1 tablespoon
  chile sambal
1¼ cups coconut milk
1¼ cups crunchy peanut butter
1 tablespoon dark soy sauce or dark
  brown sugar
1 teaspoon tamarind pulp, soaked in
  3 tablespoons warm water
coarsely crushed peanuts
salt

2 Simmer gently until the sauce thickens, then stir in the soy sauce or sugar. Strain in the tamarind juice, add salt to taste and stir well. Spoon into a bowl and sprinkle with a few coarsely crushed peanuts.

VARIATION
Quail's eggs can be used instead of normal eggs and look very attractive in this dish. Hard cook for 3 minutes and halve or leave whole.

3 To make the salad, core the cucumber and peel the pears or yam bean. Cut them into matchsticks. Finely shred the apples and sprinkle them with the lemon juice. Spread a bed of lettuce leaves on a flat platter, then pile the fruit and vegetables on top.

4 Add the sliced or quartered hard-cooked eggs, the chopped noodles and the deep-fried onions. Serve at once, with the sauce.

1 Make the peanut sauce. Put the ground chiles or chile sambal in a pan. Pour in the coconut milk, then stir in the peanut butter. Heat gently, stirring, until well blended.

BEEF RENDANG

IN INDONESIA, THIS SPICY DISH IS USUALLY SERVED WITH THE MEAT QUITE DRY; IF YOU PREFER MORE SAUCE, SIMPLY ADD MORE WATER WHEN STIRRING IN THE POTATOES.

SERVES 6–8

INGREDIENTS
2 onions or 5–6 shallots, chopped
4 garlic cloves, chopped
1-inch piece fresh galangal, peeled
  and sliced, or 1 tablespoon
  galangal paste
1-inch piece fresh ginger root, peeled
  and sliced
4–6 fresh red chiles, seeded
  and roughly chopped
lower part only of 1 lemongrass
  stem, sliced
1-inch piece fresh turmeric, peeled
  and sliced, or 1 teaspoon ground
  turmeric
2¼ pounds prime beef in one piece
1 teaspoon coriander seeds, dry fried
1 teaspoon cumin seeds, dry fried
2 kaffir lime leaves, torn into pieces
1¾ cups coconut milk
1¼ cups water
2 tablespoons dark soy sauce
1 teaspoon tamarind pulp, soaked in
  4 tablespoons warm water
8–10 small new potatoes, scrubbed
salt and ground black pepper
deep-fried onions (see below),
  sliced fresh red chiles and
  scallions, to garnish

1 Put the onions or shallots in a food processor. Add the garlic, galangal, ginger, chiles, sliced lemongrass and fresh or ground turmeric. Process to a fine paste or grind in a mortar, using a pestle.

2 Cut the meat into cubes using a large sharp knife, then place the cubes in a bowl.

3 Grind the dry-fried coriander and cumin seeds, then add to the meat with the onion, chile paste and kaffir lime leaves; stir well. Cover and leave in a cool place to marinate while you prepare the other ingredients.

COOK'S TIP
This dish is even better if you can cook it a day or two in advance of serving, which allows the flavors to mellow beautifully. Add the potatoes on reheating and simmer until tender.

4 Pour the coconut milk and water into a wok, then stir in the spiced meat and the soy sauce. Strain the tamarind water and add to the wok. Stir over medium heat until the liquid boils, then simmer gently, half-covered, for 1½ hours.

5 Add the potatoes and simmer for 20–25 minutes, or until meat and potatoes are tender. Add water if liked. Season and serve, garnished with deep-fried onions, chiles and scallions.

DEEP-FRIED ONIONS

KNOWN AS BAWANG GORENG, THESE ARE A TRADITIONAL GARNISH AND ACCOMPANY MANY INDONESIAN DISHES. ORIENTAL STORES SELL THEM READY-PREPARED, BUT IT IS EASY TO MAKE THEM. THE SMALL RED ONIONS SOLD IN ASIAN MARKETS ARE EXCELLENT AS THEY CONTAIN LESS WATER.

MAKES 1 POUND

INGREDIENTS
1 pound onions
vegetable oil, for deep frying

1 Thinly slice the onions with a sharp knife or in a food processor. Spread the slices out in a single layer on paper towels and leave them to dry, in an airy place, for 30 minutes–2 hours.

2 Heat the oil in a deep fryer or wok to 375°F. Fry the onions in batches, until crisp and golden, turning all the time. Drain well on paper towels, cool and store in an airtight container, unless using immediately.

SAMBAL GORENG <u>WITH</u> SHRIMP

SAMBAL GORENG IS AN IMMENSELY USEFUL AND ADAPTABLE SAUCE. HERE IT IS COMBINED WITH SHRIMP AND GREEN BELL PEPPER, BUT YOU COULD ADD FINE STRIPS OF CALF'S LIVER, CHICKEN LIVERS, TOMATOES, GREEN BEANS OR HARD-COOKED EGGS.

<u>SERVES 4–6</u>

INGREDIENTS

   12 ounces peeled cooked shrimp
   1 green bell pepper, seeded and
     thinly sliced
   4 tablespoons tamarind juice
   pinch of sugar
   3 tablespoons coconut milk or cream
   boiled rice, to serve
   lime rind and red onion, to garnish

For the sambal goreng
   1-inch cube shrimp paste (blachan)
   2 onions, roughly chopped
   2 garlic cloves, roughly chopped
   1-inch piece fresh galangal, peeled
     and sliced
   2 teaspoons chile sambal or 2 fresh
     red chiles, seeded and sliced
   1/4 teaspoon salt
   2 tablespoons vegetable oil
   3 tablespoons tomato paste
   2 1/2 cups vegetable stock or water

1 Make the sambal goreng. Grind the shrimp paste (blachan) with the onions and garlic using a mortar and pestle. Alternatively put in a food processor and process to a paste. Add the galangal, chile sambal or sliced chiles and salt. Process or pound to a fine paste.

COOK'S TIP
Store the remaining sauce in the refrigerator for up to 3 days or freeze it for up to 3 months.

2 Heat the oil in a wok or frying pan and fry the paste for 1–2 minutes, without browning, until the mixture gives off a rich aroma. Stir in the tomato paste and the stock or water and cook for 10 minutes. Ladle half the sauce into a bowl and leave to cool. This leftover sauce can be used in another recipe (see Cook's Tip).

3 Add the shrimp and green bell pepper to the remaining sauce. Cook over medium heat for 3–4 minutes, then stir in the tamarind juice, sugar and coconut milk or cream. Spoon into warmed serving bowls and garnish with strips of lime rind and sliced red onion. Serve at once with boiled rice.

VARIATIONS
To make tomato sambal goreng, add 1 pound peeled coarsely chopped tomatoes to the sauce mixture, before stirring in the stock or water.
To make egg sambal goreng, add 3 or 4 chopped hard-cooked eggs, and 2 peeled chopped tomatoes to the sauce.

BAMIE GORENG

THIS FRIED NOODLE DISH IS WONDERFULLY ACCOMMODATING. YOU CAN ADD OTHER VEGETABLES,
SUCH AS MUSHROOMS, TINY PIECES OF CHAYOTE, BROCCOLI, LEEKS OR BEANSPROUTS. USE WHATEVER
IS TO HAND, BEARING IN MIND THE NEED FOR A BALANCE OF COLORS, FLAVORS AND TEXTURES.

SERVES 6–8

INGREDIENTS

1 pound dried egg noodles
2 eggs
2 tablespoons butter
6 tablespoons vegetable oil
1 skinless boneless chicken
  breast, sliced
4 ounces pork tenderloin, sliced
4 ounces calf's liver, finely
  sliced (optional)
2 garlic cloves, crushed
4 ounces peeled cooked shrimp
4 ounces pak-choi
2 celery sticks, finely sliced
4 scallions, shredded
about 4 tablespoons chicken stock
dark soy sauce and light soy sauce
salt and ground black pepper
deep-fried onions and shredded
  scallions, to garnish (optional)

1 Bring a pan of lightly salted water to a boil, add the noodles and cook them for 3–4 minutes. Drain, rinse under cold water and drain again. Set aside.

2 Put the eggs in a bowl, beat and add salt and pepper to taste. Heat the butter with 1 teaspoon oil in a small pan, add the eggs and stir over low heat until scrambled but still quite moist. Set aside.

3 Heat the remaining oil in a wok and fry the chicken, pork and liver (if using) with the garlic for 2–3 minutes, until the meat has changed color. Add the shrimp, pak-choi, sliced celery and shredded scallions and toss to mix.

4 Add the noodles and toss over the heat until the shrimp and noodles are heated through and the greens are lightly cooked. Add enough stock just to moisten and season with dark and light soy sauce to taste. Finally, add the scrambled eggs and toss to mix. Spoon on to a warmed serving platter or into individual dishes and serve at once, garnished with onions.

COOK'S TIP
Pak-choi is similar to Swiss chard and is available from specialist stores and large supermarkets.

BANANA FRITTERS

KNOWN AS PISANG GORENG, *THESE DELICIOUS DEEP-FRIED BANANAS SHOULD BE COOKED AT THE LAST MINUTE, SO THAT THE BATTER IS CRISP AND THE BANANA INSIDE IS SOFT AND WARM.*

SERVES 8

INGREDIENTS
    1 cup self-rising flour
    1/4 cup rice flour
    1/2 teaspoon salt
    scant 1 cup water
    finely grated lime rind (optional)
    8 baby bananas
    vegetable oil, for deep frying
    strips of lime rind, to garnish
    superfine sugar and lime wedges,
      to serve

COOK'S TIP
Tiny bananas are available from some Asian markets and many larger supermarkets, alternatively use small bananas and cut in half lengthwise and then in half again.

1 Sift together the self-rising flour, rice flour and salt into a bowl. Add just enough water to make a smooth, coating batter. Mix well, then add the lime rind, if using.

VARIATION
Instead of lime, add finely grated orange rind to the batter.

2 Heat the oil in a deep fryer or wok to 375°F. Meanwhile, peel the bananas. Dip them into the batter two or three times until well coated, then deep fry until crisp and golden. Drain on paper towels. Serve hot, dredged with the sugar and garnished with strips of lime. Offer the lime wedges for squeezing over the bananas.

BLACK GLUTINOUS RICE PUDDING

THIS VERY UNUSUAL RICE PUDDING, KNOWN AS BUBOR PULOT HITAM, *IS FLAVORED WITH BRUISED FRESH GINGER ROOT AND IS QUITE DELICIOUS SERVED WITH COCONUT MILK OR CREAM. WHEN COOKED, BLACK RICE STILL RETAINS ITS HUSK AND HAS A LOVELY NUTTY TEXTURE.*

SERVES 6

INGREDIENTS
    2/3 cup black glutinous rice
    2 cups water
    1/2-inch piece fresh ginger root,
      peeled and bruised
    1/3 cup soft dark brown sugar
    1/4 cup superfine sugar
    1 1/4 cups coconut milk or coconut
      cream, to serve

COOK'S TIP
Canned coconut milk and cream is available, but it is easy to make at home. Blend 2 2/3 cups shredded coconut with 1 3/4 cups boiling water in a food processor for 30 seconds, then cool slightly. Tip into a cheesecloth-lined strainer and twist the cheesecloth to extract as much liquid as possible.

1 Put the black glutinous rice in a strainer and rinse it well under plenty of cold running water. Drain the rice and put it in a large pan, along with the water. Bring the water to a boil and stir it as it heats, in order to prevent the rice from settling on the base of the pan. Cover the pan and cook over very low heat for about 30 minutes.

2 Add the ginger and both types of sugar to the pan. Cook for 15 minutes more, adding a little more water if necessary, until the rice is cooked and porridge-like.

3 Remove the ginger and pour into individual bowls. Serve warm, topped with coconut milk or coconut cream.

VIETNAM AND THE PHILIPPINES

Vietnam borders China, Laos and Cambodia, in the heart of South-east Asia, and it is not surprising that its cuisine has much in common with its neighbors. In the north nearest China, stir-fries and mild curries are popular; further south there is a strong French influence. Rice, the staple, is bolstered by baguettes. Pâtés, herb salads, rare beef and casseroles feature alongside traditional dishes served with the pungent fish sauce, nuoc mam. In the Philippines, dishes such as Puchero, Escabeche and Adobo of Chicken owe much to their Spanish origins, but have their own distinct flavor.

VIETNAMESE RICE PAPER ROLLS

RICE PAPER WRAPPERS COME IN SMALL AND LARGE ROUNDS AND CAN BE BOUGHT FROM ASIAN MARKETS. THEY SOFTEN WHEN BRUSHED WITH WARM WATER, BUT THEY ARE VERY BRITTLE SO MUST BE HANDLED WITH CARE. CASUALTIES CAN BE USED FOR PATCHING OTHER PAPERS.

SERVES 8

INGREDIENTS
    8 cups water
    1 small onion, sliced
    a few fresh cilantro stems
    2 tablespoons fish sauce
    8-ounce piece pork belly, boned
      and rind removed
    2 ounces fine rice vermicelli
    4 cups beansprouts, rinsed and
      drained
    8 crisp lettuce leaves, halved
    fresh mint and cilantro leaves
    6 ounces peeled cooked shrimp,
      thawed if frozen
    16 large rice papers
    ground black pepper

For the black bean sauce
    1–2 tablespoons peanut oil
    2 garlic cloves, crushed
    1 fresh red chile, seeded and sliced
    4–5 tablespoons canned black
      salted beans
    2 tablespoons fish sauce
    1 teaspoon rice vinegar
    2–3 teaspoons light brown sugar
    1 tablespoon crunchy peanut butter
    1 tablespoon sesame seeds, dry fried
    1 teaspoon sesame oil
    6 tablespoons fish, pork or
      chicken stock

1 Mix the water, onion slices, cilantro stems and fish sauce in a large pan. Bring to a boil. Add the pork and boil for 20–30 minutes, turning the pork from time to time until it is tender when tested with a skewer. Lift the pork from the pan, leave to cool, then slice it into thin strips. (Strain the stock and reserve it for making soup.)

2 Make the sauce. Heat the peanut oil in a frying pan and fry the garlic and chile for 1 minute. Stir in all the remaining ingredients, mix well, then transfer to a food processor and process briefly. Pour into a serving bowl and leave to cool.

3 Soak the rice vermicelli in warm water until softened. Drain well, then snip into neat lengths. Bring a pan of water to a boil and add the vermicelli. As soon as the water boils again, after about 1 minute, drain the noodles, rinse them under cold water, then drain them again. Put them in a serving bowl. Put the beansprouts in a separate dish, and arrange the lettuce and herb leaves on a platter. Put the shrimp in a bowl.

4 When almost ready to serve place the rice papers two at a time on a dish towel and brush both sides with warm water to soften them.

5 Transfer two rice papers very carefully to each of eight individual serving plates. Each guest places a piece of lettuce on a rice paper wrapper at the end closest to them, topping it with some of the noodles and beansprouts, a few mint or cilantro leaves and some strips of pork.

6 Roll up one turn and then place a few shrimp on the open part of the wrapper. Continue rolling to make a neat parcel. The roll can be cut in half, if preferred, then it is dipped in the black bean sauce before being eaten. The second wrapper is filled and eaten in the same way.

CHA GIO AND NUOC CHAM

CHINESE SPRING ROLL WRAPPERS ARE USED HERE INSTEAD OF THE RICE PAPERS TRADITIONALLY USED IN VIETNAM. CHA GIO IS AN IMMENSELY POPULAR SNACK—THE VEGETABLE CONTENT OF THE FILLING CAN BE VARIED AS LONG AS THE FLAVORS ARE COMPLEMENTARY.

MAKES 15

INGREDIENTS
   1 ounce cellophane noodles soaked
      for 10 minutes in hot water to cover
   6–8 dried wood ears, soaked for
      30 minutes in warm water to cover
   8 ounces ground pork
   8 ounces fresh or canned crab meat
   4 scallions, trimmed and
      finely chopped
   1 teaspoon fish sauce
   flour and water paste, to seal
   9-ounce packet spring roll wrappers
   vegetable oil, for deep frying
   salt and ground black pepper

For the *nuoc cham* sauce
   2 fresh red chiles, seeded and
      pounded to a paste
   2 garlic cloves, crushed
   1 tablespoon sugar
   3 tablespoons fish sauce
   juice of 1 lime or 1/2 lemon

1 Make the *nuoc cham* sauce by mixing the chiles, garlic, sugar and fish sauce in a bowl and stirring in lime or lemon juice to taste. Drain the noodles and snip into 1-inch lengths. Drain the wood ears, trim away any rough stems and slice the wood ears finely.

COOK'S TIP
Serve the rolls Vietnamese-style by wrapping each roll in a lettuce leaf together with a few sprigs of fresh mint and cilantro and a stick of cucumber.

2 Mix the noodles and the wood ears with the pork and set aside. Remove any cartilage from the crab meat and add to the pork mixture with the scallions and fish sauce. Season to taste, mixing well.

3 Place a spring roll wrapper in front of you, diamond-fashion. Spoon some mixture just below the center, fold over the nearest point and roll once.

4 Fold in the sides to enclose, then brush the edges with flour paste and roll up to seal. Repeat with the remaining wrappers and filling.

5 Heat the oil in a wok or deep fryer to 375°F. Deep fry the rolls in batches for 8–10 minutes or until they are cooked through. Drain them well on paper towels and serve hot. To eat, dip the rolls in the *nuoc cham* sauce

CHICKEN, VEGETABLE AND CHILE SALAD

GOI TOM, A TYPICAL VIETNAMESE SALAD, IS FULL OF SURPRISING TEXTURES AND FLAVORS. SERVE AS A LIGHT LUNCH DISH OR FOR SUPPER WITH CRUSTY FRENCH BREAD.

SERVES 4

INGREDIENTS

  8 ounces Chinese leaves
  2 carrots, cut in matchsticks
  1/2 cucumber, cut in matchsticks
  salt
  2 fresh red chiles, seeded and cut
    into thin strips
  1 small onion, sliced into fine rings
  4 pickled gherkins, sliced, plus
    3 tablespoons of the liquid
  1/2 cup peanuts, lightly ground
  8 ounces cooked chicken,
    finely sliced
  1 garlic clove, crushed
  1 teaspoon sugar
  2 tablespoons cider or white vinegar

1 Finely slice the Chinese leaves and set aside with the carrot matchsticks. Sprinkle the cucumber matchsticks with salt and set aside for 15 minutes.

COOK'S TIP
Add a little more cider or white wine vinegar to the dressing if a sharper taste is preferred.

2 Mix together the chiles and onion rings and then add the sliced gherkins and peanuts. Tip the salted cucumber into a strainer, rinse well and pat dry.

3 Put all the vegetables into a salad bowl and add the chile mixture and chicken. Mix the gherkin liquid with the garlic, sugar and vinegar. Pour over the salad and toss lightly, then serve immediately.

ASPARAGUS AND CRAB SOUP

ASPARAGUS OWES ITS POPULARITY TO THE FRENCH INFLUENCE ON VIETNAMESE COOKING. IT IS OFTEN COMBINED WITH CRAB AND MADE INTO A DELICIOUS SOUP, CAHN CUA.

SERVES 4–6

INGREDIENTS

  12 ounces asparagus spears, trimmed
    and halved
  3 3/4 cups chicken stock, preferably
    homemade
  2–3 tablespoons sunflower oil
  6 shallots, chopped
  4 ounces crab meat, fresh or
    canned, chopped
  1 tablespoon cornstarch, mixed to a
    paste with water
  2 tablespoons fish sauce
  1 egg, lightly beaten
  snipped chives, plus extra chives
    to garnish
  salt and ground black pepper to taste

1 Cook the asparagus spears in the chicken stock for 5–6 minutes until tender. Drain, reserving the stock.

2 Heat the oil in a large wok or frying pan and stir-fry the chopped shallots for 2 minutes, without allowing them to brown. Add the asparagus spears, chopped crab meat and chicken stock.

3 Bring the mixture to a boil and cook for 3 minutes, then remove the wok or pan from the heat and spoon some of the liquid into the cornstarch mixture. Return this to the wok or pan and stir until the soup begins to thicken slightly.

4 Stir in the fish sauce, with salt and pepper to taste, then pour the beaten egg into the soup, stirring briskly so that the egg forms threads. Finally, stir the snipped chives into the soup and serve it immediately, garnished with chives.

COOK'S TIP
If fresh asparagus isn't available, use 12-ounce can asparagus. Drain and halve the spears.

FILIPINO SHRIMP FRITTERS

Ukoy are a favorite snack or starter. Unusually, they are first shallow fried, then deep fried. They are best eaten fresh from the pan, first dipped in the piquant sauce.

4 Peel and grate the sweet potato using the large holes on a grater, and add it to the batter, then stir in the crushed garlic and the drained beansprouts.

5 Pour the oil for shallow frying into a large frying pan. It should be about ¼-inch deep. Pour more oil into a wok for deep frying. Heat the oil in the frying pan. Taking a generous spoonful of the batter, drop it carefully into the frying pan so that it forms a fritter, about the size of a large drop scone.

6 Make more fritters in the same way. As soon as the fritters have set, top each one with a single shrimp and a few chopped scallions. Continue to cook over medium heat for 1 minute, then remove with a fish slice.

7 Heat the oil in the wok to 375°F and deep fry the shrimp fritters in batches until they are crisp and golden brown. Drain the fritters on paper towels and then arrange on a serving plate or platter. Offer a bowl of the sauce for dipping.

SERVES 2–4

INGREDIENTS

16 raw shrimp in the shell
2 cups all-purpose flour
1 teaspoon baking powder
½ teaspoon salt
1 egg, beaten
1 small sweet potato
1 garlic clove, crushed
2 cups beansprouts, soaked in cold water and well drained
vegetable oil, for shallow and deep frying
4 scallions, chopped

For the dipping sauce
1 garlic clove, sliced
3 tablespoons rice or wine vinegar
1–2 tablespoons water
salt, to taste
6–8 tiny fresh red chiles

1 Mix together all the ingredients for the dipping sauce and divide between two small bowls.

2 Put the whole shrimp in a pan with water to cover. Bring to a boil, then simmer for 4–5 minutes or until the shrimp are pink and tender. Lift the shrimp from the pan with a slotted spoon. Discard the heads and the body shell, but leave the tails on. Strain and reserve the cooking liquid. Allow to cool.

3 Sift the flour, baking powder and salt into a bowl. Add the beaten egg and about 1¼ cups of the shrimp stock to make a batter that has the consistency of thick cream.

VARIATION
Use cooked jumbo shrimp if you prefer. In this case, make the batter using fish stock or chicken stock.

ESCABECHE

THIS PICKLED FISH DISH IS EATEN WHEREVER THERE ARE—OR HAVE BEEN—SPANISH SETTLERS. HERE IT HAS BEEN MODIFIED IN ORDER TO REFLECT THE CHINESE INFLUENCE ON FILIPINO CUISINE.

SERVES 6

INGREDIENTS

1½–2 pounds white fish fillets, such as sole or plaice
3–4 tablespoons seasoned all-purpose flour
vegetable oil, for shallow frying

For the sauce
1-inch piece fresh ginger root, peeled and thinly sliced
2–3 garlic cloves, crushed
1 onion, cut into thin rings
2 tablespoons vegetable oil
½ large green bell pepper, seeded and cut in small neat squares
½ large red bell pepper, seeded and cut in small neat squares
1 carrot, cut into matchsticks
1½ tablespoons cornstarch
scant 2 cups water
3–4 tablespoons herb or cider vinegar
1 tablespoon light brown sugar
1–2 teaspoons fish sauce
salt and ground black pepper
1 small chile, seeded and sliced and scallions, finely shredded, to garnish (optional)
boiled rice, to serve

1 Wipe the fish fillets and leave them whole, or cut into serving portions, if you like. Pat dry on paper towels then dust lightly with seasoned flour.

2 Heat oil for shallow frying in a frying pan and fry the fish in batches until golden and almost cooked. Transfer to a baking dish and keep warm.

3 Make the sauce in a wok or large frying pan. Fry the ginger, garlic and onion in the oil for 5 minutes, until the onion is softened but not browned.

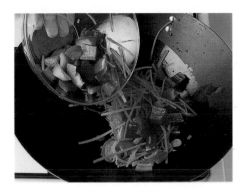

4 Add the pepper squares and carrot strips and stir-fry for 1 minute.

5 Put the cornstarch in a small bowl and add a little of the water to make a paste. Stir in the remaining water, the vinegar and the sugar. Pour the cornstarch mixture over the vegetables in the wok and stir until the sauce boils and thickens a little. Season with fish sauce and salt and pepper if needed.

6 Add the fish to the sauce and reheat briefly without stirring. Transfer to a warmed serving platter and garnish with chile and scallions, if liked. Serve with boiled rice.

COOK'S TIP
Red snapper or small sea bass could be used for this recipe, in which case ask your fishmonger to cut them into fillets.

ADOBO OF CHICKEN AND PORK

FOUR INGREDIENTS ARE ESSENTIAL IN AN ADOBO, ONE OF THE BEST-LOVED RECIPES IN THE FILIPINO REPERTOIRE. THEY ARE VINEGAR, GARLIC, PEPPERCORNS AND BAY LEAVES.

SERVES 4

INGREDIENTS

   1 chicken, about 3 pounds, or
     4 chicken quarters
   12 ounces pork leg steaks (with fat)
   2 teaspoons sugar
   4 tablespoons sunflower oil
   5 tablespoons wine or cider vinegar
   4 plump garlic cloves, crushed
   $\frac{1}{2}$ teaspoon black peppercorns,
     crushed lightly
   1 tablespoon light soy sauce
   4 bay leaves
   $\frac{1}{2}$ teaspoon annatto seeds, soaked in
     2 tablespoons boiling water, or
     $\frac{1}{2}$ teaspoon ground turmeric
   salt

For the plantain chips
   1–2 large plantains and/or
     1 sweet potato
   vegetable oil, for deep frying

1 Wipe the chicken and cut into eight even-size pieces, or halve the chicken quarters, if using. Cut the pork into neat pieces. Spread out all the meat on a board, sprinkle lightly with sugar and set aside.

2 Heat the oil in a wok or large frying pan and fry the chicken and pork pieces, in batches if necessary, until they are golden on both sides.

3 Add the vinegar, garlic, peppercorns, soy sauce and bay leaves and stir well.

4 Strain the annatto seed liquid and stir it into the pan or stir in the turmeric. Add salt to taste. Bring to a boil, cover, lower the heat and simmer for 30–35 minutes. Remove the lid and simmer for 10 minutes more.

5 Meanwhile, prepare the plaintain chips. Heat the oil in a deep fryer to 390°F. Peel the plantains or sweet potato (or both), if liked, and slice them into rounds or chips. Deep fry them, in batches if necessary, until cooked but not brown. Drain on paper towels. When ready to serve, reheat the oil and fry the plantains or sweet potato until crisp—it will only take a few seconds. Drain. Spoon the adobo into a serving dish and serve with the chips.

COOK'S TIP
Sprinkling the chicken lightly with sugar turns the skin beautifully brown when fried, but do not have the oil too hot to begin with or they will over-brown.

SINIGANG

MANY FILIPINOS WOULD CONSIDER THIS SOUR SOUP-LIKE STEW TO BE THEIR NATIONAL DISH. IT IS ALWAYS SERVED WITH NOODLES OR RICE, AND FISH—SHRIMP OR THIN SLIVERS OF FISH FILLET—IS OFTEN ADDED FOR GOOD MEASURE.

3 Pour the prepared fish stock into a large pan and add the diced mooli. Cook the mooli for 5 minutes, then add the beans and continue to cook for 3–5 minutes more.

SERVES 4–6

INGREDIENTS

1 tablespoon tamarind pulp
²/₃ cup warm water
2 tomatoes
4 ounces spinach or Chinese kangkong leaves
4 ounces peeled cooked jumbo shrimp, thawed if frozen
5 cups prepared fish stock (see Cook's Tip)
¹/₂ mooli, peeled and finely diced
4 ounces green beans, cut into ¹/₂-inch lengths
8-ounce piece of cod or haddock fillet, skinned and cut into strips
fish sauce, to taste
squeeze of lemon juice, to taste
salt and ground black pepper
boiled rice or noodles, to serve

1 Put the tamarind pulp in a bowl and pour over the warm water. Set aside while you peel and chop the tomatoes, discarding the seeds. Strip the spinach or kangkong leaves from the stems and tear into small pieces.

2 Remove the heads and shells from the shrimp, leaving the tails intact.

4 Add the fish strips, tomato and spinach. Strain in the tamarind juice and cook for 2 minutes. Stir in the shrimp and cook for 1–2 minutes to heat. Season with salt and pepper and add a little fish sauce and lemon juice to taste. Transfer to individual serving bowls and serve immediately, with rice or noodles.

COOK'S TIP

A good fish stock is essential for Sinigang. Ask your fishmonger for about 1¹/₂ pounds fish bones. Wash them, then place in a large pan with 8 cups water. Add half a peeled onion, a piece of bruised peeled ginger root, and a little salt and pepper. Bring to a boil, skim, then simmer for 20 minutes. Cool slightly, then strain. Freeze unused fish stock.

PUCHERO

A FILIPINO POT-AU-FEU WITH SPANISH CONNECTIONS. SOMETIMES IT IS SERVED AS TWO COURSES, FIRST SOUP, THEN MEAT AND VEGETABLES WITH RICE, BUT IT CAN HAPPILY BE SERVED AS IS, ON RICE IN A WIDE SOUP BOWL. EITHER WAY IT IS VERY SATISFYING AND A SIESTA AFTERWARDS IS RECOMMENDED.

SERVES 6–8

INGREDIENTS

generous 1 cup chick-peas, soaked
  overnight in water to cover
3 pounds chicken, cut into 8 pieces
12 ounces pork belly, rinded and
  cubed, or pork tenderloin, cubed
2 chorizo sausages, thickly sliced
2 onions, chopped
10 cups water
4 tablespoons vegetable oil
2 garlic cloves, crushed
3 large tomatoes, peeled, seeded
  and chopped
1 tablespoon tomato paste
1–2 sweet potatoes, cut into
  ½-inch cubes
2 plantains, sliced (optional)
salt and ground black pepper
chives or chopped scallions,
  to garnish
½ head Chinese leaves, shredded,
  and boiled rice, to serve

For the eggplant sauce
1 large eggplant
3 garlic cloves, crushed
4–6 tablespoons wine or
  cider vinegar

1 Drain the chick-peas and put them in a large saucepan. Cover with water, bring to a boil and boil rapidly for 10 minutes. Reduce the heat and simmer for 30 minutes until the chick-peas are half tender. Drain.

2 Put the chicken pieces, pork, sausage and half of the onions in a large pan. Add the chick-peas and pour in the water. Bring to a boil and lower the heat, cover and simmer for 1 hour or until the meat is just tender when tested with a skewer.

3 Meanwhile, make the eggplant sauce. Preheat the oven to 400°F. Prick the eggplant in several places, then place it on a baking sheet and bake for 30 minutes or until very soft.

4 Cool slightly, then peel away the eggplant skin and scrape the flesh into a bowl. Stir in the crushed garlic, season to taste and add just enough vinegar to sharpen the sauce, which should be quite piquant. Set aside.

5 Heat the oil in a frying pan and fry the remaining onion and garlic for 5 minutes, until soft but not brown. Stir in the tomatoes and tomato paste and cook for 2 minutes, then add this mixture to a large pan with the diced sweet potato. Add the plantains, if using. Cook over gentle heat for about 20 minutes until the sweet potato is thoroughly cooked. Add the Chinese leaves for the last minute or two.

6 Spoon the thick meat soup into a soup tureen, and put the vegetables in a separate serving bowl. Garnish both with whole or chopped chives or scallions and serve with boiled rice and the eggplant sauce.

ENSAIMADAS

THESE SWEET BREAD ROLLS ARE A POPULAR SNACK IN THE PHILIPPINES AND COME WITH VARIOUS FILLINGS, SEVERAL OF THEM SAVORY. THIS VERSION INCLUDES CHEESE.

2 Cream the softened butter with the remaining sugar in a large bowl. When it is fluffy, beat in the egg yolks and a little of the sifted flour. Gradually stir in the remaining flour with the yeast mixture and enough milk to form a soft but not sticky dough. Transfer to an oiled plastic bag. Close the bag loosely, leaving plenty of room for the dough to rise. Leave in a warm place for about 1 hour, until the dough doubles in bulk.

3 On a lightly floured surface, punch down the dough, then roll it out into a large rectangle. Brush the surface with half the melted butter, scatter with the cheese, then roll up from a long side like a Swiss roll.

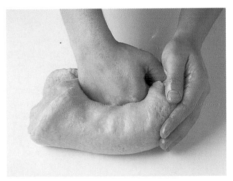

4 Knead the dough thoroughly to distribute the cheese, then divide the dough into 10–12 pieces.

5 Roll each piece of dough into a thin rope, about 15 inches long. On greased baking sheets, coil each rope into a loose spiral, spacing them well apart. Tuck the loose ends under to seal. Leave to rise, in a warm place, for about 45 minutes or until doubled in size. Meanwhile, preheat the oven to 425°F.

MAKES 10–12

INGREDIENTS
  2 tablespoons superfine sugar, plus extra for sprinkling
  2/3 cup warm water
  1 tablespoon dried yeast
  4 cups white bread flour
  1 teaspoon salt
  1/2 cup butter, softened, plus 2 tablespoons melted butter for the filling
  4 egg yolks
  6–8 tablespoons warm milk
  1 cup grated Cheddar cheese (or similar well-flavored hard cheese)

1 Dissolve 1 teaspoon of the sugar in the warm water, then sprinkle in the dried yeast. Stir, then set aside for 10 minutes or until frothy. Sift the flour and salt into a large bowl.

6 Bake the ensaimadas in the oven for 15–20 minutes, until golden and cooked through. Remove from the oven, then immediately brush with the remaining melted butter and sprinkle with caster sugar. Serve warm.

CHURROS

THESE IRRESISTIBLE FRITTERS, SERVED AT EVERY OPPORTUNITY WITH HOT CHOCOLATE OR COFFEE, CAME TO THE PHILIPPINES WITH THE SPANISH WHO WERE KEEN TO KEEP MEMORIES OF HOME ALIVE.

MAKES ABOUT 24

INGREDIENTS
   1 cup water
   1 tablespoon olive oil
   1 tablespoon sugar, plus extra
     for sprinkling
   ½ teaspoon salt
   1½ cups all-purpose flour
   1 large egg
   sunflower oil, for deep frying
   superfine sugar, for sprinkling

COOK'S TIP
If you don't have a piping bag, you could fry teaspoons of mixture in the same way. Don't try to fry too many churros at a time as they swell a little during cooking.

1 Mix the water, oil, sugar and salt in a large pan and bring to a boil. Remove from the heat, and then sift in the flour. Beat well with a wooden spoon until smooth.

2 Beat in the egg to make a smooth, glossy mixture with a piping consistency. Spoon into a pastry bag fitted with a large star nozzle.

3 Heat the oil in a wok or deep fryer to 375°F. Pipe loops of the mixture, two at a time, into the hot oil. Cook the loops for 3–4 minutes till they are golden. Lift out the churros with a slotted spoon and drain them on paper towels. Dredge them with sugar and serve warm.

LECHE FLAN

SERVE THIS DELICIOUS DESSERT HOT OR COLD WITH WHIPPED CREAM. THE USE OF EVAPORATED MILK REFLECTS THE FIFTY YEARS OF AMERICAN PRESENCE IN THE PHILIPPINES.

SERVES 8

INGREDIENTS
   5 large eggs
   2 tablespoons sugar
   few drops vanilla extract
   1¾ cups evaporated milk
   1¼ cups milk
   1 teaspoon finely grated lime rind
   strips of lime rind, to decorate

For the caramel
   1 cup sugar
   ½ cup water

1 Make the caramel. Put the sugar and water in a heavy-based pan. Stir to dissolve the sugar, then boil without stirring until golden. Quickly pour into eight ramekins, rotating them to coat the sides. Set aside to set.

2 Preheat the oven to 300°F. Beat the eggs, sugar and vanilla essence in a bowl. Mix the evaporated milk and fresh milk in a pan. Heat to just below boiling point, then pour on to the egg mixture, stirring all the time. Strain the custard mixture into a pitcher, add the grated lime rind and cool. Pour into the caramel-coated ramekins.

3 Place the ramekins in a roasting pan and pour in enough warm water to come halfway up the sides of the dishes.

4 Transfer the roasting pan to the oven and cook the custards for 35–45 minutes or until they just shimmer when the ramekins are gently shaken. Serve the custards in their ramekin dishes or by inverting on to serving plates, in which case break the caramel and use as decoration. The custards can be served warm or cold, decorated with strips of lime rind.

COOK'S TIPS
Make extra caramel, if liked, for the decoration. Pour on to lightly oiled foil and let set, then crush with a rolling pin.

JAPAN AND KOREA

Japanese food is unique. The 200 year ban on foreigners from 1640 meant that food in Japan remained true to its origins and exquisitely refined. Artistry is evident in even the simplest dish. Eating out is the norm, and restaurants specialize in dishes such as Sushi, Sukiyaki, Sashimi or Tempura. Korean food features seven basic flavors—garlic, ginger, pepper, soy sauce, scallions, sesame oil and toasted sesame seeds.

SASHIMI

THIS JAPANESE SPECIALITY—SLICED RAW FISH—EMPLOYS THE CUTTING TECHNIQUE KNOWN AS HIRA ZUKURI. THE PERFECTLY CUT FISH CAN BE ARRANGED IN MANY ATTRACTIVE WAYS AND IS THEN SERVED WITH WASABI—JAPANESE HORSERADISH—AND SOY SAUCE.

<u>SERVES 4</u>

INGREDIENTS
   2 fresh salmon fillets, skinned and
      any stray bones removed, total
      weight about 14 ounces
   Japanese soy sauce and wasabi
      paste, to serve

For the garnish
   2 ounces mooli, peeled
   shiso leaves

1 Put the salmon fillets in a freezer for 10 minutes to make them easier to cut, then lay them skinned side up with the thick end to your right and away from you. Use a long sharp knife and tilt it to the left. Slice carefully towards you, starting the cut from the point of the knife, then slide the slice away from the fillet, to the right. Always slice from the far side towards you.

2 Finely shred or grate the mooli and place in a bowl of cold water. Leave for 5 minutes, then drain well.

3 Arrange the salmon in an attractive way on a serving platter, or divide the salmon among four serving plates.

4 Give guests their own platter, together with a garnish of mooli and shiso leaves. The fish is eaten dipped in soy sauce and wasabi paste.

COOK'S TIP
Salmon and tuna are among the most popular choices for sashimi, although almost any type of fish can be used. If you are making sashimi for the first time, choose salmon or tuna and make sure you buy from a reputable fishmonger where you can be sure the fish is absolutely fresh.

YAKITORI CHICKEN

THESE ARE JAPANESE-STYLE KEBABS. THEY ARE EASY TO EAT AND IDEAL FOR BARBECUES OR PARTIES.
MAKE EXTRA YAKITORI SAUCE IF YOU WOULD LIKE TO SERVE IT WITH THE KEBABS.

SERVES 4

INGREDIENTS
   6 boneless chicken thighs
   bunch of scallions
   shichimi (seven-flavor spice), to serve
     (optional)

For the yakitori sauce
   ²/₃ cup Japanese soy sauce
   scant ¹/₂ cup sugar
   1¹/₂ tablespoons sake or dry
     white wine
   1 tablespoon all-purpose flour

3 Cut the scallions into 1¹/₄-inch pieces. Preheat the broiler or light the barbecue.

4 Thread the chicken and scallions alternately on to the drained skewers. Broil under medium heat or cook on the barbecue, brushing generously several times with the sauce. Allow 5–10 minutes, until the chicken is cooked but still moist.

5 Serve with a little extra yakitori sauce, offering shichimi (seven-flavor spice) with the kebabs if available.

COOK'S TIP
Paprika can be used instead of shichimi, if that is difficult to obtain.

1 Soak 12 bamboo skewers in water for at least 30 minutes to prevent them from scorching under the broiler. Make the sauce. Stir the soy sauce, sugar and sake or wine into the flour in a small saucepan and bring to a boil, stirring. Lower the heat and simmer the mixture for 10 minutes, until the sauce is reduced by a third. Set aside.

2 Cut each chicken thigh into bite-size pieces and set aside.

ROLLED OMELET

THIS IS A FIRMLY SET, ROLLED OMELET, CUT INTO NEAT PIECES AND SERVED COLD. THE TEXTURE SHOULD BE SMOOTH AND SOFT, NOT LEATHERY, AND THE FLAVOR IS SWEET-SAVORY. PICKLED GINGER, SOMETIMES CALLED GARI, MAKES AN ATTRACTIVE GARNISH.

SERVES 4

INGREDIENTS
  8 eggs
  4 tablespoons sugar
  4 teaspoons Japanese soy sauce,
    plus extra, to serve
  6 tablespoons sake or dry white wine
  vegetable oil, for cooking
  wasabi and pickled ginger, to garnish

COOK'S TIP
Wasabi, which can be bought from Asian stores, is a very hot and peppery, bright green paste. Use it sparingly.

1 Put the eggs in a large bowl and stir them together, using a pair of chopsticks and a cutting action.

2 Mix the sugar with the soy sauce and sake or wine in a small bowl. Lightly stir this mixture into the eggs. Pour half the mixture into another bowl.

3 Heat a little oil in a frying pan, then wipe off the excess. Pour a quarter of the mixture from one bowl into the pan, tilting the pan to coat it thinly. When the edge has set, but the middle is moist, roll up the omelet towards you.

4 Moisten a paper towel with oil and grease the empty side of the pan. Pour a third of the remaining egg into the pan. Lift the rolled egg up with your chopsticks and let the raw egg run underneath it. When the edge has set, roll up in the opposite direction, tilting the pan away from you.

5 Slide the roll towards you, grease the pan and pour in half the remaining mixture, letting the egg run under. When set, insert chopsticks in the side of the rolled omelet, then flip over towards the opposite side. Cook the remainder in the same way. Slide the roll so that its join is underneath. Cook for 10 seconds.

6 Slide the roll out on to a bamboo mat and roll up tightly, then press neatly into a rectangular shape. Leave to cool. Cook the second batch in the same way. Slice the cold omelets into 1-inch pieces, arrange on a platter and garnish with a little wasabi and with a pickled ginger flower. Serve with soy sauce.

FIVE-FLAVOR NOODLES

THE JAPANESE NAME FOR THIS DISH IS GOMOKU YAKISOBA, *MEANING FIVE DIFFERENT INGREDIENTS; HOWEVER, YOU CAN ADD AS MANY DIFFERENT INGREDIENTS AS YOU WISH TO MAKE AN EXCITING AND TASTY NOODLE STIR-FRY.*

SERVES 4

INGREDIENTS
11 ounces dried Chinese thin egg
   noodles or 1¼ pounds fresh yakisoba noodles
7 ounces lean boneless pork,
   thinly sliced
4½ teaspoons sunflower oil
¼ ounce grated fresh ginger root
1 garlic clove, crushed
7 ounces green cabbage, roughly
   chopped
2 cups beansprouts
1 green bell pepper, seeded and cut
   into fine strips
1 red bell pepper, seeded and cut
   into fine strips
salt and ground black pepper
4 teaspoons ao-nori seaweed, to
   garnish (optional)

For the seasoning mix
4 tablespoons Worcestershire sauce
1 tablespoon Japanese soy sauce
1 tablespoon oyster sauce
1 tablespoon sugar
½ teaspoon salt
ground white pepper

1 Cook the noodles according to the instructions on the packet. Drain well and set aside.

2 Cut the pork into 1¼–1½-inch strips and season with salt and pepper.

3 Heat 1½ teaspoons of the oil in a large wok or frying pan. Stir-fry the pork until just cooked, then remove it from the pan.

4 Wipe the wok with paper towels, and heat the remaining oil in it. Add the ginger, garlic and cabbage and stir-fry for 1 minute.

5 Add the beansprouts, stir until softened, then add the peppers and stir-fry for 1 minute more.

6 Return the pork to the pan and add the noodles. Stir in all the ingredients for the seasoning mix and stir-fry for 2–3 minutes. Serve immediately, sprinkled with ao-nori seaweed (if using).

CHICKEN AND EGG WITH RICE

OYAKO-DON, *THE JAPANESE NAME FOR THIS DISH MEANS PARENT* (OYA), *CHILD* (KO) *AND BOWL* (DON); *IT IS SO CALLED BECAUSE IT USES BOTH CHICKEN MEAT AND EGG. A CLASSIC DISH, IT IS EATEN THROUGHOUT THE YEAR.*

2 Place the onion, dashi, sugar, soy sauce and mirin (sweet rice wine) in a saucepan and bring to a boil. Add the chicken and cook over medium heat for about 5 minutes, or until cooked. Skim off any scum that rises to the surface of the liquid.

3 Ladle a quarter of the chicken and stock mixture into a frying pan and heat until the liquid comes to a boil.

4 Pour a quarter of the beaten egg over the mixture in the frying pan and sprinkle over 1 tablespoon of the peas.

5 Cover and cook over medium heat until the egg is just set. Slide the egg mixture on to a large plate and keep it warm while cooking the other omelets in the same way. Transfer to serving dishes and serve with boiled rice.

COOK'S TIP
Ideally use either Japanese rice or Thai fragrant rice for this meal and allow 2–3 ounces raw rice per person.

SERVES 4

INGREDIENTS
11 ounces skinless boneless
 chicken breasts
1 large mild onion, thinly sliced
scant 1 cup freshly made dashi
 (kombu and bonito stock) or
 instant dashi
4½ teaspoons sugar
4 tablespoons Japanese soy sauce
2 tablespoons mirin (sweet rice wine)
4 eggs, beaten
4 tablespoons frozen peas, thawed
boiled rice, to serve

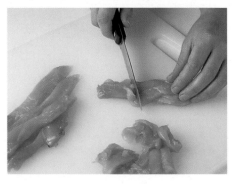

1 Slice the chicken breasts diagonally with a sharp knife, then cut the slices into 1¼-inch lengths.

RICE TRIANGLES

PICNICS ARE VERY POPULAR IN JAPAN AND RICE SHAPES—ONIGIRI—ARE IDEAL PICNIC FARE.
YOU CAN PUT ANYTHING YOU LIKE IN THE RICE, SO YOU COULD INVENT YOUR OWN ONIGIRI.

SERVES 4

INGREDIENTS
  1 salmon steak
  1 tablespoon salt
  4 cups freshly cooked
    sushi rice
  4 umeboshi (plum pickles)
  ¹/₂ sheet yaki-nori seaweed, cut into
    four equal strips
  white and black sesame seeds,
    for sprinkling

1 Broil the salmon steak for 4–5 minutes on each side, until the flesh flakes easily when it is tested with the tip of a sharp knife. Set aside to cool while you make other *onigiri*. When the salmon is cold, flake it, discarding any skin and bones.

2 Put the salt in a bowl. Spoon a quarter of the warm cooked rice into a small rice bowl. Make a hole in the middle of the rice and put in one umeboshi. Smooth the rice over to cover.

3 Wet the palms of both hands with cold water, then rub the salt evenly on to your palms.

4 Empty the rice and umeboshi from the bowl on to one hand. Use both hands to shape the rice into a triangular shape, using firm but not heavy pressure. Make three more rice triangles in the same way.

5 Mix the flaked salmon into the remaining rice, then shape it into triangles as before.

6 Wrap a strip of yaki-nori around each of the umeboshi triangles. Sprinkle sesame seeds on the salmon triangles.

COOK'S TIP
Always use warm rice to make the triangles. Allow them to cool completely and wrap each in foil or plastic wrap.

MISO SOUP

THIS SOUP IS ONE OF THE MOST COMMONLY EATEN DISHES IN JAPAN, AND IT IS USUALLY SERVED WITH EVERY MEAL THAT INCLUDES RICE.

SERVES 4

INGREDIENTS
 ½ packet silken beancurd (tofu),
  drained weight about 5 ounces
 4 cups freshly made dashi (kombu
  and bonito stock) or instant dashi
 ¼ ounce dried wakame seaweed
 4 tablespoons white or red
  miso paste
 2 scallions, shredded, to garnish

COOK'S TIP
Reduce the heat when the stock boils, as the delicate flavor of the soup will be lost if it is boiled for too long.

1 Cut the beancurd into ½-inch cubes. Bring the dashi to a boil, lower the heat and add the wakame seaweed. Simmer for 1–2 minutes.

2 Pour a little of the soup into a bowl and add the miso paste, stirring until it dissolves. Pour the mixture back into the pan.

3 Add the beancurd and heat through for 1 minute. Pour the soup into warmed serving dishes and serve immediately, garnished with the shredded scallions.

VARIATION
Wakame is a young, dark-colored seaweed that can be found dried and in Japanese supermarkets. Nori seaweed could be used instead.

SWEET ADUKI BEAN SOUP WITH RICE CAKES

DON'T ASSUME FROM THE WORD SOUP THAT THIS IS A SAVORY DISH—ZENZAI IS ACTUALLY A CLASSIC AND POPULAR JAPANESE DESSERT, SERVED WITH THE READY-TO-EAT RICE CAKES (MOCHI) THAT ARE SOLD IN JAPANESE SUPERMARKETS. JAPANESE GREEN TEA MAKES A GOOD ACCOMPANIMENT.

SERVES 4

INGREDIENTS
 scant 1 cup dried aduki beans
 1 cup sugar
 pinch of salt
 4 ready-to-eat rice cakes (mochi)

1 Put the aduki beans in a strainer, wash them under cold running water, then drain them and tip them into a large pan. Add 4 cups water and bring to a boil. Drain the aduki beans and return them to the rinsed out pan.

2 Add a further 5 cups water to the pan and bring to a boil, then add a further 5 cups water and bring to a boil again. Lower the heat and simmer for 30 minutes until the beans are soft.

3 Skim the surface of the broth regularly to remove any scum, if left, it would give the soup an unpleasant bitter taste.

4 When the beans are soft enough to be mashed between your fingers, add half the sugar and simmer for a further 20 minutes.

5 Add the remaining sugar and the salt to the pan, stirring until the sugar has completely dissolved.

6 Heat the broiler, then broil both sides of the rice cakes until softened, but not browned. Add the rice cakes to the soup and bring to a boil. Serve the soup immediately in deep warmed bowls.

Simple Rolled Sushi

These simple rolls, known as Hosomaki, are an excellent way of learning the art of rolling sushi. They are very good for picnics and canapés and are always served cold. You will need a bamboo mat (makisu) for the rolling process.

MAKES 12 ROLLS OR 72 SLICES

INGREDIENTS
   2 cups sushi rice, soaked for
      20 minutes in water to cover
   3½ tablespoons rice vinegar
   1 tablespoon sugar
   ½ teaspoon salt
   6 sheets yaki-nori seaweed
   7 ounces tuna, in one piece
   7 ounces salmon, in one piece
   wasabi paste
   ½ cucumber, quartered lengthwise
      and seeded
   pickled ginger, to garnish (optional)
   Japanese soy sauce, to serve

1 Drain the rice, then put in a pan with 2¼ cups water. Bring to a boil, then lower the heat, cover and simmer for 20 minutes, or until all the liquid has been absorbed. Meanwhile, heat the vinegar, sugar and salt, stir well and cool. Add to the hot rice, then remove the pan from the heat and allow to stand (covered) for 20 minutes.

2 Cut the yaki-nori sheets in half lengthwise. Cut the tuna and salmon into four long sticks, each about the same length as the long side of the yaki-nori, and about ½-inch square if viewed from the side.

3 Place a sheet of yaki-nori, shiny side down, on a bamboo mat. Divide the rice into 12 portions. Spread one portion over the yaki-nori, leaving a ½-inch clear space at the top and bottom.

4 Spread a little wasabi paste in a horizontal line along the middle of the rice and lay one or two sticks of tuna on this.

5 Holding the mat and the edge of the yaki-nori nearest to you, roll up the yaki-nori and rice into a cylinder with the tuna in the middle. Use the mat as a guide—do not roll it into the food. Roll the rice tightly so that it sticks together and encloses the filling firmly.

6 Carefully roll the sushi off the mat. Make 11 more rolls in the same way, four for each filling ingredient, but do not use wasabi with the cucumber. Use a wet knife to cut each roll into six slices and stand them on a platter. Garnish with pickled ginger, if you wish, and serve with soy sauce.

ASSORTED TEMPURA

TEMPURA IS ONE OF JAPAN'S MOST FAMOUS AND DELICIOUS DISHES. FISH, RATHER THAN MEAT, IS TRADITIONALLY USED, BUT CHOOSE ANY VEGETABLE YOU LIKE. THE ESSENCE OF GOOD TEMPURA IS THAT IT SHOULD BE COOKED AND SERVED IMMEDIATELY.

SERVES 4–6

INGREDIENTS

1 small sweet potato, about 4 ounces
8 large jumbo shrimp
1 small squid, cleaned
vegetable oil, for deep frying
all-purpose flour, for coating
1 small carrot, cut into matchsticks
4 shiitake mushrooms, stems removed
2 ounces French beans, trimmed
1 red bell pepper, seeded and sliced
    into ¾-inch thick strips

For the dip
    scant 1 cup water
    3 tablespoons mirin (sweet rice wine)
    ¼ ounce bonito flakes
    3 tablespoons Japanese soy sauce

For the batter
    1 egg
    6 tablespoons iced water
    ¾ cup all-purpose flour
    ½ teaspoon baking powder
    2 ice cubes

2 Peel the shrimp, leaving the tail shells intact, and de-vein. Lay a shrimp on its side. Make three or four diagonal slits, about two-thirds of the way in towards the spine, leaving all the pieces attached. Repeat with the rest. Flatten with your fingers. Cut the body of the squid into 1¼-inch thick strips.

3 Put the egg in a large bowl, stir without beating and set half aside. Add the water, flour and baking powder. Stir two or three times, leaving some flour unblended. Add the ice cubes.

4 Heat the oil in a deep fryer to 365°F. Dust the shrimp lightly with flour. Holding each in turn by the tail, dip them into the batter, then carefully lower them into the hot oil; cook until golden. Fry the remaining shrimp and the squid in the same way. Keep warm.

5 Reduce the temperature of the oil to 340°F. Drain the sweet potato and pat dry. Dip the vegetables into the batter and deep fry (see Cook's Tip). Drain well, then keep warm. As soon as all the tempura are ready, serve with the dip.

1 Mix the dip ingredients in a pan. Bring to a boil, cool, then strain. Divide among 4–6 bowls. Slice the unpeeled sweet potato thinly. Put in a bowl with cold water to cover.

COOK'S TIP
Batter and deep fry the carrots and beans in small bunches. The mushrooms look best if only the undersides are dipped. Cut a cross in the upper side of the mushroom cap, if you like.

GREEN AND YELLOW LAYERED CAKES

THIS COLORFUL TWO-TONE DESSERT IS MADE BY MOLDING CONTRASTING MIXTURES IN A SMALL POUCH. THE JAPANESE TITLE IS DERIVED FROM THE PREPARATION TECHNIQUE: CHAKIN-SHIBORI, IN WHICH CHAKIN MEANS A POUCH SHAPE AND SHIBORI MEANS A MOLDING ACTION.

MAKES 6

INGREDIENTS
For the yolk mixture (kimi-an)
   6 small hard-cooked eggs
   1/4 cup sugar

For the pea mixture (endo-an)
   1 3/4 cups frozen peas
   3 tablespoons sugar

1 Make the yolk mixture. Shell the eggs, cut them in half and scoop the yolks into a sifter placed over a bowl. Using a wooden spoon, press the yolks through the sifter. Add the sugar and mix well.

2 To make the pea mixture, cook the peas in lightly salted boiling water for about 3–4 minutes, until softened. Drain and place in a mortar, then crush with a pestle. Transfer the paste to a saucepan. Add the sugar and cook over low heat until thick. Stir constantly so that the mixture does not burn.

3 Spread out the pea paste in a shallow dish so that it cools as quickly as possible. Divide both mixtures into six portions.

COOK'S TIP
Use a food processor instead of a mortar and pestle if preferred. Process for a few seconds to make a coarse paste.

4 Wet a piece of cheesecloth or thin cotton and wring it out well. Place a portion of the pea mixture on the cloth and put a similar amount of the yolk mixture on top. Wrap the mixture up and twist the top of the cloth to join the mixtures together and mark a spiral pattern on the top. Unwrap and place on a plate. Make five more cakes in the same way. Serve cold.

SUKIYAKI

YOU WILL NEED A SPECIAL CAST-IRON SUKIYAKI PAN (SUKIYAKI-NABE) AND BURNER OR A SIMILAR TABLE-TOP COOKER FOR THIS DISH. IT IS GREAT FUN BECAUSE GUESTS CAN COOK THEIR OWN DINNER IN FRONT OF THEM, AND THEN HELP THEMSELVES TO THE DELICIOUS MORSELS OF FOOD.

SERVES 4

INGREDIENTS
   2¼ pounds beef topside, thinly
     sliced
   lard, for cooking
   4 leeks or scallions, sliced diagonally
     into ½-inch pieces
   bunch of shungiku leaves, stems
     removed, chopped (optional)
   bunch of enoki mushrooms, brown
     roots cut off (optional)
   8 shiitake mushrooms, stems
     removed
   11 ounces shirataki noodles, boiled
     for 2 minutes, drained and halved
   2 pieces grilled beancurd (yaki tofu),
     about 4 × 2¾-inches, cut into
     1¼-inch cubes
   4 fresh eggs, to serve

For the sukiyaki stock
   scant ½ cup mirin (sweet rice wine)
   3 tablespoons sugar
   7 tablespoons Japanese soy sauce

For the seasoning mix
   scant 1 cup dashi (kombu and bonito
     stock) or instant dashi
   scant ½ cup sake or dry white wine
   1 tablespoon Japanese soy sauce

2 To make the seasoning mix, heat the dashi, sake or wine and soy sauce in a small pan. As soon as the mixture boils, remove from the heat and set aside.

3 Fan out the beef slices on a large serving plate. Put the lard for cooking on the same plate. Arrange all the remaining ingredients, except the eggs, on one or more large plates.

4 Stand the portable cooker on a suitably heavy mat to protect the dining table and ensure that it can be heated safely. Melt the lard, add three or four slices of beef and some leeks or scallions, and then pour in the sukiyaki stock. Gradually add the remaining ingredients, except the eggs.

5 Place each egg in a ramekin and beat lightly with chopsticks. Place one before each diner. When the beef and vegetables are cooked, diners help themselves to whatever they fancy, dipping their chosen piece of meat, vegetable or grilled beancurd (yaki tofu) in the raw egg before eating.

6 When the stock has thickened, gradually stir in the seasoning mix and carry on cooking until all the ingredients have been eaten.

1 Make the sukiyaki stock. Pour the mirin (sweet rice wine) into a pan and bring to a boil. Stir in the sugar and soy sauce, bring to a boil, then remove from the heat and set aside.

CHAP CHAE

A KOREAN STIR-FRY OF MIXED VEGETABLES AND NOODLES GARNISHED ATTRACTIVELY WITH THE YELLOW AND WHITE EGG SHAPES THAT ARE SO TYPICALLY KOREAN.

SERVES 4

INGREDIENTS
8 ounces rump or sirloin steak
4 ounces cellophane noodles, soaked
   for 20 minutes in hot water to cover
4 Chinese dried mushrooms, soaked
   for 30 minutes in warm water
peanut oil, for stir-frying
2 eggs, separated
1 carrot, cut into matchsticks
1 onion, sliced
2 zucchini or ½ cucumber, cut
   into sticks
½ red bell pepper, seeded and cut
   into strips
4 button mushrooms, sliced
1½ cups beansprouts, washed
   and drained
1 tablespoon light soy sauce
salt and ground black pepper
sliced scallions and sesame seeds,
   to garnish

1 Put the steak in the freezer until it is firm enough to cut into thin slices and then into 2-inch strips.

2 Mix the ingredients for the marinade in a shallow dish (see Cook's Tip), stir in the steak strips. Drain the noodles and cook them in boiling water for 5 minutes. Drain again, then snip into short lengths. Drain the mushrooms, cut off and discard the stems; slice the caps.

3 Prepare the garnish. Heat the oil in a small frying pan. Beat the egg yolks together and pour into the pan. When set, slide them on to a plate. Add the egg whites to the pan and cook until set. Cut both yolks and whites into diamond shapes and set aside.

COOK'S TIP
To make the marinade, blend together 1 tablespoon sugar, 2 tablespoons light soy sauce, 3 tablespoons sesame oil, 4 finely chopped scallions, 1 crushed garlic clove and 2 teaspoons crushed toasted sesame seeds.

4 Drain the beef. Heat the oil in a wok or large frying pan and stir-fry the beef until it changes color. Add the carrot and onion and stir-fry for 2 minutes, then add the other vegetables, tossing them until just cooked.

5 Add the noodles and season with soy sauce, salt and pepper. Cook for 1 minute. Spoon into a serving dish and garnish with egg, scallions and sesame seeds.

KIMCHI

NO SELF-RESPECTING KOREAN MOVES FAR WITHOUT THE BELOVED KIMCHI. IN THE PAST, LARGE STONE POTS WERE FILLED WITH THIS PICKLED CABBAGE, AND BURIED IN THE GROUND FOR THE WINTER.

SERVES 6–8

INGREDIENTS
1½ pounds Chinese leaves, shredded
1 large or 2 medium yam beans,
   total weight about 1½ pounds or
   2 hard pears, peeled and thinly
   sliced
4 tablespoons salt
scant 1 cup water
4 scallions, finely chopped
4 garlic cloves, crushed
1-inch piece fresh ginger root, peeled
   and finely chopped
2–3 teaspoons chili powder

1 Place the Chinese leaves and yam beans or pears in a bowl and sprinkle evenly with salt. Mix well, then press down into the bowl.

2 Pour the water over the vegetables, then cover the bowl and leave overnight in a cool place. Next day, drain off the brine from the vegetables and set it aside. Mix the brined vegetables with the scallions, garlic, ginger and chili powder (use rubber gloves if you have sensitive hands). Pack the mixture into a 2-pound jar or two smaller ones. Pour over the reserved brine.

3 Cover with plastic wrap and place on a sunny window-sill or in an airing cupboard for 2–3 days. Thereafter store in the refrigerator, where the mixture can be kept for several weeks.

MARINATED BEEF STEAKS

BULGOGI *IS A VERY POPULAR DISH FOR OUTDOOR ENTERTAINING. TRADITIONALLY IT WOULD HAVE BEEN COOKED ON A GENGHIS KHAN BROILER, WHICH IS SHAPED LIKE THE CROWN OF A HAT, BUT A RIDGED HEAVY FRYING PAN OR WOK WORKS ALMOST AS WELL.*

SERVES 3–4

INGREDIENTS
    1 pound fillet of beef or rump
      steak, in the piece
    sesame oil, for frying

For the marinade
    $2/3$ cup dark soy sauce
    2 tablespoons sesame oil
    2 tablespoons sake or dry white wine
    1 garlic clove, cut into thin slivers
    1 tablespoon sugar
    2 tablespoons crushed roasted
      sesame seeds
    4 scallions, cut into long lengths
    salt and ground black pepper

1 Put the meat into the freezer until it is firm enough to slice very thinly and evenly. Arrange the slices of beef in a shallow glass dish.

2 Make the marinade. Mix the soy sauce, oil, sake or wine, garlic, sugar and sesame seeds in a bowl and add the scallions. Season to taste.

3 Pour the marinade over the slices of beef and mix well. Cover the dish and transfer to the refrigerator. Chill for at least 3 hours or overnight.

4 Heat the merest slick of oil in a ridged heavy frying pan or wok. Drain the beef slices and fry over high heat for a few seconds, turning once. Serve at once.

PORK <u>AND</u> SCALLION PANCAKES

BINDAEDUK *IS SOMETIMES REFERRED TO AS* KOREA'S *ANSWER TO THE PIZZA, ALTHOUGH IT IS REALLY A BEANCAKE. THE FILLING CAN INCLUDE* KIMCHI *(PICKLED CABBAGE), CARROT AND GINGER, BUT PORK AND SCALLIONS ARE MORE TRADITIONAL INGREDIENTS.*

SERVES 4–6

INGREDIENTS

1¼ cups skinned, split mung beans
⅓ cup glutinous rice
1 tablespoon light soy sauce
1 tablespoon roasted sesame
  seeds, crushed
½ teaspoon baking soda
½ cup beansprouts, blanched
  and dried
1 garlic clove, crushed
4 scallions, chopped
4 ounces cooked lean pork, shredded
2 tablespoons sesame oil, plus extra
  for drizzling
salt and ground black pepper
fresh chives, to garnish
light soy sauce, to serve

1 Pick over the mung beans and put them in a bowl. Add the glutinous rice and pour in water to cover. Leave to soak for at least 8 hours. After this time, tip the beans and rice into a strainer, rinse under cold water, then drain. Put the mixture into a food processor and process to a batter with the consistency of thick cream.

2 Add the soy sauce, sesame seeds and bicarbonate of soda and process briefly to mix. When ready to cook, tip the batter into a bowl and add the beansprouts, garlic, scallions and pork. Season to taste.

3 Heat about 2 teaspoons of the sesame oil in a large frying pan. Spoon or ladle in half the batter, and, using the back of a spoon, spread it into a thick pancake.

4 Drizzle a little more sesame oil over the surface of the pancake, cover and cook over medium heat until the underside is cooked. Invert a lightly oiled plate over the pan. Remove the pan from the heat and, holding both plate and pan tightly together, turn both over carefully so that the pancake is transferred to the plate. Slide it back into the pan and cook on the other side for 3–4 minutes more. Keep this first pancake hot while cooking a second pancake in the same way. Place the pancakes on serving plates and garnish with chives. Cut into wedges and serve with soy sauce.

SHOPPING FOR ASIAN INGREDIENTS

General

99 Ranch Market
5150 Buford Highway, B-199
Doraville, GA 30340
Tel: (770) 458-8899

Asian Food Market
6450 Market Street
Upper Darby, PA 19082
Tel: (610) 352-4433

Asian Foods, Etc.
1375 Prince Avenue
Atlanta, GA 30341
Tel: (404) 543-8624

Asian Foods Ltd.
260-280 West Lehigh
Avenue
Philadelphia, PA 19133
Tel: (215) 291-9500

Asian Market
2513 Stewart Avenue
Las Vegas, NV 89101
(702) 387-3373

Asian Market
18815 Eureka Road
South Gate, MI 48195
Fax: (734) 246-4795
www.asianmarket.qpg.com

Augusta Market Oriental Foods
2117 Martin Luther King Jr.
Boulevard
Altanta, GA 30901
Tel: (706) 722-4988

Bharati Food & Spice
 Center
6163 Reynolds Road Suite G
Morrow, GA 30340
Tel: (770) 961-9007

First Asian Food Center
3420 East Ponce De Leon
Avenue
Scottsdale, GA 30079
Tel: (404) 292-6508

The House of Rice Store
3221 North Hayden Road
Scottsdale, AZ 85251
Tel: (480) 947-6698
www.houserice.com

Han Me Oriental Food
 & Gifts
2 E. Derenne Avenue
Savannah, GA 31405
Tel: (912) 355-6411

Hong Tan Oriental Food
2802 Capitol Street
Savannah, GA 31404
Tel: (404) 233-9184

Huy Fong Foods Inc.
5001 Earle Avenue
Rosemead, CA 91770
Tel: (626) 286-8328
Fax: (626) 286-8522
www.huyfong.com

Khanh Tam Oriental Market
4051 Buford Highway, NE
Atlanta, GA 30345
Tel: (404) 728-0393

May's American Oriental
 Market
422 West University
 Avenue
Saint Paul, MN 55103
Tel: (651) 293-1118
www.maysamoriental.qpg.com

Norcross Oriental Market
6062 Norcross-Tucker
 Road
Chamblee, GA 30341
Tel: (770) 496-1656

Oriental Grocery
11827 Del Amo Boulevard
Cerritos, CA 90701
Tel: (310) 924-1029

Oriental Market
670 Central Park Avenue
Yonkers, NY 10013
(212) 349-1979

The Oriental Pantry
423 Great Road
Acton, MA 01720
Tel: (978) 264-4576
www.orientalpantry.com

Saigon Asian Market
10090 Central Avenue
Biloxi, MS 39532
Tel: (228) 392-8044
Fax: (228) 392-8039
www.saigonor.qpg.com

Siam Market
27266 East Baseline Street
Highland, CA 92346
Tel: (909) 862-8060

Unimart American and Asian
 Groceries
1201 Howard Street
San Francisco, CA 94103
Tel: (415) 431-0362

Chinese

Chinese Oriental Market
300 South Bruce Street
Las Vegas, NV 89101
(702) 382-7295

DIHO Market
655 Pasquinelli Drive
Westmont, IL 60559
Tel: (630) 323-1668
Fax: (630) 323-8180
www.pcmax.net/Chinese/food/
diho.html

Pearl River Chinese Products
 Emporium
277 Canal Street
New York, NY
Tel: (212) 431-4770

Indian

Alhambra, CA 91801
Tel: (626) 576-2455
Fax: (626) 284-2756
kajala@GTE.net

Bombay Sweets
1401 University Boulevard
Langley Park, MD 20783
(Indian candies and desserts)

Cherian Indian Groceries
1707 Church Street
Decatur, GA 30030
Tel: (404) 299-0842

Indian Asian Bazaar
159 North 72nd Street
Omaha, NE 68127
Tel: (402) 556-3309

Indian Grocery
4535 Fredricksburg Road
San Antonio, TX 78200
Tel: (210) 737-0556

Indian International Mart
6391 S. Sheridan Road
Tulsa, OK 74133

Indian Spices and Gifts
3901 Wilson Boulevard
Arlington, VA 22203
Tel: (703) 522-0149
Fax: (703) 528-5603

Indo-Pak Spices
422 Elden Street
Herndon, VA 22070
(Indian/Pakistani spices)

Kajala Imports
23 East Main Street
Alhambra, CA 91801
Tel: (626)576-2455
Fax: (626) 284-2756
kalaja@GTE.net

Patel Brothers
2080 University Boulevard
Langley Park, MD 20783
Tel: (301) 422-1555

Spice & Sweets Mahal
431 South Frederick
   Avenue
Gaithersburg, MD 20877

Spice Mahal
3621 Kirkwood Highway
Wilmington, DE
Tel: (302) 994-8144

Subzi Mandi
Twin Oaks Center
757 Hungerford Drive
Rockville, MD 20850

Sushma Emporium
480-A Blossom Hill Road
San Jose, CA
Tel: (408) 281-0392
www.indolink.com/SFO/sushm
a.html

TAJ International Foods
7334 Lee Highway
Chattanooga, TN 37421
Tel: (423) 892-0259

Indonesian

Bachri's Chili & Spice Gourmet
5617 Villa Haven
Pittsburgh, PA 15236
Tel: (412) 831-1131
Fax: (412) 831-2542
email: chris@telerama.lm.com

Japanese

Daido
1385 16th Street
Fort Lee, NJ 07024
Tel: (201) 944-0020

Katagiri Speciality
224 East 59th Street
New York, NY 10022
Tel: (212) 755-3566
Fax: (212) 752-4197
www.katagiri.com

Maruwa Foods Company of
   America
1737 Post Street
San Francisco, CA 94115
Tel: (415) 563-1901
Fax: (415) 563-0716
www.maruwa.com

Sea Rance
3223 West Lake Avenue
Wilmette, IL 60091
(708) 256-4404

Suruki Super Market
71 East 4th Avenue
San Maleo, CA 94401
Tel: (415) 347-5288
Fax: (415) 347-7548
www.americandreams.com

Yaohan
595 River Road
Edgewater, NJ 07020
Tel: (201) 941-9113

Korean

Lotte
2030 Will Ross Court
Chamblee, GA 30341
Tel: (770) 454-7569

Thai/Laos

Ai Hoa
860 North Hill Street
Los Angeles, CA 90026
Tel (213) 482-48

Bangkok Market
4757 Melrose Avenue
Los Angeles, CA 90029
Tel: (203) 662-7990

Modern Thai
   Incorporated
135 Yacht Club Way #210
Hypuluxo, FL 33462
Tel: (888) THAI-8888

Thai Market
3297 Las Vegas Boulevard
Las Vegas, NV 89030
Tel: (702) 643-8080

Thai Market
916 Harrelson Street
Fort Walton Beach,
FL 32547
Tel: (904) 863-2013

Thai Number One Market
5927 Cherry Avenue
Long Beach, CA 90805
Tel: (310) 422-6915

Thai-Lao Market
1721 West La Palma Avenue
Anaheim, CA 92801
Tel: (714) 535-2656

**Author's
Acknowledgements**

Sallie Morris would like
to thank her family:
Johnnie, Alex and James
for their support; Beryl
Castles for her help in
typing the manuscript;
Beth Ware for advice on
recipes from the
Phillipines and Rupert
Welchman for his advice
on Japanese recipes.

Deh-ta Hsiung would
like to thank Sallie
Morris and Emi Kazuko
for their advice and help
in writing about South-
east Asian and Japanese
foods for the ingredients
section.

INDEX